Communications in Computer and Information Science 2767

Rationale
The CCIS series is devoted to the publication of proceedings of computer science conferences. Its aim is to efficiently disseminate original research results in informatics in printed and electronic form. While the focus is on publication of peer-reviewed full papers presenting mature work, inclusion of reviewed short papers reporting on work in progress is welcome, too. Besides globally relevant meetings with internationally representative program committees guaranteeing a strict peer-reviewing and paper selection process, conferences run by societies or of high regional or national relevance are also considered for publication.

Topics
The topical scope of CCIS spans the entire spectrum of informatics ranging from foundational topics in the theory of computing to information and communications science and technology and a broad variety of interdisciplinary application fields.

Information for Volume Editors and Authors
Publication in CCIS is free of charge. No royalties are paid, however, we offer registered conference participants temporary free access to the online version of the conference proceedings on SpringerLink (http://link.springer.com) by means of an http referrer from the conference website and/or a number of complimentary printed copies, as specified in the official acceptance email of the event.

CCIS proceedings can be published in time for distribution at conferences or as post-proceedings, and delivered in the form of printed books and/or electronically as USBs and/or e-content licenses for accessing proceedings at SpringerLink. Furthermore, CCIS proceedings are included in the CCIS electronic book series hosted in the SpringerLink digital library at http://link.springer.com/bookseries/7899. Conferences publishing in CCIS are allowed to use our online conference service (Meteor) for managing the whole proceedings lifecycle (from submission and reviewing to preparing for publication) free of charge.

Publication process
The language of publication is exclusively English. Authors publishing in CCIS have to sign the Springer CCIS copyright transfer form, however, they are free to use their material published in CCIS for substantially changed, more elaborate subsequent publications elsewhere. For the preparation of the camera-ready papers/files, authors have to strictly adhere to the Springer CCIS Authors' Instructions and are strongly encouraged to use the CCIS LaTeX style files or templates.

Abstracting/Indexing
CCIS is abstracted/indexed in DBLP, Google Scholar, EI-Compendex, Mathematical Reviews, SCImago, Scopus. CCIS volumes are also submitted for the inclusion in ISI Proceedings.

How to start
To start the evaluation of your proposal for inclusion in the CCIS series, please send an e-mail to ccis@springer.com

Ali Abbasov · Aleksander Sładkowski ·
Tofig Babayev
Editors

Problems of Logistics, Management and Operation in the East-West Transport Corridor

4th International Conference, PLMO 2025
Baku, Azerbaijan, May 13–15, 2025
Proceedings

Springer

Editors
Ali Abbasov
Institute of Control Systems
Baku, Azerbaijan

Tofig Babayev
Institute of Control Systems
Baku, Azerbaijan

Aleksander Sładkowski
Silesian University of Technology
Katowice, Poland

ISSN 1865-0929 ISSN 1865-0937 (electronic)
Communications in Computer and Information Science
ISBN 978-3-032-13671-8 ISBN 978-3-032-13672-5 (eBook)
https://doi.org/10.1007/978-3-032-13672-5

This Springer imprint is published by the registered company Springer Nature Switzerland AG
The registered company address is: Gewerbestrasse 11, 6330 Cham, Switzerland

Preface

These conference proceedings are a collection of the best papers accepted by the 4th International Conference on Problems of Logistics, Management and Operation in the East-West Transport Corridor, PLMO 2025, held in Baku, Azerbaijan, on May 13–15, 2025.

The conference was organized by the Institute of Control Systems, ICS, of the Ministry of Science and Education of the Republic of Azerbaijan, Silesian University of Technology of Poland, Guangzhou University of China, the Technical University of Georgia, Tashkent State Transport University of Uzbekistan, and Azerbaijan Technological University. The conference, which covered a wide geographical area, was attended by representatives of the Azerbaijani scientific community, as well as scientists from 12 foreign countries.

The East-West Transport Corridor is an integral part of the ancient Silk Road and an initiative that requires the development of new mechanisms for regional economic partnership. It stimulates economic prosperity, cultural exchange, and communication between the member countries. Moreover, it serves as a tool to promote peace and create sustainable development.

Being an integral part of the "One Belt One Road" concept, the East-West Corridor is aimed at improving trade routes, transport, and economic corridors and creating new trade routes. The East-West Corridor is also considered to be the shortest trade route that connects Europe and China.

The main goal of PLMO 2025 was to bring together researchers and relevant representatives from the public and private sectors, universities, and international organizations to discuss scientific and practical issues such as problems in the transportation of goods through different transportation methods. Taking into consideration the achievements of 4th Industrial Revolution, the introduction of digital technologies and digital economy could tackle the problem.

115 participants, including presenters registered to attend the conference. In total 57 papers were submitted. The papers were submitted and reviewed through the EasyABS system. All the papers were single-blind peer reviewed by leading transport and information technology experts, with submissions receiving three reviews on average. The reviewers evaluated the compliance of research papers with the conference topic, their scientific novelty, and practical value. Out of 57 papers submitted to the conference, 56 were included in the conference program. Presentations were made in a hybrid format: on-line and in person, in 4 sections in Baku and in an off-site session at Azerbaijan Technological University in Ganja. The opening ceremony of the conference was dedicated to the 90th anniversary of the birth of Academician Telman Aliyev, Advisor to Azerbaijan National Academy of Sciences, Senior Researcher of the Institute of Control Systems, who headed the Institute of Control Systems for 32 years.

Fifteen papers evaluated by the reviewers as the best of the presented papers and approved by the Program Committee were selected to be included in these Conference Proceedings.

October 2025

Ali Abbasov
Aleksander Sładkowski
Tofig Babayev

Organization

Organizing Committee

Organizing Committee Chairs

Ali Abbasov (Chair)	Institute of Control Systems, Azerbaijan
Xingfa Gu (Co-chair)	Guangzhou University, China
Tamaz Natriashvili (Co-chair)	Institute of Machine Mechanics, Georgia
Yashar Omarov (Co-chair)	Azerbaijan Technological University, Azerbaijan
Tofig Babayev (Executive Secretary)	Institute of Control Systems, Azerbaijan

Organizing Committee Members

Abdullayeva, Gulchin	Institute of Control Systems, Azerbaijan
Ahmedov, Heybatulla	Azerbaijan Technical University, Azerbaijan
Aliyev, Elchin	Institute of Control Systems, Azerbaijan
Amirgaliyev, Edilkhan	Institute of Information and Computing Technologies, Kazakhstan
Apostolov, Mario	United Nations Economic Commission for Europe, Switzerland
Chaudhary, Prince Shiva	Intel, USA
Ćwiek, Janusz	Silesian University of Technology, Poland
Gogiashvili, Phridon	Akaki Tsereteli State University, Georgia
Gulamov, Abdulaziz	Tashkent State Transport University, Uzbekistan
Ibrahimov, Bayram	Azerbaijan Technical University, Azerbaijan
Imanov, Azer	Ministry of Digital Development and Transport, Azerbaijan
Imanov, Gorkhmaz	Institute of Control Systems, Azerbaijan
Mamedov, Ilgar	Institute of Control Systems, Azerbaijan
Mammadova, Masuma	Institute of Information Technology, Azerbaijan
Mansimov, Kamil	Institute of Control Systems, Azerbaijan
Musaeva, Naila	Institute of Control Systems, Azerbaijan
Norkulov, Sukhrob	Center for Training and Retraining of Railway Transport workers of Legal Entities owning their own railways, Uzbekistan
Nuriyev, Urfat	Ege University, Türkiye
Piliponis, Arturas	Ernst &Young, Lithuania

Renying, Li	Belt and Road Alliance for Science & Technology, China
Rzayev, Ramin	Institute of Control Systems, Azerbaijan
Sabziev, Elkhan	Institute of Control Systems, Azerbaijan
Shahbazova, Shahnaz	Azerbaijan State University of Economics, Azerbaijan
Sipos, Tibor	Budapest University of Technology and Economics, Hungary
Turaev, Bakhodir	Tashkent State Transport University, Uzbekistan
Virkovski, Valery	Institute of Control Systems, Azerbaijan

Program Committee

Program Committee Chairs

Rasim Alguliyev (Chair)	Institute of Information Technologies, Azerbaijan
Aleksander Sładkowski (Co-chair)	Silesian University of Technology, Poland
Adil Bagirov (Co-chair)	Federation University, Australia
Said Shaumarov (Co-chair)	Tashkent State Transport University, Uzbekistan

Program Committee Members

Abdullayev, Seidulla	School of Transport Engineering and Logistics after M. Tynyshpaev, Kazakhstan
Abramović, Borna	University of Zagreb, Croatia
Aida-Zade, Kamil	Institute of Control Systems, Azerbaijan
Aliev, Telman	Institute of Control Systems, Azerbaijan
Asenov, Asen	University of Ruse, Bulgaria
Bačkalic, Todor	University of Novi Sad, Serbia
Božičnik, Stane	University of Maribor, Slovenia
Bureika, Gintautas	Vilnius Gediminas Technical University, Lithuania
Carnis, Laurent	UPE, IFSTTAR, AME, DEST, France
Droździel, Paweł	Lublin University of Technology, Poland
Elemesov, Kasym	Kazakh National Technical University, Kazakhstan
Faraslis, Ioannis	University of Thessaly, Greece
Gasimov, Sayavush	Baku Eurasian University, Azerbaijan
Gašparík, Jozef	Slovak University of Technology in Bratislava, Slovakia
Gitolendia, Boris	Georgian Technical University, Georgia

Hajiyev, Chingiz	Istanbul Technical University, Türkiye
Hasanov, Fakhri	King Abdullah Petroleum Studies and Research Center, Saudi Arabia
Ivanov, Rosen	University of Ruse, Bulgaria
Juwet, Marc	KU Leuven, Belgium
Kikvidze, Omar	Akaki Tsereteli State University, Georgia
Kirtadze, Shalva	Akaki Tsereteli State University, Georgia
Krupp, Thomas	TH Köln (University of Applied Sciences), Germany
Malenkovska Todorova, Marija	University "St. Kliment Ohridski" in Bitola, North Macedonia
Mansurov, Yulbarshon	Tashkent State Transport University, Uzbekistan
Melikov, Agassi	Bakı Mühəndislik Universiteti, Azerbaijan
Mezitis, Marek	Transport Academy, Latvia
Mocan, Marian	Polytechnic University of Timişoara, Romania
Mukhitdinov, Akmal	Tashkent State Transport University, Uzbekistan
Pencheva, Velizara	University of Ruse, Bulgaria
Pogodzinski, Joseph	San José State University, USA
Poliak, Miloš	Žilina University, Slovakia
Prentkovskis, Olegas	Vilnius Gediminas Technical University, Lithuania
Providas, Efthimios	University of Thessaly, Greece
Radjibaev, Davron	Uzbekistan University of Economics and Pedagogy, Uzbekistan
Rakhimov, Rustam	Tashkent State Transport University, Uzbekistan
Ricci, Stefano	Sapienza University of Rome, Italy
Ruzmetov, Yadgor	Tashkent State Transport University, Uzbekistan
Sierpiński, Grzegorz	Silesian University of Technology, Poland
Staniek, Marcin	Silesian University of Technology, Poland
Švadlenka, Libor	University of Pardubice, Czech Republic
Török, Ádám	UAB İNTA, Hungary
Tumanishvili, Georgy	Georgian Technical University, Georgia
Vitkauskas, Vytautas	INTA, Lithuania
Wojnar, Grzegorz	Silesian University of Technology, Poland

Contents

Prospects of Using Technologies for Adaptive Control of the Latent Period of Accidents in Facilities of the East-West Transport Corridor

Telman Aliev[1,2], Tofig Babayev[2(✉)], Naila Musaeva[1,2], Ana Mammadova[1,2], and Rauf Gadimov[2]

[1] Azerbaijan University of Architecture and Construction, Ayna Sultanova 11, Baku, Azerbaijan
director@cyber.az

[2] Institute of Control Systems of Ministry of Science and Education, 68 B.Vahabzade, Baku AZ1141, Azerbaijan
tbabayev@bk.ru

Abstract. It is shown that increasing the level of safety of the East-West transport corridor first of all requires developing technologies, means and a system for adaptive control of the onset of malfunctions on rolling stock, railroads, bridges, tunnels and key communications along the entire route. At present, the number of unexpected accidents in rail transport largely depends on the qualification of the driver, who intuitively determines the current technical condition of the object and the beginning of possible accidents on the basis of accumulated experience and information received from control systems. Despite this, sometimes the driver's decision is delayed and accidents occur. Usually, these accidents occur as a result of emergence and development of various malfunctions. Here facilities enter the latent period of an emergency state, noises emerge that are correlated with the controlled signal $g(t)$, the dynamics of facility operation changes, causing the spectra of the useful signal $X(t)$ and the noise $\varepsilon(t)$, which is filtered according to traditional technologies, to change as well. In this paper, while allowing the traditional control technology to stand, we additionally propose an adaptive technology for controlling the beginning of the latent period of the accident. Here the estimate of the relay cross-correlation function between the following the useful signal $X(t)$ and the noise $\varepsilon(t)$ is used as an informative attribute. In addition, the use of positional binary technology is considered.

Keywords: Adaptive Control · Rail Transport · Informative Attributes · Diagnostic Information · Useful Signal · Noise · Signaling · Safety · Transport Corridor

1 Introduction

Analysis has shown that at present, ensuring the safety of the East-West transport corridor first of all requires increasing the level of control over the dynamics of the latent period of accidents. For this purpose, it is necessary to create effective technologies that allow

A. Abbasov et al. (Eds.): PLMO 2025, CCIS 2767, pp. 1–10, 2026.
https://doi.org/10.1007/978-3-032-13672-5_1

adequate control of the beginning and development of the emergency situation of the transport corridor facilities. Currently, various technologies and diagnostic tools are successfully used in rail transport safety systems. In this case, to form informative attributes of malfunctions, the technologies for analyzing vibration, pressure, force, current, voltage, resistance, time intervals, etc. are used. Of these parameters the most information is contained in vibration signals, as in most of the rolling stock equipment the occurrence of a malfunction leads to the emergence of mechanical vibrations. Thanks to this, it is possible to control the dynamics of the change in the latent period of damage in real time [1–9].

In this case, of particular importance is the control and diagnosis of malfunction of the density of the supply and brake lines, malfunction of the brake valve, malfunction of the brake cylinders, malfunction of the compressor, bearing defects, lack and shortage of lubrication, mounting defects, imbalance of rotating parts, gearbox defects.

2 Problem Statement

As is known, in the correlation analysis of noisy random signals $g(t) = X(t) + \varepsilon_1(t)$ it is assumed that there is no correlation between the noise $\varepsilon_1(t)$ and the useful signal $X(t)$ and to eliminate the influence of the noise on the result of control, filtering of the noise $\varepsilon(t)$ is used. Due to this we get the estimate $R_{xx}(\tau)$ that is close enough to the estimates $R_{XX}(\tau)$ of the useful signals $X(t)$, i.e. the equality

$$R_{XX}(\tau) \approx R_{xx}(\tau)$$

is true, thereby ensuring the adequacy of control results.

However, at the beginning of the latent period of the emergency state of the object T_1 a noise $\varepsilon_2(t)$ emerges, which is correlated with the useful signal $X(t)$, the inequality $R_{X\varepsilon}(t) \neq 0$ takes place and a part of the spectrum of the useful signal $X(t)$ overlaps with the spectrum of the noise $\varepsilon(t)$ and for this reason the following inequality takes place:

$$\begin{cases} R_{XX}(\mu) > R_{xx}(\mu) \\ R_{XX}(\mu) < R_{xx}(\mu) \end{cases}.$$

Because of this, if in the process of operation, the estimate $R_{xx}(\mu)$ is greater than the one set by the regulation, the information of the control system about the beginning of the accident will be questionable.

However, after that, during the period of transition of the facility to the emergency state T_2, the readings of measuring devices will correspond to reality and the estimation $R_{xx}(\tau)$ will be steadily different from the one set by the regulations. Due to this, the driver is able to eliminate the cause of accidents and return the object to the normal technical state T_0. However, in cases where this information may be delayed, he may not have time to return the object from the emergency state to the normal state. In this case, i.e., when objects transition to the latent emergency period T_1, depending on the nature of the malfunction, the dynamics of technological processes changes, which also changes the spectra of useful signals $X(i\Delta t)$ and noise $\varepsilon(i\Delta t)$. In this regard, in order to increase the safety level, it is necessary to create an additional alternative adaptive technology for controlling the latent period of accidents on rolling stock, railroads, bridges and tunnels.

3 Technology of Adaptive Determination of the Sampling Interval of the Analyzed Signals

It is known that in order to improve the adequacy of the control results in the latent period of the emergency state of objects it is necessary to ensure the adaptability of determining the sampling interval of the signals $g(i\Delta t)$. Our studies have shown that to this end, it is possible to use the frequency properties of the least significant digit $q_0(i\Delta t)$ of the samples $g(i\Delta t)$ of noisy signals [1, 5]. Since during the analog-to-digital conversion of these signals in real time the coefficients of the k relations N_{i0} and N are easily determined according to the formula

$$k = \frac{N_{i0}}{N},$$

where N_{i0} is the number of state changes of the least significant digit of the samples over time T_a^*, N is the total number of samples of the signal $g(t)$ during its conversion into a digital code $g(i\Delta t)$ over time T_a^*.

Obviously, formula (1) for adaptive determination of the sampling interval Δt_a can be represented as an algorithm:

$$\Delta t_a = \begin{cases} \Delta t_a + 1, & \text{when} \quad \frac{N_{i0}}{N} \leq 2 \\ \Delta t_a - 1, & \text{when} \quad \frac{N_{i0}}{N} > 2 \end{cases}, \tag{1}$$

which is easy to implement in terms of hardware.

For example, in rail transportation, the spectrum of vibration signals $g(i\Delta t)$ received at the output of vibration sensors changes depending on the change in train speed. Here, the frequency of change in the state of binary digits of the samples $g(i\Delta t)$ of the analyzed signals will also change in proportion to the train speed. Because of this, there will be an error in the estimates obtained as a result of analyzing the signals. It is obvious that using the algorithm for adaptive determining the sampling interval Δt_a, it is possible to increase the degree of adequacy of the control results.

4 Technologies for Monitoring the Beginning of the Latent Period of Accidents

Our analysis showed that one of the possible solutions to the problem of monitoring the beginning of the latent period of accidents T_1 comes down to the use of the noise $\varepsilon(t)$ of the analyzed noisy signals $g(t)$ as a carrier of diagnostic information [10–13]. In this regard, let us consider this issue in detail. It is known that the estimate of the correlation function $R_{gg}(0)$ at $\tau = 0$ is determined from the formula

$$\begin{gathered} R_{gg}(0) \approx \tfrac{1}{N}\textstyle\sum_{i=1}^{N}[X(i\Delta t) + \varepsilon(i\Delta t)][X(i\Delta t) + \varepsilon(i\Delta t)] \\ = \tfrac{1}{N}\textstyle\sum_{i=1}^{N} X^2(i\Delta t) + \tfrac{1}{N}\sum_{i=1}^{N} X(i\Delta t)\varepsilon(i\Delta t) + \tfrac{1}{N}\sum_{i=1}^{N} X(i\Delta t)\varepsilon(i\Delta t) \\ +\tfrac{1}{N}\textstyle\sum_{i=1}^{N} \varepsilon^2(i\Delta t). \end{gathered} \tag{2}$$

From the analysis of this expression it is obvious that if there is a correlation between $X(t)$ and $\varepsilon(t)$, the inequalities.

$$R_{X\varepsilon}(0) = \frac{2}{N}\sum_{i=1}^{N} X(i\Delta t)\varepsilon(i\Delta t) \neq 0,$$

take place and in this case the estimate $R_{gg}(0)$ is determined from the formula

$$R_{gg}(0) = D_{XX}(0) + 2R_{X\varepsilon}(0) + R_{\varepsilon\varepsilon}(0). \tag{3}$$

In those cases where there no correlation between $X(t)$ and $\varepsilon(t)$, the estimate of the cross-correlation function between the useful signal $X(t)$ and the noise $\varepsilon(t)$ is zero, i.e.

$$R_{X\varepsilon}(0) = \frac{2}{N}\sum_{i=1}^{N} X(i\Delta t)\varepsilon(i\Delta t) \approx 0,$$

and in this case, the estimate $R_{gg}(0)$ is determined from the formula

$$R_{gg}(0) = R_{XX}(0) + R_{\varepsilon\varepsilon}(0). \tag{4}$$

Comparing formula (3) and (4), it is obvious that monitoring the beginning of the latent period of accidents T_1 can be easily implemented by determining the beginning of time of emergence of the correlation $R_{X\varepsilon}(0)$ between the useful signal $X(i\Delta t)$ and the noise $\varepsilon(i\Delta t)$ of the analyzed noisy signals $g(i\Delta t)$ [11–13].

The conducted experimental studies confirmed the effectiveness of this variant of the problem under consideration. It was revealed that for real objects the estimate of the relay cross-correlation function $R^*_{X\varepsilon}(\mu)$ between the useful signal $X(i\Delta t)$ and noise $\varepsilon(i\Delta t)$ is the most reliable informative attribute of monitoring the onset of accidents. From the literature [1–9] it is known that its estimates $R^*_{X\varepsilon}(\mu)$ can be determined from the expression

$$R^*_{X\varepsilon}(\mu = 0) = R^*_{gg}(\mu = 0) - 2R^*_{gg}(\mu = 1) + R^*_{gg}(\mu = 2).$$

It can be shown that the estimate obtained by this formula will ensure the adequacy of the control results. For this purpose, taking into account the condition

$$\operatorname{sgn} g(i\Delta t) = \begin{cases} +1 \text{ when } g(i\Delta t) > 0 \\ 0 \text{ when } g(i\Delta t) = 0 \\ -1 \text{ when } g(i\Delta t) < 0 \end{cases}$$

we consider the validity of formula (2) which can also be represented as

$$\begin{gathered} R^*_{x\varepsilon} \approx \tfrac{1}{N}\textstyle\sum_{i=1}^{N}\big[\operatorname{sgn} g(i\Delta t)g(i\Delta t) - 2\operatorname{sgn} g(i\Delta t) \\ \times g((i+1)\Delta t) + \operatorname{sgn} g(i\Delta t)g((i+2)\Delta t)\big]. \end{gathered} \tag{5}$$

Using the known equalities

$$\begin{cases} sgng(i\Delta t) = sgnX(i\Delta t) \\ sgng(i\Delta t)\cdot g(i\Delta t) = sgnX(i\Delta t)\ \cdot [X(i\Delta t) + \varepsilon(i\Delta t)] \\ R^*_{gg}(0) = \tfrac{1}{N}\sum_{i=1}^{N}\operatorname{sgn} g(i\Delta t)\ \cdot \big[g((i+\mu)\Delta t)\big] \end{cases}$$

expression (5) can also be reduced to the form

$$\begin{array}{c} R^*_{x\varepsilon}(\mu) \approx \frac{1}{N}\sum_{i=1}^{N} \mathrm{sgn}[X(i\Delta t)][X(i\Delta t) + \varepsilon(i\Delta t)] \\ -\frac{1}{N}\sum_{i=1}^{N} 2\mathrm{sgn}[X(i\Delta t)] \\ \times[X((i+1)\Delta t) + \varepsilon((i+1)\Delta t)] \\ +\frac{1}{N}\sum_{i=1}^{N} \mathrm{sgn}[X(i\Delta t)][X((i+2)\Delta t) + \varepsilon((i+2)\Delta t)] \end{array} \tag{6}$$

which, taking into account the equalities,

$$\left.\begin{array}{c} R^*_{XX}(0) + R^*_{XX}(2\Delta t) - 2R^*_{XX}(\Delta t) \approx 0 \\ R^*_{X\varepsilon}(\Delta t) = \frac{1}{N}\sum_{i=1}^{N} \mathrm{sgn}\, X(i\Delta t)\varepsilon((i+1)\Delta t) \approx 0 \\ R^*_{X\varepsilon}(2\Delta t) = \frac{1}{N}\sum_{i=1}^{N} X(i\Delta t)\varepsilon((i+2)\Delta t) \approx 0 \end{array}\right\}$$

can be considered true for expressions (6). Therefore, the beginning of the latent period of accidents can be determined based on the estimate $R^*_{X\varepsilon}(\mu\Delta t)$ of the relay cross-correlation function between the useful signal $X(i\Delta t)$ and the noise $\varepsilon(i\Delta t)$. Here, it is necessary to use the technology of adaptive sampling of the noisy signals $g(i\Delta t)$ according to formula (1).

Thus, in the process of operation of the object, from the initiation of various defects preceding accidents in the time period T1, as a result of the occurrence of the noise $\varepsilon_2(i\Delta t)$ $(\varepsilon(i\Delta t) = \varepsilon_1(i\Delta t) + \varepsilon_2(i\Delta t))$ the value of the estimate obtained by formula (5) will be different from zero, i.e.$R^*_{X\varepsilon}(\tau) \neq 0$, which can be used as an informative attribute for adaptive control the beginning of the latent period of accidentsT_1. In this case, the traditional control technology remains valid. The driver is additionally provided with an alternative technology to identify the beginning of the possible accident. It allows the driver to prevent an emergency situation by taking measures ahead of time. For this purpose, he is provided with information on the monitor on both existing and alternative technology. In the first variant, with the combination of signals on the driver's monitor

$$\begin{cases} T_{0C} = 0, T_{1C} = 0, T_{2C} = 0, T_{3C} = 0 \\ T_{0A} = 0, T_{1A} = 0, T_{2A} = 0, T_{3A} = 0 \end{cases}$$

it follows that the object is in normal state. In the second variant from the combination on the monitor

$$\begin{cases} T_{0C} = 0, T_{1C} = 0, T_{2C} = 0, T_{3C} = 0 \\ T_{0A} = 1, T_{1T} = 0, T_{2T} = 0, T_{3T} = 0 \end{cases}$$

it follows that the object, according to the alternative technology, has entered an emergency state; from the combination in the third case on the monitor

$$\begin{cases} T_{0C} = 1, T_{1c} = 0, T_{2C} = 0, T_{3C} = 0 \\ T_{0A} = 1, T_{1A} = 1, T_{2A} = 0, T_{3A} = 0 \end{cases}$$

it follows that the object, according to both technologies, has entered a latent emergency state.

Thus, according to the proposed technologies, the driver on the monitor of both existing and alternative technologies will receive information about the beginning of the latent period of an emergency state of the facility in advance. As a result, he will be able to reliably eliminate the cause of the beginning of the emergency state in a timely manner.

5 Possibility of Monitoring the Onset of Malfunctions Using the Positional Binary Technology

Studies [1–5] have shown that it is advisable to use the positional binary technology (PBT) for analyzing noisy vibration signals in systems of rail transport control and diagnostic systems to analyze vibration signals. [1].

It is known that in practice, when measuring signals $g(t)$, there is a minimum value of the increment Δx, which depends on the resolution of the instruments used. The values of the binary codes of the corresponding digits q_k of the samples of the sampled signal $X(i\Delta t)$ with a sampling interval Δt here are calculated based on the following algorithm [1–5]:

$$q_k(i\Delta t) = \begin{cases} 1 & \text{when} \quad x_{rem(k)}(i\Delta t) \geq \Delta x 2^k \\ 0 & \text{when} \quad x_{rem(k)}(i\Delta t) < \Delta x 2^k \end{cases}, \tag{7}$$

$$x_{rem(k)}(i\Delta t) = x_k(i\Delta t) - \left[q_{k+1}(i\Delta t) + q_{k+2}(i\Delta t) + \ldots + q_{(n-1)}(i\Delta t)\right],$$

where

$$X(i\Delta t) > 2^n,$$

$$x_{rem(n-1)}(i\Delta t) = X(i\Delta t),$$

$$n \geq \log \frac{x_{max}}{\Delta x}, \; k = n-1, n-2, \ldots, 1, 0.$$

In accordance with this algorithm, at each sampling interval Δt, the equality $x_{rem(n-1)}(i\Delta t) = X(i\Delta t)$ is initially assumed, and according to condition (7), signals $q_k(i\Delta t)$ are iteratively formed in the form of code 1 or 0. In the first step, $X(i\Delta t)$ is compared with the value $2^{n-1}\Delta x$. According to (7), if $X(i\Delta t) \geq 2^{n-1}\Delta x$, then the digit $q_{n-1}(i\Delta t)$ is set as equal to 1, and based on the difference

$$X(i\Delta t) - 2^{n-1}\Delta x = x_{rem(n-2)}$$

the value of the remainder $x_{rem(n-2)}$ is calculated. When $X(i\Delta t) < 2^{n-1}\Delta x$, the digit $q_{n-1}(i\Delta t)$ is set as equal to zero, and the difference remains unchanged. The same thing happens in the next iteration. As a result, in each conversion cycle with a sampling interval Δt, the signal $X(i\Delta t)$ is decomposed into signals $q_k(i\Delta t)$,, which take values of 1 or 0 and have weights corresponding to their positions. During the sampling process, the codes remain unchanged over time when the value of the original signal $X(i\Delta t)$ does not change. Hereinafter, these signals will be referred to as position-binary signals (PBS). Consequently, position-binary technology (PBT) for vibration signal analysis is a set of processing procedures based on the decomposition of the vibration signal into a position-binary signal PBS.

According to algorithm (7), in the process of analog-to-digital conversion, the width of the PBS will be proportional to the quantity of Δt when $q_k(i\Delta t)$ remains unchanged. Depending on the shape of $X(i\Delta t)$, the same signal $q_k(i\Delta t)$ can change its value several times at corresponding time intervals. Note that here $T_{k1_1}, T_{k1_2}, \ldots$ correspond to the time intervals when the condition $q_k(i\Delta t) = 2^k(\Delta x = 1)$; $T_{k0_1}, T_{k0_2}, \ldots$ correspond to the time intervals when the condition $q_k(i\Delta t) = 2^k(\Delta x = 0)$. is satisfied. Naturally, if the technical condition of an object operating in a cyclic mode remains unchanged, then the combinations of time intervals $T_{k1_1}, T_{k0_1}, T_{k1_2}, T_{k0_2}, \ldots$ of PBS in each cycle will be constant values and will be repeated. Otherwise, they will also change. According to expression (7), in each cycle, the sum of all PBS will be equal to the initial signal, i.e.

$$X(i\Delta t) \approx q_{n-1}(i\Delta t) + q_{n-2}(i\Delta t) + \ldots + q_1(i\Delta t) + q_0(i\Delta t) = g^*(i\Delta t).$$

Each $q_k(i\Delta t)$ here can be taken as a separate signal, and combinations of time interval sequences when $q_k(i\Delta t)$ are in the unit and zero states can be considered as informative attributes. Due to this, for vibration signals, these PBS $q_k(i\Delta t)$ will represent periodic rectangular pulses with corresponding unit T_1 and zero T_0 half-periods.

Due to the above, a change in the technical condition of the object leads to a change in the corresponding samples $X(i\Delta t)$ of the vibration signal by a quantity greater than Δx,, and this will be reflected in its corresponding digits $q_k(i\Delta t)$. Consequently, already at the initial stage of the malfunction, during the formation of the PBS in the form of a combination of the corresponding time intervals $q_{n-1}(i\Delta t), q_{n-2}(i\Delta t), \ldots, q_0(i\Delta t)$ of the current time instants, their difference from similar parameters of previous time instants will be detected, which will allow the formation and presentation of information about the beginning of a latent period of change in the technical condition of the controlled object. To do this, it is only necessary to calculate the average frequency $\langle f_k \rangle$ and period $\langle T_k \rangle$ of position-binary signals.

At the same time, the algorithms for their calculation are quite simple to implement in practice, since each position-vibration signal takes only two values. It is intuitively clear that for random and periodic noisy signals $g(i\Delta t)$, the average value of 0 and 1 half-periods of position signals $q_k(i\Delta t)$ with sufficient observation time T can be calculated using the formula

$$\langle T_{q_k} \rangle = \langle T_{1q_k} \rangle + \langle T_{0q_k} \rangle, \tag{8}$$

where

$$\begin{cases} \langle T_{1q_k} \rangle = \frac{1}{\gamma} \sum_{j=1}^{\gamma} T_{1q_{kj}} \\ \langle T_{0q_k} \rangle = \frac{1}{\gamma} \sum_{j=1}^{\gamma} T_{0q_{kj}} \end{cases}. \tag{9}$$

Here, γ is the number of 0 and 1 half-periods of PBS over observation time T, j is the sequence number of the q_k-th position of PBS.

In [1], it is shown that for a sufficient observation time, subject to the condition of stationarity, the estimate of the average duration of periods $\langle T_k \rangle$ and the average frequency f_{q_k} of PBS will be non-random values. Due to this, they can be used as an informative attribute to control the onset of changes in the technical condition of an object. At the same time, due to the simplicity of their calculation, the solution of control problems, which is traditionally solved using estimates of the correlation or spectral characteristics of random processes, is greatly simplified. In general, under normal stable technical conditions of a cyclic object, a set of combinations of average frequencies $q_k(i\Delta t)$. of the PBS can be formed from the signal $g(i\Delta t)$. Obviously, a change in the technical condition of the object will lead to a change in the combination of estimates of their average frequencies $\overline{f}_{q0}, \overline{f}_{q1}, \ldots, \overline{f}_{qm}$, which are determined by the expressions

$$\overline{f}_{q0} = \frac{1}{T_{q0}}, \overline{f}_{q1} = \frac{1}{T_{q1}}, \overline{f}_{q2} = \frac{1}{T_{q2}}, \ldots, \overline{f}_{qm} = \frac{1}{T_{qm}}.$$

and are non-random values.

Now let us consider the possibility of using the relationship between the beginning of the latent period of accidents and the estimates of the characteristics of positional binary signals [1–3]. For this purpose, according to expressions (8) and (9), combinations of estimates are determined by expressions

$$\begin{cases} \overline{f}_{q0} = \frac{1}{\langle T_{q0}\rangle}, \overline{f}_{q1} = \frac{1}{\langle T_{q1}\rangle}, \overline{f}_{q2} = \frac{1}{\langle T_{q2}\rangle}, \ldots, \overline{f}_{qm} = \frac{1}{\langle T_{qm}\rangle} \\ k_{fq_0} = \frac{f_{q1}}{f_{q0}}, k_{fq_1} = \frac{f_{q2}}{f_{q1}}, k_{fq_2} = \frac{f_{q3}}{f_{q2}}, \ldots, k_{fq_m} = \frac{f_{qm}}{f_{q_{m-1}}} \\ k_{q0} = \frac{\langle T_{q1}\rangle}{\langle T_{q2}\rangle}, k_{q1} = \frac{\langle T_{q2}\rangle}{\langle T_{q3}\rangle}, k_{q2} = \frac{\langle T_{q3}\rangle}{\langle T_{q4}\rangle}, \ldots, k_{qm} = \frac{\langle T_{qm}\rangle}{\langle T_{q_{m-1}}\rangle} \end{cases}$$

As a result, combinations of PBS frequencies $\overline{f}_{q0}, \overline{f}_{q1}, \overline{f}_{q2}, \ldots, \overline{f}_{qm}$ and combinations of ratios $k_{fq_0}, k_{fq_1}, k_{fq2}, \ldots, k_{fm}$ and $k_{q0}, k_{q1}, k_{q2}, \ldots, k_{qm}$ are formed. It is easy to see that by forming a set of reference informative attributes from them during the training process, it is possible to create intelligent technologies for monitoring the onset of a latent period of malfunctions on the railroad track.

Over time, the above informative attributes form a knowledge base consisting of a set W_j, by analyzing vibration signals received from all controlled objects during the day:

$$W_j = \left\{ \begin{array}{l} \overline{f}_{q0}^{max}, \overline{f}_{q1}^{max}, \ldots, \overline{k}_{fq0}^{max}, \overline{k}_{fq_1}^{max}, \ldots, \overline{k}_{q0}^{max}, \overline{k}_{q1}^{max} \\ \overline{f}_{q0}^{max}, \overline{f}_{q2}^{max}, \ldots, \overline{k}_{fq0}^{max}, \overline{k}_{fq_2}^{max}, \ldots, \overline{k}_{q0}^{max}, \overline{k}_{q2}^{max} \\ \overline{f}_{q0}^{max}, \overline{f}_{q3}^{max}, \ldots, \overline{k}_{fq0}^{max}, \overline{k}_{fq_3}^{max}, \ldots, \overline{k}_{q0}^{max}, \overline{k}_{q3}^{max} \\ \cdots\cdots\cdots\cdots\cdots\cdots\cdots\cdots\cdots\cdots \\ \cdots\cdots\cdots\cdots\cdots\cdots\cdots\cdots\cdots\cdots \\ \overline{f}_{q0}^{max}, \overline{f}_{qm}^{max}, \ldots, \overline{k}_{fq0}^{max}, \overline{k}_{fq_m}^{max}, \ldots, \overline{k}_{q0}^{max}, \overline{k}_{qm}^{max} \end{array} \right\}$$

As a result, within 24 h, based on information received from real objects, an array W_j is formed, reflecting their technical condition. After some time, the formation of another similar set W_{j+1} begins, and after another 8 h, this process is repeated and another set W_{j+2} is formed. Consequently, when the onset of a malfunction is established based on the estimates obtained, a set of informative attributes is formed. This makes it possible to increase the reliability of detecting the onset of a malfunction that causes concern and therefore requires unscheduled control.

Thus, information received from objects that generate "alarming" information is formed and transmitted to the control system. This process is repeated cyclically, ensuring the continuous operation of the system and thereby increasing the reliability of the objects.

6 Conclusion

1. Control systems of technical facilities do not provide monitoring and control of the beginning of the latent period of accidents. During this period the dynamics of operation of technological processes and the spectrum of analyzed signals change. In these cases, to ensure accident-free operation of technical facilities, it is necessary to control the beginning and dynamics of accident development. In vibration diagnostics the adequacy of the control result depends to a great extent on fulfillment of this condition. In this period noise has a significant diagnostic potential. To ensure the adequacy of vibration control results it is advisable to use it. Ignoring the noise as a carrier of diagnostic information makes it difficult to ensure the effectiveness of vibration control in practice. If this condition is fulfilled, it is possible to determine reliably enough the initial stages of malfunctions, which usually precede catastrophic accidents, based on the estimates of several informative attributes obtained from the analysis of various vibration signals.
2. In rail transport control and diagnostic systems, the most informative signals are vibration signals obtained at the outputs of vibration sensors, which can be installed in the most informative units of the rolling stock. As a rule, they have a highly noisy and abruptly changing step-wise shape. At the same time, the noises of these signals also carry diagnostic information, and their spectrum changes depending on the speed of the train.
3. In the East-West transport corridor, the railroad route is several thousand km long. For such cases, the method of scheduled control by track-testing cars becomes unreasonably expensive and hence unsatisfactory. Hence, for such cases it is necessary to reduce the number of track-testing cars. Therefore, it is advisable to create technologies for identifying suspicious track sections using the rolling stock itself in the time interval between two scheduled inspections. The implementation of this technology should be uncomplicated, inexpensive and reliable. At the same time, it should be maximally adapted to the specific features of the railroad track as a control object.
4. Analysis of accident causes has shown [14–17] that during rail transport operation, the occurrence of the latent period of malfunction is due to the fact that under conditions of continuous movement of rolling stock with heavy loads on the railroad track, the latter is subjected to destruction, fatigue cracks, residual stresses, fatigue damage, fatigue, wear, friction, and abrasions. To increase the reliability of operation, it is advisable to use control technology based on the estimate of the correlation function between the useful signal and the noise, as well as the estimates obtained by positional-binary analysis of vibration signals. For practical application of the proposed technology, it will be necessary to select the most suitable vibration sensors, controllers, and communication means, taking into account the specifics of railroad tracks. Only after further numerous experiments and improvements will the proposed technology find wide application in the rail transport safety system.

References

1. Aliev, T.: Noise control of the Beginning and Development Dynamics of Accidents, p. 201. Springer, Cham (2019)

2. Aliev, T., Babayev, T., Alizada, T., Rzayeva, N.: Control of the beginning of accidents in railroad operation safety systems in seismically active regions using the noise technology. Transp. Probl.: Int. Sci. J. **14**(3), 155–162 (2019)
3. Aliev, T., Babayev, T., Alizada, T., Rzayeva, N.: Noise control of the beginning and development dynamics of faults in the running gear of the rolling stock. Transp. Probl.: Int. Sci. J. **15**(2), 83–91 (2020)
4. Aliev, T., Babayev, T., Alizada, T., Rzayeva, N., Alibayli, E., Ahmedov, H.: Intelligent system of noise control of the technical condition of railroad tracks. Transp. Probl.: Int. Sci. J. **16**(1), 65–73 (2021)
5. Aliev, T., Musaeva, N., Babayev, T., Mammadova, A., Alibayli. E.: Technologies and intelligent systems for adaptive vibration control in rail transport. Transp. Probl.: Int. Sci. J. **17**(3), 31–38 (2022)
6. Musaeva, N.F.: A robust method of estimation under 'polluting' rough errors. Autom. Control. Comput. Sci. **6**, 50–64 (2003)
7. Musaeva, N.F.: Technology for determining the magnitude of robustness as an estimate of statistical characteristic of noisy signal. Autom. Control. Comput. Sci. **39**(5), 64–74 (2005)
8. Musaeva, N., Aliyev, E., Sattarova, U., Gadimov, R.: Technology and algorithms for monitoring of the technical condition of high-rise buildings, construction and strategic objects in seismically active regions by means of sets of informative attributes. In: 4th International Conference "Problems of Cybernetics and Informatics", PCI 2012 - Proceedings, vol. II, pp. 109–115, Baku (2012)
9. Musaeva, N., Aliyev, E., Sattarova, U., Rzayeva, N.: Correlation matrices in problems of identification of seismic stability and technical condition of high-rise buildings and building structures. In: 4th International Conference "Problems of Cybernetics and Informatics", PCI 2012 - Proceedings, vol. 2, pp. 116–123 (2012)
10. Collacott, R.A.: Mechanical fault diagnosis and condition monitoring, p. 506 (1977)
11. Thompson, D.: Railway Noise and Vibration: Mechanisms, Modelling and Means of Control, 1st edn. Kindle edn., p. 845 (2008)
12. Anderson, D., Gautier, P., Iida, M., et al.: Noise and vibration mitigation for rail transportation systems. In: Proceedings of the 12th International Workshop on Railway Noise, Terrigal, Australia, 12–16 September 2016 (2016)
13. Sun, C., Gao, L.: Medium-to-low-speed freight rail transport induced environmental vibration and analysis of the vibration isolation effect of building slope protection piles. J. Vibroeng. **19**(6), 4531–4549 (2017)
14. Машины и Оборудование для Диагностики Пути. Региональный Центр Инновационных Технологий. Путевые Машины, Применяемые ОАО "РЖД" Конструкция, Теория и Расчет, Глава 11
15. Ashpiz, Y.S.: Methods and Tools of Roadbed Diagnostics. Zheleznodorozhniy Put (2013)
16. Mikhalkin, I.K., Simakov, O.B., Sedelkin, Y.A., Atapin, V.V.: New Approaches to Monitoring the Railroad Track. NPTS INFOTRANS. (in Russian)
17. Осадчий, Г., Лыков, А.: Система Диагностики и Удаленного Мониторинга Состояния Железнодорожного Пути. Открытое Образование, Изд. Федеральное государственное бюджетное образовательное учреждение высшего образования "Российский экономический университет имени Г.В. Плеханова", pp. 221–224 (2011)

Technologies for Controlling the Rate of Railroad Track Malfunction Development Based on Ratios of Estimates of High-Order Characteristics

Telman Aliev[1,2], Naila Musaeva[1,2](✉), and Matanat Suleymanova[1,2]

[1] Institute of Control Systems, 68, B. Vahabzada, Baku 1141, Azerbaijan
musanaila@gmail.com

[2] Azerbaijan University of Architecture and Construction, 11, A. Sultanova, Baku 1073, Azerbaijan

Abstract. A railroad track requires continuous monitoring of its technical condition. In the previously proposed work, an intelligent system for identifying track sections requiring unscheduled inspection, installed in one of the rolling stock cars of a railroad bed, has been developed. A noisy vibration signal enters the system, and the characteristics of the noise are computed, which are further used as informative attributes to identify the initial latent period of malfunction initiation. For this purpose, the noise characteristics are transmitted via radio channel to the control station, where a knowledge base reflecting the technical condition of each section is formed.

In this paper, in order to increase the adequacy of the control results, we propose using ratios of the estimates of the high-order characteristics of the useful signal and noise as informative attributes. Due to the complexity of implementation of these characteristics, it is recommended to send the control result to the control station, where technical means are installed that allow to perform such calculations. Introduction of the proposed ratios in the knowledge base allows to reveal the dynamics of malfunction development. The use of the proposed technologies increases the degree of train traffic safety.

Keywords: railroad track · vibration signal · useful signal · noise · high-order moments · rate of malfunction development · informative attribute

1 Introduction

It is known that rail transport transports goods and people over long sections [1]. Compared to other modes of transport, it is a reliable, safe, environmentally friendly and economical means of transportation. For the movement of rail transport, a railroad bed is constructed, which includes the earth bed, sand cushion, ballast layer, sleepers, rails and track fastenings. At the same time, railroad tracks are subjected to significant wear and tear as a result of operation. In addition, the technical condition of railroad tracks is also greatly affected by such weather conditions as rain, snow, fog, strong wind, icing,

A. Abbasov et al. (Eds.): PLMO 2025, CCIS 2767, pp. 11–22, 2026.
https://doi.org/10.1007/978-3-032-13672-5_2

etc. [2]. Therefore, during the operation of the railroad bed, the quality and construction of the ballast layer changes, serious damages, cracks, malfunctions, defects, etc. of sleepers, rails, track fastenings, the condition of the subgrade, sand cushion, etc. emerge [3, 4].

To ensure the safe movement of trains, it is necessary to regularly monitor the technical condition of the railroad bed [2–4]. For this purpose, specialized track-testing cars, track recording cars and flaw detector cars are used on railroads [1, 2]. They work according to the schedule, periodically inspecting the condition of the track at each section. However, changes in the technical condition of track elements can occur hourly, daily due to various external influences.

In [5], an intelligent system for detecting railroad track sections requiring urgent immediate inspection is proposed. It states that the vibration signal arriving at the track testing car from ground vibrations contains a useful component and a noise, which cannot be separated from each other. The main indicators indicating early track defects are the estimates of the cross-correlation function, the Rayleigh cross-correlation function between the useful signal and the noise, the spectral characteristics of the noise, the estimates of the variance of the noise and the useful component, and the ratio of the variance of the useful signal to the noise. These noise characteristics are calculated by the controller of the intelligent system installed in the train car and transmitted via radio channel to the control station. In the control station, a knowledge base is formed from the values of the listed characteristics collected during the day. The characteristics included in the knowledge base are used as informative attributes of the initial latent stage of the malfunction occurrence at the corresponding section. Thus, by analyzing the knowledge base, the technical condition of the railroad track at each level section is assessed.

The analysis has shown that in order to improve the adequacy of the results of control of sections requiring unscheduled control, the knowledge base of informative attributes should be supplemented with new more sensitive characteristics that allow not only to identify the initial latent period of malfunction initiation, but also the dynamics of its development. Therefore, in this work we propose supplementing the knowledge base with new informative attributes in the form of estimates of the ratio of high order moments of the useful signal and the noise. However, the algorithms for calculating these features are quite complex and require a more powerful computer for implementation. Therefore, this paper proposes sending the noisy vibration signal to the control station for further processing using the algorithms developed below.

The use of estimates of the ratio of high-order moments of the useful signal and noise in the form of informative attributes improves the knowledge base described in [5]. Further development of technologies for analyzing the noise characteristics leads to the addition of the knowledge base and its improvement. As a result, it becomes possible to prevent serious damage and accidents, to ensure reliability and safety of railroad communication, to increase the efficiency of train traffic by increasing the number of informative attributes for assessing the technical condition of the railroad bed.

2 Problem Statement

As mentioned above, in order to ensure effective and continuous monitoring of the technical condition of the railroad bed, it is necessary to analyze the vibration signal that emerges from ground vibrations during the movement of rail vehicles [5–8]. Typically, the vibration signal $G(t)$ includes a useful component $X(t)$ and a noise $\mathrm{E}(t)$ [5, 9–12]:

$$G(t) = X(t) + \mathrm{E}(t).$$

$G(t)$, $X(t)$ and $\mathrm{E}(t)$ are stationary random processes with normal distribution law, mathematical expectations and variances

$$m_G = \sum_{i=1}^{N} G(i\Delta t),\ m_X = \sum_{i=1}^{N} X(i\Delta t),\ m_{\mathrm{E}} = 0, \tag{1}$$

$$D_G = \frac{\sum_{i=1}^{N} (G(i\Delta t) - m_G)^2}{N}, \tag{2}$$

$$D_X = \frac{\sum_{i=1}^{N} (X(i\Delta t) - m_X)^2}{N}, \tag{3}$$

$$D_{\mathrm{E}} = \frac{\sum_{i=1}^{N} (\mathrm{E}(i\Delta t) - m_{\mathrm{E}})^2}{N}. \tag{4}$$

In [5] it is noted that it is reasonable to use coefficients as informative attributes about the beginning of a malfunction on the railroad track:

$$K_{D-X\mathrm{E}} = \frac{D_X}{D_{\mathrm{E}}},$$

$$K_{D-G\mathrm{E}} = \frac{D_G}{D_{\mathrm{E}}},$$

$$K_{D-GX} = \frac{D_G}{D_X}. \tag{5}$$

These coefficients determine the noise content in the useful and noisy signals: the greater the values of coefficients (5), the lower the noise content. These coefficients are calculated by the intelligent system controller in the track testing car.

It is shown in [5, 9–15] that the noise consists of two components $\mathrm{E}_1(t)$ and $\mathrm{E}_2(t)$. The noise $\mathrm{E}_1(t)$ is caused by changes in external influences such as seismic effects, landslide processes, heavy rains, snow, hail, etc. [3, 4, 9]. This noise $\mathrm{E}_1(t)$ is not correlated with $X(t)$, i.e., correlation coefficient [5, 9–15]:

$$r_{X\mathrm{E}} = 0, \tag{6}$$

where

$$r_{X\mathrm{E}} = \frac{\sum_{i=1}^{N} (X(i\Delta t) - m_X)(\mathrm{E}(i\Delta t) - m_{\mathrm{E}})}{\sqrt{\sum_{i=1}^{N} (X(i\Delta t) - m_X)^2} \sqrt{\sum_{i=1}^{N} (\mathrm{E}(i\Delta t) - m_{\mathrm{E}})^2}}. \quad (7)$$

Noise $\mathrm{E}_2(t)$ is caused by damage, cracks, malfunctions, defects and other problems on sleepers, rails, track fastenings, as well as in the condition of the earth bed, sand cushion and other elements. It is shown in [5, 9–15] that in this case the correlation coefficient is non-zero:

$$r_{X\mathrm{E}} \neq 0. \quad (8)$$

Therefore, condition (8) is an indicator of the occurrence of a malfunction in the latent period at the railroad section. And conditions (5) allow us to judge the degree of contamination of $G(t)$ with the noise $\mathrm{E}(t)$.

However, a malfunction can develop very slowly, slowly, at an average rate, quickly, very quickly, rapidly. A defect that is insignificant in the initial period can quickly progress to a dangerous malfunction leading to an emergency condition, or vice versa. A defect that is significant may remain unchanged for quite a long time.

Therefore, in this paper, in order to determine the rate of malfunction development at each railroad section, it is proposed to use, in addition to conditions (5), the ratios of central moments of order q as informative attributes:

$$\begin{aligned} K_{\mu q-X\mathrm{E}} &= \frac{\mu_{Xq}}{\mu_{\mathrm{E}q}}, \\ K_{\mu q-G\mathrm{E}} &= \frac{\mu_{Gq}}{\mu_{\mathrm{E}q}}, \\ K_{\mu q-GX} &= \frac{\mu_{Gq}}{\mu_{Xq}}, \end{aligned} \quad (9)$$

$$\mu_{Xq} = \frac{\sum_{i=1}^{N} (X(i\Delta t) - m_X)^q}{N}, \quad (10)$$

$$\mu_{\mathrm{E}q} = \frac{\sum_{i=1}^{N} (\mathrm{E}(i\Delta t) - m_{\mathrm{E}})^q}{N}, \quad (11)$$

$$\mu_{Gq} = \frac{\sum_{i=1}^{N} (G(i\Delta t) - m_G)^q}{N}. \quad (12)$$

The analysis has shown that ratios (9) are more sensitive informative attributes determining the dynamics of malfunction development. However, the calculation of informative attributes (9) is rather complicated. Therefore, they should be calculated not by means of the intelligent system controller installed in the train car, but in the control station where the noisy vibration signal is sent.

The knowledge base described in [5] and updated with new informative attributes (9) can be used not only to identify the initial latent stage of a malfunction at the corresponding railroad section, but also to determine the rate of development of this malfunction. As a result, it becomes possible to evaluate the technical condition of the railroad track at each section more fully and accurately. Therefore, let us consider the issue of calculating informative attributes (9) and the possibility of using them to determine the period of defect initiation and intensity of its development at each railroad track section in more detail.

3 Technologies for Calculating Informative Attributes for Assessing the Technical Condition of Each Railroad Track Section

Informative attributes to assess the technical condition of each railroad track section can be divided into two categories: 1) those indicating the beginning of defects, damages, cracks, etc.; 2) those indicating the dynamics of malfunction development at the initial stage [9–11].

Let us consider the first category of informative attributes. It was noted above that an indicator of the occurrence of a defect, damage, crack, etc. on the railroad track is the presence of correlation between $X(t)$ and $\mathrm{E}(t)$. . To verify the fulfillment of condition (8), it would be necessary to calculate the correlation coefficient $r_{X\mathrm{E}}$ using formula (7). However, in practice, it is impossible to separate the samples $X(i\Delta t)$ and $\mathrm{E}(i\Delta t)$ from $G(i\Delta t)$. It was proved in [5] that the following formula can be used to calculate the correlation coefficient between $X(t)$ and $\mathrm{E}(t)$:

$$r^*_{X\mathrm{E}} = \frac{R^{r*}_{X\mathrm{E}}(0)}{\sqrt{\frac{2}{\pi} \cdot D^*_{\mathrm{E}}}}, \tag{13}$$

where $R^{r*}_{X\mathrm{E}}(\mu)$ is the relay cross-correlation function between $X(t)$ and $\mathrm{E}(t)$:

$$R^{r*}_{X\mathrm{E}}(0) = R^r_{GG}(0) - 2R^r_{GG}(1) + R^r_{GG}(2), \tag{14}$$

$R^r_{GG}(\mu)$ is the relay correlation function of $G(t)$:

$$R^r_{GG}(\mu) = \frac{1}{N}\sum_{i=1}^{N} \operatorname{sgn} \overset{\circ}{G}(i\Delta t)\, \overset{\circ}{G}((i+\mu)\Delta t), \tag{15}$$

$$\mathrm{sgnG}(i\Delta t) = \begin{cases} +1 \; \textit{if} \;\; \overset{\circ}{G}(i\Delta t) > 0 \\ 0 \; \textit{if} \;\; \overset{\circ}{G}(i\Delta t) = 0 \\ -1 \; \textit{if} \;\; \overset{\circ}{G}(i\Delta t) < 0 \end{cases},$$

$$\overset{\circ}{G}(i\Delta t) = G(i\Delta t) - m_G,$$

D^*_{E} is the variance of $\mathrm{E}(t)$:

$$D^*_{\mathrm{E}} = R_{GG}(0) - 2R_{GG}(\Delta t) + R_{GG}(2\Delta t), \tag{16}$$

$R_{GG}(\mu)$ is the autocorrelation function of $G(t)$:

$$R_{GG}(\mu) = \frac{1}{N}\sum_{i=1}^{N} \overset{\circ}{G}(i\Delta t)\,\overset{\circ}{G}((i+\mu)\Delta t). \tag{17}$$

3.1 Technologies for Calculating the Indicator of the Dynamics of Railroad Track Malfunction Development

Let us consider the possibility of calculating the indicator of determining the dynamics of the development of the malfunction of the railroad track on the ratios of high-order moments of useful signal and noise. To calculate ratios (9) it is necessary to know the central moments of the high-order of the noisy signal, the useful signal and the noise. It is known that for ergodic stationary random normally distributed processes $G(t)$, $X(t)$, $\mathrm{E}(t)$ it is always possible to calculate the high-order central moments using recurrence ratios:

$$\mu_{Gq} = (q-1)D_G\mu_{G(q-2)},$$

$$\mu_{Xq} = (q-1)D_X\mu_{X(q-2)},$$

$$\mu_{\mathrm{E}q} = (q-1)D_{\mathrm{E}}\mu_{\mathrm{E}(q-2)}. \tag{18}$$

The variances D_G, D_{E} can be calculated using formulas (2), (16), and for D_X taking into account expressions (13) and (17) at $\mu = 0$ we obtain:

$$D^*_X = D_G - 2r^*_{X\mathrm{E}} - D^*_{\mathrm{E}}. \tag{19}$$

Then we have:

$$\mu_{Gq} = (q-1)D_G\mu_{G(q-2)},$$

$$\mu^*_{Xq} = (q-1)D^*_X\mu^*_{X(q-2)},$$

$$\mu^*_{\mathrm{E}q} = (q-1)D^*_{\mathrm{E}}\mu^*_{\mathrm{E}(q-2)}, \tag{20}$$

$$K^*_{\mu q-X\mathrm{E}} = \frac{\mu^*_{Xq}}{\mu^*_{\mathrm{E}q}},$$

$$K^*_{\mu q-G\mathrm{E}} = \frac{\mu_{Gq}}{\mu^*_{\mathrm{E}q}},$$

$$K^*_{\mu q-GX} = \frac{\mu_{Gq}}{\mu^*_{Xq}}. \tag{21}$$

Ratios (21) can be used for more accurate and effective assessment of the technical condition of the railroad track taking into account the dynamics of the malfunction development at the initial stage.

4 Technologies for Assessing the Dynamics of Malfunction Development at Each Railroad Track Section

It is said in [5] that in addition to the value of the correlation coefficient between $X(t)$ and $\mathrm{E}(t)$ and ratios (5), the ratios of the relay cross-correlation function $R^{r*}_{X\mathrm{E}}(\mu)$ and the cross-correlation function $R^{*}_{X\mathrm{E}}(\mu)$ between $X(t)$ and $\mathrm{E}(t)$ to D^{*}_{X} and D^{*}_{E} can also be used as informative attributes of malfunction initiation on a railroad track section:

$$K^{*}_{R-D\mathrm{E}} = \frac{R^{*}_{X\mathrm{E}}(\mu)}{D^{*}_{\mathrm{E}}},$$

$$K^{*}_{R-X} = \frac{R^{*}_{X\mathrm{E}}(\mu)}{D^{*}_{X}}, \quad (22)$$

$$K^{*}_{Rr-\mathrm{E}} = \frac{R^{r*}_{X\mathrm{E}}(\mu)}{D^{*}_{\mathrm{E}}},$$

$$K^{*}_{Rr-X} = \frac{R^{r*}_{X\mathrm{E}}(\mu)}{D^{*}_{X}}, \quad (23)$$

which are calculated by the intelligent system controller in the track testing car.

Indicators (5), (22), (23) are compared with the reference ones obtained as a result of training. If for a day m out of n rolling stock that passed along the same section recorded that condition (8) is fulfilled with the ratio

$$\frac{m}{n} \geq 0,5$$

and (5), (22), (23) do not exceed critical values

$$K^{*}_{D-X\mathrm{E}} = \frac{D^{*}_{X}}{D^{*}_{\mathrm{E}}} \leq K^{*}_{D-X\mathrm{E},c},$$

$$K^{*}_{D-G\mathrm{E}} = \frac{D_{G}}{D^{*}_{\mathrm{E}}} \leq K^{*}_{D-G\mathrm{E},c},$$

$$K^{*}_{D-GX} = \frac{D_{G}}{D^{*}_{X}} \leq K^{*}_{D-GX,c}, \quad (24)$$

$$K^{*}_{R-D\mathrm{E}} \neq K_{R-D\mathrm{E},c},$$

$$K^{*}_{R-X} \neq K_{R-X,c},$$

$$K^{*}_{Rr-\mathrm{E}} \neq K_{Rr-\mathrm{E},c},$$

$$K^{*}_{Rr-X} \neq K_{Rr-X,c}, \quad (25)$$

then a signal is generated about the occurrence of a malfunction at the current railroad section. This information is sent to the control station.

In this paper it is proposed to send the vibration signal itself to the control station simultaneously with the estimates of characteristics (13), (5), (22), (23). The values of ratios (24) are recorded in the control station for the current railroad track section. These values are considered as initial estimates for analyzing the dynamics of malfunction development.

Let us consider the technology of determining the dynamics of malfunction development on the example of the ratio K^*_{D-XE}. Suppose that at the moment t_0 of vibration signal arrival the value of this relation is:

$$K^*_{D-X\mathrm{E},c,t0} = \frac{D^*_{X,t0}}{D^*_{\mathrm{E},t0}}. \tag{26}$$

Then the control station, taking into account formula (20), calculates ratios (21):

$$K^*_{\mu q-X\mathrm{E},t0} = \frac{\mu^*_{Xq,t0}}{\mu^*_{\mathrm{E}q,t0}}. \tag{27}$$

After some time at the time t_1, new values of ratios (24) are received in the control station, and $K^*_{\mu q-X\mathrm{E},t1}$ are calculated for t_1.

If

$$K^*_{D-X\mathrm{E},c,t0} = K^*_{D-X\mathrm{E},c,t1},$$

it means that the content of $\mathrm{E}(t)$ in $G(t)$ has remained the same, the malfunction on the railroad section under investigation is not progressing, and the dynamics is zero.

If

$$K^*_{D-X\mathrm{E},c,t0} \approx K^*_{D-X\mathrm{E},c,t1},$$

it means that the content of $\mathrm{E}(t)$ in $G(t)$ has changed insignificantly.

Then we should compare the ratios of the fourth-order moments

$$\Delta K^*_{\mu 4-X\mathrm{E},t0-t1} = \left| K^*_{\mu 4-X\mathrm{E},t0} - K^*_{\mu 4-X\mathrm{E},t1} \right|, \tag{28}$$

then we should calculate:

$$\Delta K^*_{\mu 6-X\mathrm{E},t0-t1} = \left| K^*_{\mu 6-X\mathrm{E},t0} - K^*_{\mu 6-X\mathrm{E},t1} \right| \tag{29}$$

and compare it with the reference value

$$\Delta K^*_{\mu 6-X\mathrm{E},t0-t1} \leq ET^*_{\mu 6-X\mathrm{E},t0-t1}. \tag{30}$$

This process should be continued until, at some q, the difference of the moment ratio exceeds the reference value

$$\Delta K^*_{\mu q-X\mathrm{E},t0-t1} = \left| K^*_{\mu q-X\mathrm{E},t0} - K^*_{\mu q-X\mathrm{E},t1} \right| > ET^*_{\mu q-X\mathrm{E},t0-t1}. \tag{31}$$

Then it is necessary to fix the order of moments in ratios (21), and to establish the relationship between this order and the degree of malfunction development. Obviously, the higher the order of moments in (31), the lower the dynamics of malfunction development.

If the following conditions are met:

$$K^*_{D-X\mathrm{E},c,t0} - K^*_{D-X\mathrm{E},c,t1} = ET^*_{D-X\mathrm{E},c,t0-t1}, \tag{32}$$

then the content of $\mathrm{E}(t)$ in $G(t)$ is significant. Then the conditions (28), (30), (31) should be checked again, the order should be fixed and the relationship with the degree of malfunction hazard should be established.

If the following conditions are met:

$$K^*_{D-X\mathrm{E},c,t0} - K^*_{D-X\mathrm{E},c,t1} >> ET^*_{D-X\mathrm{E},c,t0-t1}, \tag{33}$$

then the malfunction development is unacceptably intensive and urgent emergency repair of the railroad section is required.

A similar analysis is performed for the ratios $K^*_{D-G\mathrm{E},c}$, $K^*_{D-GX,c}$ from expression (24):

$$K^*_{D-G\mathrm{E},c,t0} = \frac{D_{G,t0}}{D^*_{\mathrm{E},t0}},\ K^*_{\mu q-G\mathrm{E},t0} = \frac{\mu_{Gq,t0}}{\mu^*_{\mathrm{E}q,t0}},$$

$$K^*_{D-G\mathrm{E},c,t0} = K^*_{D-G\mathrm{E},c,t1},\ K^*_{D-G\mathrm{E},c,t0} \approx K^*_{D-G\mathrm{E},c,t1},$$

$$\Delta K^*_{\mu 4-G\mathrm{E},t0-t1} = \left|K^*_{\mu 4-G\mathrm{E},t0} - K^*_{\mu 4-G\mathrm{E},t1}\right|,\ \Delta K^*_{\mu 6-G\mathrm{E},t0-t1} = \left|K^*_{\mu 6-G\mathrm{E},t0} - K^*_{\mu 6-G\mathrm{E},t1}\right|,$$

$$\Delta K^*_{\mu 6-G\mathrm{E},t0-t1} \le ET^*_{\mu 6-G\mathrm{E},t0-t1},$$

$$\Delta K^*_{\mu q-G\mathrm{E},t0-t1} = \left|K^*_{\mu q-G\mathrm{E},t0} - K^*_{\mu q-G\mathrm{E},t1}\right| > ET^*_{\mu q-G\mathrm{E},t0-t1},$$

$$K^*_{D-G\mathrm{E},c,t0} - K^*_{D-G\mathrm{E},c,t1} = ET^*_{D-G\mathrm{E},c,t0-t1},$$

$$K^*_{D-G\mathrm{E},c,t0} - K^*_{D-G\mathrm{E},c,t1} >> ET^*_{D-G\mathrm{E},c,t0-t1}$$

and

$$K^*_{D-GX,c,t0} = \frac{D_{G,t0}}{D^*_{X,t0}},\ K^*_{\mu q-GX,t0} = \frac{\mu_{Gq,t0}}{\mu^*_{Xq,t0}},$$

$$K^*_{D-GX,c,t0} = K^*_{D-GX,c,t1},\ K^*_{D-GX,c,t0} \approx K^*_{D-GX,c,t1},$$

$$\Delta K^*_{\mu 4-GX,t0-t1} = \left|K^*_{\mu 4-GX,t0} - K^*_{\mu 4-GX,t1}\right|,\ \Delta K^*_{\mu 6-GX,t0-t1} = \left|K^*_{\mu 6-GX,t0} - K^*_{\mu 6-GX,t1}\right|,$$

$$\Delta K^*_{\mu 6-GX,t0-t1} \le ET^*_{\mu 6-GX,t0-t1},$$

$$\Delta K^*_{\mu q-GX,t0-t1} = \left|K^*_{\mu q-GX,t0} - K^*_{\mu q-GX,t1}\right| > ET^*_{\mu q-GX,t0-t1},$$

$$K^*_{D-GX,c,t0} - K^*_{D-GX,c,t1} = ET^*_{D-GX,c,t0-t1},$$

$$K^*_{D-GX,c,t0} - K^*_{D-GX,c,t1} >> ET^*_{D-GX,c,t0-t1}.$$

Thus, the knowledge base of the technical state of the railroad track section is supplemented in the control station with new characteristics in the form of ratios of moments of high orders of useful signal and noise, characterizing the dynamics of malfunction development:

$$D = \begin{pmatrix} K^*_{D-X\mathrm{E},c,t0} & K^*_{D-X\mathrm{E},c,t1} & \cdots & K^*_{D-X\mathrm{E},c,tn} \\ K^*_{\mu q-X\mathrm{E},t0} & K^*_{\mu q-X\mathrm{E},t1} & \cdots & K^*_{\mu q-X\mathrm{E},tn} \\ K^*_{D-G\mathrm{E},c,t0} & K^*_{D-G\mathrm{E},c,t1} & \cdots & K^*_{D-G\mathrm{E},c,tn} \\ K^*_{\mu q-G\mathrm{E},t0} & K^*_{\mu q-G\mathrm{E},t1} & \cdots & K^*_{\mu q-G\mathrm{E},tn} \\ K^*_{D-GX,c,t0} & K^*_{D-GX,c,t1} & \cdots & K^*_{D-GX,c,tn} \\ K^*_{\mu q-GX,t0} & K^*_{\mu q-GX,t1} & \cdots & K^*_{\mu q-GX,tn} \end{pmatrix}. \tag{34}$$

Based on the knowledge base (34), warning messages are generated in the control station: the dynamics of malfunction development is zero, weak, medium, intensive, emergency-hazardous.

5 Conclusion

This paper proposes to extend the already existing knowledge base of an intelligent system designed to identify railroad track sections in need of unscheduled inspection. This extension consists in the calculation of new characteristics of the vibration noisy signal that determine the dynamics of the malfunction development. These include the ratios of high-order moments of the useful signal and the noise. The combined use of technologies for calculating the noise characteristics [16–19] that identify the initial latent period of a malfunction, as well as determining the rate of progression of the malfunction, allows the traffic safety center to service the most dangerous sections of railroad track out of turn, without waiting for scheduled inspections. As a result, the reliability of railroad track condition monitoring is improved.

References

1. Fomenko, A., Vyshnia, V.: Specialized automated system for control and support of rail cargo transportation. Int. J. Comput. **18**(2), 191–200 (2019). https://doi.org/10.47839/ijc.18.2.1417
2. Manakov, A.L., Abramov, A.D., Ilinykh, A.S., Bekher, S.A., Igumnov, A.A., Kolarz, S.A.: The stabilization control of the railroad track. Transp. Res. Procedia **61**, 681–690 (2022). https://doi.org/10.1016/j.trpro.2022.01.108

3. Toosi, T., Sirola, M., Laukkanen, J., van Heeswijk, M., Karhunen, J.: Method for detecting aging related failures of process sensors via noise signal measurement. Int. J. Comput. **18**(2), 135–146 (2019). https://doi.org/10.47839/ijc.18.2.1412
4. Metin, M., Guclu, R.: Rail vehicle vibrations control using parameters adaptive PID controller. Math. Probl. Eng. 1–10 (2014). https://doi.org/10.1155/2014/728946
5. Aliev, T.A., Babayev, T.A., Musaeva, N.F., Gadimov, R.M., Mammadova, A.I.: An intelligent system for identifying track hauls requiring out-of-turn control of the railroad bed. Mekhatronika, Avtomatizatsiya, Upravlenie **25**(5), 223–230 (2024). https://doi.org/10.17587/mau.25.223-230
6. Prodeus, A., Didkovska, M.: Audio signals clipping detection using kurtosis and its transforms. Int. J. Comput. **19**(3), 411–417 (2020)
7. Anderson, D., Gautier, P.E., Iida, M., et al.: Noise and vibration mitigation for rail transportation systems. In: Proceedings of the 12th International Workshop on Railway Noise, Terrigal, Australia, 12–16 September 2016. https://doi.org/10.1007/978-3-319-73411-8
8. Dudkin, E.P., Andreeva, L.A., Sultanov, N.N.: Methods of noise and vibration protection on urban rail transport. Procedia Eng. **189**, 829–835 (2017). https://doi.org/10.1016/j.proeng.2017.05.129
9. Aliev, T.: Noise control of the Beginning and Development Dynamics of Accidents, p. 201. Springer, Cham (2019). https://doi.org/10.1007/978-3-030-12512-7
10. Aliev, T., Musaeva, N., Babayev, T., Mammadova, A., Alibayli, E.: Technologies and intelligent systems for adaptive vibration control in rail transport. Transp. Probl.: Int. Sci. J. **17**(3), 31–38 (2022). https://doi.org/10.20858/tp.2022.17.3.03
11. Aliev, T.A., Musaeva, N.F.: Technologies for monitoring the technical condition of transport infrastructure objects based on the coefficient of correlation between critical values of noise and useful signals. Transp. Probl.: Int. Sci. J. **17**(2), 213–224 (2022). https://doi.org/10.20858/tp.2022.17.2.18
12. Aliev, T.A., Musaeva, N.F., Suleymanova, M.T., Gazizade, B.I.: Technology for calculating the parameters of the density function of the normal distribution of the useful component in a noisy process. J. Autom. Inf. Sci. **48**(4), 39–55 (2016). https://doi.org/10.1615/JAutomatInfScien.v48.i4.50
13. Aliev, T.A., Musaeva, N.F., Sattarova, U.E.: Robust technologies for calculating normalized correlation functions. Cybern. Syst. Anal. **46**(10), 153–166 (2010). https://doi.org/10.1007/s10559-010-9194-1
14. Aliev, T.A., Musaeva, N.F.: Technologies for early monitoring of technical objects using the estimates of noise distribution density. J. Autom. Inf. Sci. **51**(9), 12–23 (2019). https://doi.org/10.1615/JAutomatInfScien.v51.i9.20
15. Aliev, T.A., Musaeva, N.F., Gazizade, B.I.: Calculation algorithms of the high order moments of interference of noisy signals. J. Autom. Inf. Sci. **50**(6), 1–13 (2018). https://doi.org/10.1615/JAutomatInfScien.v50.i6.10
16. Musaeva, N.F.: A robust method of estimation under 'polluting' rough errors. Autom. Control Comput. Sci. **6**, 50–64 (2003). https://www.scopus.com/record/display.uri?eid=2-s2.0-1542579519&origin=recordpage
17. Musaeva, N.F.: Technology for determining the magnitude of robustness as an estimate of statistical characteristic of noisy signal. Autom. Control Comput. Sci. **39**(5), 64–74 (2005). https://www.scopus.com/record/display.uri?eid=2-s2.0-25144507620&origin=recordpage
18. Musaeva, N., Aliyev, E., Sattarova, U., Gadimov, R.: Technology and algorithms for monitoring of the technical condition of high-rise buildings, construction and strategic objects in seismically active regions by means of sets of informative attributes. In: 4th International Conference "Problems of Cybernetics and Informatics", PCI 2012 - Proceedings, Baku, vol. II, pp. 109–115 (2012). https://www.scopus.com/record/display.uri?eid=2-s2.0-84876004916&origin=recordpage

19. Musaeva, N., Aliyev, E., Sattarova, U., Rzayeva, N.: Correlation matrices in problems of identification of seismic stability and technical condition of high-rise buildings and building structures. In: 4th International Conference "Problems of Cybernetics and Informatics", PCI 2012 - Proceedings, vol. 2, pp. 116–123 (2012). https://www.scopus.com/record/display.uri?eid=2-s2.0-84875984284&origin=recordpage

Managing Possible Risks in the Field of Transport and Logistics

Aygun Aliyeva[1,2](✉) and Sayyad Agayev[1,3,4]

[1] Institute of Control Systems of Ministry of Science and Education, 68 B.Vahabzade, Baku AZ1141, Azerbaijan
aliyevaaygun1978@gmail.com
[2] Azerbaijan University of Architecture and Construction, Ayna Sultanova 11, Baku, Azerbaijan
[3] Academy of State Customs Committee, Baku, Azerbaijan
[4] Azerbaijan State Oil and Industry University, Azadliq Avenue 34, Baku, Azerbaijan

Abstract. Logistics plays a vital role in sustaining business competitiveness by enhancing customer satisfaction and reducing costs through process efficiency improvements. It serves as a critical link between internal business functions and external partners—both upstream (suppliers) and downstream (distributors/customers) to achieve synergistic outcomes within operational constraints.

As businesses expand globally, they are increasingly challenged to balance customer service excellence with the growing complexity of logistics networks. Globalization forces enterprises to navigate trade-offs between responsiveness and operational efficiency, often under tight timelines and resource limitations.

In today's era of globalized business operations, logistics systems face numerous uncertainties and disruptions. Serious transportation accidents and natural disasters are reported worldwide on an almost monthly basis, highlighting the vulnerability of these systems. Consequently, the development of effective and efficient risk management strategies has become a top priority for logistics professionals. This paper provides a concise exploration of risk management in logistics systems across several key areas: disruption risk management, operational risk control, disaster and emergency response, and logistics service risk analysis. Additionally, it reviews the contributions of the papers featured in this special issue. The paper concludes by proposing a range of future research directions aimed at enhancing risk management practices in logistics systems.

The article also provides an econometric assessment of the dependence of freight transportation on the volume of investment in fixed capital. Understanding the elasticity between investments in fixed capital and cargo transportation volumes provides important insights for risk management in the transport and logistics sector.

Keywords: Risk Management · Logistic · Transport · Financial Impact · Economic Growth

A. Abbasov et al. (Eds.): PLMO 2025, CCIS 2767, pp. 23–32, 2026.
https://doi.org/10.1007/978-3-032-13672-5_3

1 Introduction

Logistics is a critical process that links product manufacturing activities from suppliers to end customers. The "Journal of Business Logistics" defines logistics as "the process of planning, implementing, and controlling the efficient, effective flow and storage of goods, services, and related information from the point of origin to the point of consumption, for the purpose of conforming to customer requirements." Traditionally, logistics focused on managing the physical delivery and storage of goods in a cost-effective manner to meet business needs [1]. However, increasing market competition has compelled businesses to adopt strategies aimed at achieving the "seven rights" of logistics: delivering the right product, to the right customer, in the right place, at the right time, in the right quantity, with the right quality, and at the right price. Coordinating all seven elements is a complex task that requires seamless integration across internal departments and external partners to achieve a synergistic outcome.

In global business operations, achieving the "seven rights" of logistics heavily depends on collaboration with external resources, including both upstream suppliers and downstream partners. The key to successful logistics management lies in the integration of activities, cooperation, coordination, and effective information sharing throughout the entire supply chain—from suppliers to end customers. Rapid advancements in information technology have significantly supported logistics management by enabling seamless data exchange and communication across process flows. Technologies such as barcodes, RFID, point-of-sale systems, EDI, VPNs, and ERP systems not only help reduce the complexity of physical operations but also lower uncertainty through improved information visibility and sharing among supply chain partners [2].

Beyond managing internal operations, logistics outcomes are also influenced by a range of external and internal disruptions. For instance, the eruption of Iceland's volcano disrupted airline schedules, while rising labor costs have forced manufacturers to relocate—both of which can increase logistics complexity and costs.

However, disruptions do not necessarily lead to losses unless an enterprise's vulnerabilities increase its exposure to risk. In general, sources of threats or disruptions can be categorized as either exogenous (external) or endogenous (internal). Enterprises cannot entirely avoid uncertainty from either category; instead, the extent of potential losses depends on how effectively risks are identified and mitigated before they occur. Furthermore, the more complex a process becomes, the greater the likelihood of vulnerability to risk. In today's global business environment, enterprises must expand their operations and networks across countries to serve customers in local markets. This naturally extends logistics processes and adds more activities, which in turn increases exposure to various risks [3].

At the same time, any disruption occurring at a single node within the logistics flow can impact the performance of the entire logistics system. Moreover, logistics complexity is closely tied to the nature of business relationships with partners and the deployment of business strategies. For instance, in a lean production model, inventory holding costs are minimized to reduce waste and improve efficiency. In contrast, a rapid response strategy may require maintaining higher inventory levels as a trade-off to ensure flexibility and responsiveness. Therefore, all logistics activities must be carefully planned and executed in alignment with the overall strategy. Any unplanned disruption can compromise the intended performance outcomes. To sustain logistics performance, risk management should be integrated into the broader enterprise risk management framework.

Just as business development evolves to meet changing demands, logistics must also adapt to support new business requirements. Naturally, these changes introduce additional risks throughout the supply chain. As a result, adaptive logistics systems are essential to remain competitive in the market, and a commitment to continuous improvement in risk management must be established.

In the following sections, we will explore the various risks present in logistics systems and outline ongoing risk management processes. Techniques for risk identification and assessment will also be described for reference.

Logistics, by definition, is a process that connects product manufacturing activities from suppliers to end customers. It involves the planning, implementation, and control of the efficient and effective flow and storage of goods, services, and related information from the point of origin to the point of consumption, with the goal of meeting customer requirements.

From a logistics function perspective, logistics was initially defined as the management of physical delivery and storage, focused on efficiency to meet enterprise business requirements. However, increasing market competition has driven changes in business strategies, leading to the provision of additional services such as Vendor Managed Inventory (VMI) and cross-docking warehouse operations. Furthermore, globalization has introduced more complex supply chain structures, including configuration assembly and multiple dispatching centers, resulting in intricate logistics networks and increased inventory within the logistics pipeline. As a result, managing logistics effectively and efficiently has evolved from an operational necessity into a core business strategy essential for the long-term sustainability and competitiveness of enterprises [4].

According to the Council of Supply Chain Management Professionals, logistics management should aim to achieve the "seven rights": delivering the right product, to the right customer, in the right place, at the right time, in the right quantity, with the right quality, and at the right price. Coordinating all seven elements is a complex task that requires seamless integration across internal departments and external partners to produce a synergistic outcome. In a global business environment, achieving these objectives depends heavily on collaboration with external resources, including both upstream suppliers and downstream distribution partners. Therefore, the key to successful logistics management lies in the integration of activities, strong cooperation, effective coordination, and consistent information sharing throughout the entire supply chain—from suppliers to end customers [8].

Continuous advancements in information technology have significantly supported logistics management by enhancing data exchange and communication across the entire process flow. Technologies such as barcodes, RFID, point-of-sale systems, Electronic Data Interchange (EDI), Virtual Private Networks (VPN), and Enterprise Resource Planning (ERP) systems not only help reduce the complexity of physical logistics processes but also minimize uncertainty through real-time information sharing among supply chain partners [5].

2 Risk Management

In recent years, risk management has gained significant attention, particularly in light of various global disruption events such as earthquakes, the eruption of Iceland's volcano, rising labor wages in China, and the BP oil spill. Each of these incidents has demonstrated the vulnerability of global supply chains and the necessity for businesses to adjust their logistics systems in response to unexpected disturbances. The impact of such accidental events can be significantly minimized if an enterprise has proactive risk management plans in place [6].

Generally, risk management in logistics can be classified into two main approaches:

- Mitigation Strategy: This approach focuses on managing and reducing risk at its source. The goal is to prevent risks from occurring or to reduce their likelihood and potential impact. This includes actions such as diversifying suppliers, improving infrastructure, investing in forecasting systems, and enhancing quality control processes.
- Contingency Strategy: This approach involves managing the consequences of a risk event once it has occurred. It includes having predefined response plans, backup suppliers, emergency logistics arrangements, and crisis communication strategies to ensure business continuity and minimize disruption [7].

Both strategies are essential and should be integrated into a comprehensive risk management framework to enhance resilience and adaptability in logistics systems.

3 Theoretical Aspects of the Impact of Investment in Fixed Capital on Freight Transportation Volume

Fixed capital investments represent investments in long-term assets required to maintain and expand the production base of the economy. In the transport industry, this includes financing road construction, fleet modernization, renovation of railway infrastructure, ports, airports, etc.

The impact of investment on freight transportation is manifested through several key channels:

1. *Increased infrastructure capacity.* Investments in expanding and upgrading transportation infrastructure increase the physical capacity to move large volumes of freight. For example, the construction of new highways, rail lines, and port terminals allows more freight to be moved in less time and at lower costs [8].
2. *Increased efficiency of transportation facilities.* Updating fleets and rolling stock results in lower operating costs, higher payload capacity, and faster delivery speeds. Modern vehicles are more reliable and fuel efficient, making transportation more economical.
3. *Reduced logistics costs.* Quality infrastructure and modernized transportation reduces the cost of delivering goods, time wastage and spoilage of goods. This en-courages companies to increase the volume of goods transported as transportation costs become less burdensome.
4. *Increased economic activity.* Transportation investments are often accompa-nied by a multiplier effect - an increase in economic activity.

4 Econometric Assessment of the Dependence of Freight Transportation on the Volume of Investment in Fixed Capital

In addition to the oil sector, Azerbaijan is also rapidly developing the transportation sector, as well as the spheres included in the non-oil sector. By 2024, Azerbaijan's transport enterprises transported 229,897 thousand tons of cargo [13]. Improving the quality of cargo transportation, timely delivery of cargo to the destination point, minimization of travel time, compliance with environmental requirements are priority tasks in the transport industry [14].

Data for econometric evaluation of the dependence of freight transportation in the Republic of Azerbaijan on the volume of investment in fixed capital were taken from the website of the State Statistical Committee of the Republic of Azerbaijan [15, 16].

Based on the data in Table 1, the econometric evaluation of the dependence of freight transportation on the volume of investment in fixed capital was carried out.

Table 1. Parameters of econometric estimation, tests of their reliability.

Variable	Coefficient	Std. Error	t-Statistic	Prob.
FCIT (-2)	0.216408	0.013772	15.71358	0.0000
C	3.711565	0.093597	39.65461	0.0000
R-squared	0.918190	Mean dependent var		5.149209
Adjusted R-squared	0.914472	S.D. dependent var		0.330786
S.E. of regression	0.096739	Akaike info criterion		-1.753939
Sum squared resid	0.205887	Schwarz criterion		-1.655768
Log likelihood	23.04727	Hannan-Quinn criter		-1.727894
F-statistic	246.9166	Durbin-Watson stat		1.206122
Prob(F-statistic)	0.000000			

Source: Results of calculations performed using the software package "EViews 13".

Quantitative characteristics of the impact of investment in fixed capital on freight transportation were estimated econometrically based on the data in Table 1. Based on the statistical base given in [15, 16], a logarithmic-logarithmic model of the dependence of freight transportation on the volume of investment in fixed capital was built. The mathematical representation of the model obtained in the program complex "EViews 13" is as follows [17–20]:

$$LN\_CT = 3.71156483989 + 0.21640805826 * LN\_FCIT\ (-2) \tag{1}$$

Here CT represents the volume of cargo transported by all modes of transportation, and CIT represents fixed capital investment in transportation.

The statistical characteristics of model (1) and the corresponding tests showed that the model is adequate, in other words, the values of the parameters of the regression

Eq. (1) found by the least squares method are unbiased and efficient [21, 22]. The main statistical characteristics of model (1) are summarized in Table 1.

Thus, model (1) shows that a 1% change in fixed capital investment in the country's transport leads to a 0.2% increase in the volume of cargo transportation by all types of transport with a lag of 2 years.

The Durbin-Watson coefficient according to the results of calculations performed using the EViews 13 software package is equal to 1.21.

According to the found value of the coefficient of determination (R-square = 0.918190) we can say that about 92 percent of the change in the amount of cargo transportation by all types of transport in the country is explained by the volume of investment in fixed capital.

Statistical characteristics of the found parameters and the results of tests for model adequacy in general show that model (1) is quite adequate. In Fig. 1, the difference (Residual) between the (Fitted) price and the actual (Actual) price found by model (1) of the freight transportation dependence on the volume of investment in fixed capital is characterized by a significantly small value.

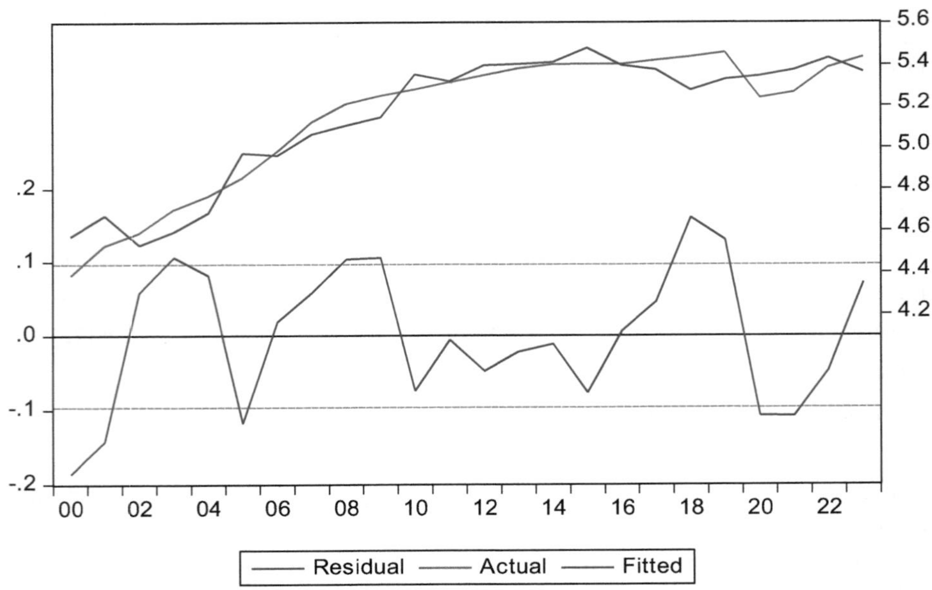

Fig. 1. Fitted, actual and residual values.

5 The Role of Risk Management in Logistic Processes

Risk, in the context of logistics, is defined as the likelihood of damage or income loss, with a calculable probability. Since the occurrence of risk events can often be predicted, various control methods can be applied proactively to prevent such events or to effectively address their consequences when they arise.

Effective risk management in logistics begins with identifying and evaluating several critical elements within logistics systems and processes. Risks can be broadly categorized as internal or external, with internal risks typically associated with intra-regional supply systems and self-sufficiency-related operations [10].

Common causes of internal risks include:

- A reduction in projected traffic volumes or freight capacity,
- Increased costs of transport services (to meet either primary or secondary needs),
- Rising fares and taxes within regional transportation systems,
- Decreased demand for transport services, often due to reduced household or business income.

One of the most critical consequences of such risks is delays, which can result in the breach of supply contracts due to failure to meet key conditions: quantity, quality, or delivery time.

In the broader domain of commerce, additional risks arise from both trade and transportation operations. The development of an integrated regional transport and logistics system can help reduce these risks—a concern shared by all stakeholders, regardless of the level or method of insurance coverage.

Uncertainty and risk often increase when logistics terms such as "just-in-time," "lowest cost," "required quality," and "required quantity" are strictly applied. These conditions leave little room for flexibility or error. However, in logistics operations, managers must consider more than three potential state conditions due to the dynamic and complex nature of supply chains [9].

Therefore, managing risk in logistics not only involves predicting and mitigating risk factors but also requires building flexible systems capable of adapting to a range of potential disruptions and uncertainties.

6 Scope and Significance of the Study

This study aims to explore the strategic role of risk management in logistics, examining how businesses can proactively identify, evaluate, and mitigate risks to maintain service quality, reduce operational disruptions, and adapt to a rapidly changing global environment.

To effectively manage and minimize risks within logistics and supply chain operations, organizations should begin by identifying high-risk areas. A thorough assessment of different aspects of the business—such as procurement, transportation, warehousing, and vendor relationships—can reveal potential vulnerabilities and areas of exposure [11].

Understanding the nature and frequency of risks, as well as their financial impact, allows organizations to proactively adjust workflows and implement targeted mitigation strategies. Establishing a structured risk management framework enables businesses to respond swiftly and efficiently to unexpected disruptions.

7 Conclusion

Logistics systems and transportation are deeply interdependent. Logistics management relies heavily on transportation to carry out daily operations, while an efficient logistics system can, in turn, contribute to the development of a better traffic and transportation environment. Since transportation typically accounts for the highest cost within logistics systems, improving transportation efficiency has a direct and significant impact on the overall performance of logistics operations.

Transportation is a critical component of the logistics process, appearing across multiple stages—from procurement and warehousing to distribution and delivery. Without seamless integration with transportation, even the most well-planned logistics strategy cannot achieve its full potential [12].

To gain a competitive edge in today's global and fast-paced market, businesses must adopt the latest technologies and embrace innovative approaches. The ultimate goal of effective logistics management is to enhance operational efficiency, ensure customer satisfaction, and drive productivity. A robust and forward-thinking logistics strategy—supported by risk management and technological integration—will empower organizations to stay resilient, responsive, and competitive in an increasingly complex supply chain landscape.

A number of mathematical methods were used in the course of the study, and during the econometric evaluation of the dependence of freight transportation in the Republic of Azerbaijan on the volume of investment in fixed capital using statistical-econometric methods it was found that the parameters of econometric evaluation given in Table 2 and their tests for reliability, heteroscedasticity and stationarity show that model (1) is quite adequate.

Thus, as a result, it was found that the volume of cargo transportation by all types of transport in Azerbaijan closely depends on investment in fixed capital, and the elasticity coefficient is equal to 0.21640805826.

The obtained elasticity coefficient of approximately 0.2164 indicates a positive, yet inelastic relationship between the volume of cargo transportation and investments in fixed capital in Azerbaijan. Specifically, a 1% increase in investment in fixed capital is associated, on average, with a 0.216% increase in the volume of cargo transported by all types of transport.

The positive sign of the coefficient suggests that increased investment contributes to the expansion of transportation capacity and infrastructure efficiency, thereby facilitating a higher volume of cargo movements. However, the fact that the elasticity is less than one reflects that the responsiveness of cargo transportation to changes in investment is relatively moderate. This implies that while investments play a significant role in enhancing transport activity, other factors—such as economic growth rates, trade flows, sectoral demand, regulatory frameworks, and operational efficiencies—also substantially influence the dynamics of cargo transportation volumes.

In summary, the analysis confirms that investments in fixed capital are an important driver of cargo transportation development, but their impact is partial and mediated by broader economic and structural variables. This elasticity analysis helps managers and policymakers anticipate the limits of investment-driven growth, optimize investment decisions, and design more comprehensive, multi-factorial risk management strategies for the transport and logistics sector.

References

1. J. Bus. Logist. **22**(2) (2001)
2. http://www.logisticsworld.com/logistics.htm. Accessed 1 June 2010
3. Lourenco, H.R.: Logistics management: an opportunity for metaheuristics. In: Sharda, R., Voß, S., Rego, C., Alidaee, B. (eds.) Metaheuristics Optimization via Memory and Evolution (2005)
4. Trkman, P., McCormack, K.: Supply chain risk in turbulent environments—a conceptual model for managing supply chain network risk. Int. J. Prod. Econ. **119**(2), 247–258 (2009)
5. Nilsson, F., Waidringer, J.: Toward adaptive logistics management. In: Proceedings of the 38th Hawaii International Conference on System Science. IEEE (2005). http://www.computer.org/portal/web/csdl. https://doi.org/10.1109/HICSS.2005.629
6. Munawar, H.S., Mojtahedi, M., Hammad, A.W., Kouzani, A., Mahmud, M.P.: Disruptive technologies as a solution for disaster risk management. **806**, Part 3 (2022)
7. Bowersox, D.J., Closs, D.J., Drayer, R.W.: The digital transformation technology and beyond. Supply Chain Manage. Rev. 22–29 ((2005))
8. Mentzer, J.T., Stank, T.P., Esper, T.L.: Supply chain management and its relationship to logistics, marketing, production, and operations management. J. Bus. Logist. **29**(1), 31–46 (2008)
9. Autry, C.W., Zacharia, Z.G., Lamb, C.W.: A logistics strategy taxonomy. J. Bus. Logist. **29**(2), 27–51 (2008)
10. Hofer, A.R., Knemeyer, A.M.: Controlling for logistics complexity: scale development and validation. Int. J. Logist. Manag. **20**(2), 187–200 (2009)
11. Willersdorf, R.G.: Adding value through logistics management. Logist. Inf. Manag. **3**(4), 6–8 (1993)
12. Aliyeva, A., Agayev, S.: Assessment of the impact of tourism logistics on the economy of Azerbaijan in line with the development of the East-West corridor. In: 3rd International Conference on Problems of Logistics, Management and Operation in the East-West Transport Corridor (2024)
13. https://www.stat.gov.az/source/transport/?lang=en
14. Agayev, S.: Estimation of the influence of transportations in transport sector to ecological pollutions in Azerbaijan. In: 37th International Scientific Conference on Economic and Social Development–"Socio Economic Problems of Sustainable Development", Baku, 14–15 February 2019, pp. 772–778 (2019)
15. https://www.stat.gov.az/source/transport/az/002_1.xls
16. http://www.stat.gov.az/source/transport/az/001_1.xls
17. Asteriou, D., Hall, S.G.: Applied Econometrics, p. 518. Palgrave, New York (2016)
18. Gujarati, D.N.: Basic Econometrics, 3rd edn. McGraw-Hill Inc., New York (1995)
19. Agayev, S.: Assessment of the dependence of passenger transportation on the volume of investments in fixed assets in the Republic of Azerbaijan. In: The 7th International Conference on Control and Optimization with Industrial Applications (COİA-2020), Baku, Azerbaijan, 26–28 August 2020, pp. 38–40 (2020)
20. Agayev, S.: Econometric assessment of the impact of transport system of the Republic of Azerbaijan on macroeconomic indicators. In: The 7th International Conference on Control and Optimization with Industrial Applications (COİA-2020), Baku, Azerbaijan, 26–28 August 2020, pp. 41–43 (2020)

21. Gorkhmaz, I., Yadulla, H.: Models of socio economic development of Azerbaijan, Elm, Baku, Azerbaijan (2001)
22. Yadulla, H.: Statistics: with practical examples. Baku, Azerbaijan, p. 564 (2014)

Analysis of the Results of Parallel Calculation of the Coefficients of the Trigonometric Fourier Series

Tahir Alizada(✉) and Akshin Mustafayev

Institute of Control Systems, Baku, Azerbaijan
tahiralizada1973@gmail.com

Abstract. Nowadays, the usage of parallel computing in modern information systems becomes a necessity, to eliminate computational challenges. Recently, new optimization techniques have been developed, and a parallel programming framework became available that opened new prospects for solving numerically complex problems. This work proposes a method of computation for the Fourier coefficients that has been developed to take into consideration multi-core processors to enhance effectiveness and reduce processing times. Performance will be scalable and reliable; hence, it provides further insight into exploration for high-performance computing in signal analysis.

Keywords: Parallel Computing · Fourier Coefficients · Optimization Techniques · Multi-Core Processors · Signal Analysis

1 Introduction

A periodic signal can be represented over a certain interval of time in terms of the linear combination of orthogonal functions, if these orthogonal functions are trigonometric functions, then the Fourier series representation is known as trigonometric Fourier series. For a continuous function f(x) defined on the interval $[-\pi, \pi]$ with period 2π, the following Fourier series equation formula is being used.

$$f(x) = a_0 + \sum_{n=1}^{\infty} (a_n \cos(nx) + b_n \sin(nx)) \tag{1}$$

where a_0 – is a mean value of the function (zero coefficient), $a_{n,} b_n$ – are the Fourier coefficients corresponding to cosine and sine terms, respectively. These coefficients are derived from the orthogonality of trigonometric functions over the interval and are calculated using definite integrals as follows:

- For the mean value of a_0:

$$a_0 = \frac{1}{2\pi} \int_{-\pi}^{\pi} f(x)dx \tag{2}$$

A. Abbasov et al. (Eds.): PLMO 2025, CCIS 2767, pp. 33–44, 2026.
https://doi.org/10.1007/978-3-032-13672-5_4

- For a_n cosine coefficients:

$$a_n = \frac{1}{\pi} \int_{-\pi}^{\pi} f(x)dx \cos(nx)dx, \ n \geq 1 \tag{3}$$

- For b_n cosine coefficients:

$$b_n = \frac{1}{\pi} \int_{-\pi}^{\pi} f(x)dx \sin(nx)dx, \ n \geq 1 \tag{4}$$

The Fourier series is always periodic by its nature even if the original function $f(x)$ is not. The periods of $sin(2\pi nx/T)$ and $cos(2\pi nx/T)$ are $2\pi/n$ so the largest period, $T = 2\pi$, comes from the $n = 1$ terms and the Fourier series has period 2π. This means that the series should be able to represent functions that are periodic of period 2π. However, calculating these coefficients analytically is often impractical for real-world signals, requiring numerical approximations using sampled data.

In practical computing, continuous integrals are evaluated by summing over a limited number of sample points. For a discrete signal f(x) which is sampled at N number of equally spaced points x_i over $[-\pi, \pi]$, the coefficients can be calculated using formulas given below [4–10]:

- For the mean value of a_0:

$$a_0 = \frac{1}{N} \sum_{i=0}^{N-1} f(x_i) \tag{5}$$

- For a_n cosine coefficients:

$$a_n = \frac{2}{N} \sum_{i=0}^{N-1} f(x_i) \cos(nx_i), \ \ n = 1, 2, \ldots \tag{6}$$

- For b_n cosine coefficients:

$$b_n = \frac{2}{N} \sum_{i=0}^{N-1} f(x_i) \sin(nx_i), n = 1, 2, \ldots \tag{7}$$

where $x_i = -\pi + i\frac{2\pi}{n}$, and n is the frequency index [4–10]. This discrete approach allows for numerical evaluation but becomes increasingly intensive from a computational point of view, as the number of members or sample points increases.

In this paper the computational challenges of calculating Fourier coefficients are being addressed by using modern multi-core processors and various parallel programming techniques. The suggested method optimizes these discrete computations, distributing the workload across multiple threads to increase efficiency and reduce processing time. By using parallelism, the approach scales effectively with signal size and complexity, which offers insights into high-performance computing for signal analysis applications.

2 Understanding Signal Processing and Performance Optimization

Hardware vendors provide tools, libraries and environments for development, testing, validating and scaling of parallel algorithms and workloads for real-world applications as well as for research purposes. For example, the Hewlett Packard Enterprise (HPE) provides a Cray Compiler Environment compatible with many standards including OpenMP standard, that performs code analysis during compilation and automatically generates highly optimized code [11].

The technical specifications of the hardware equipment used to perform calculations and testing are listed in Table 1 [12]:

Table 1. Technical specifications of the hardware equipment.

Technical specifications	HP ProLiant DL 360 Gen9 Server
Processor	Intel Xeon e5-2660 v3 2.6GHZ
Socket	Intel Socket 2011
OS	Windows Server 2016
Microarchitecture	Sandy Bridge-EP
Memory	256 GB
Number of cores	8
Number of threads	16
L1 Cache	64 KB (per core)
L2 Cache	256 KB (per core)
L3 Cache	20 MB (shared)

Signal processing plays an important role in a variety of fields, from telecommunications and sound analysis to biomedical engineering and radar technology. A key technique used in this discipline is the Fourier transform, commonly used to study the frequency components of a signal. As the signal size increases, this operation becomes more computationally demanding. Processing of big signals on modern hardware without optimizations is problematic due to the complexity of these computations [13].

To address this problem, many algorithms have been developed, however, as datasets and real-time processing requirements continue to grow, even using those algorithms may not be so effective. This is where parallelism comes into play. By using the capabilities of modern multi-core processors, parallelism allows us to divide computations into small chunks and distribute the load across many cores, significantly reducing execution times.

In this part we will explore the implementation and optimization of signal processing algorithms in C++ [14], focusing on:

- Generating test signals that simulates actual signals.
- Implementing sequential version.
- Implementing parallelized version using OpenMP library.

- Implementing parallelized version using MPI library.
- Evaluating the performance to show the benefits of parallelism.

2.1 Generating Test Signals

The *generateSignal* function returns a result of a discrete version of a continuous function f(x) by sampling it at regular intervals within a specific range. This action begins by dividing the range into *numPoints* equally spaced intervals. Each of these intervals correlates with a step size (step). For each sampling point, the function calculates the x coordinate and evaluates f(x), and after that it stores the result in a vector named signal. This implementation was chosen because unlike generating random numbers, this would provide adequate results for the intended analysis. Code snippet is specified below:

```
std::vector<double> generateSignal(int numPoints)
{
   std::vector<double> signal(numPoints);
   double step = 2 * PI / numPoints;
   for (int i = 0; i < numPoints; ++i)
   {
      double x = -PI + i * step;
      signal[i] = f(x);
   }
   return signal;
}
```

Here, f(x) is defined as an example signal, such as:

$$1 + 2*\cos(x) + 3*\sin(x) + 4*\cos(2*x) +$$
$$5*\sin(2*x) + 6*\cos(3*x) + 7*\sin(3*x) \tag{8}$$

to simulate real-world periodic behavior.

2.2 Sequential Version

The simplest way to compute Fourier coefficients from the generated signal is implemented in the *computeFourierCoefficients* function. This function performs all calculations sequentially without any parallelization. The code snippet is provided below:

```
void computeFourierCoefficients(const std::vector<double>&signal, int maxN,
std::vector<double>&an, std::vector<double>&bn)
{
   int numPoints = signal.size();
   double step = 2 * PI / numPoints;
   // Compute a0
   an[0] = 0.0;
   for (int i = 0; i < numPoints; ++i)
   {
      an[0] += signal[i];
```

```
    }
    an[0] *= step / (2 * PI);
    // Compute an and bn
    for (int n = 1; n <= maxN; ++n)
    {
        double an_local = 0.0;
        double bn_local = 0.0;
        for (int i = 0; i < numPoints; ++i)
        {
            double x = -PI + i * step;
            an_local += signal[i] * cos(n * x);
            bn_local += signal[i] * sin(n * x);
        }
        an[n] = (2.0 / numPoints) * an_local;
        bn[n] = (2.0 / numPoints) * bn_local;
    }
}
```

2.3 Parallelized Version Using OpenMP Library

computeFourierCoefficientsParallel function increases efficiency by dividing the computation across multiple threads. The outer loop, which calculates coefficients is split among the threads. The number of threads is determined automatically by the OpenMP, which is usually equals the number of cores by default. Each thread calculates a specific range of frequencies independently. This method makes optimal use of multi-core processors, which speeds up calculations, specifically for large signals [15–18]:

```
void computeFourierCoefficientsParallel(const std::vector<double>&signal, int maxN, std::vector<double>&an, std::vector<double>&bn)
{
    int numPoints = signal.size();
    double step = 2 * PI / numPoints;
    // Compute a0. Parallelizing a0 computation may introduce overhead
    // a0 is computed differently from an and bn
    an[0] = 0.0;
    for (int i = 0; i < numPoints; ++i)
    {
        an[0] += signal[i];
    }
    an[0] *= step / (2 * PI);
    // Compute an and bn (parallelized outer loop over n)
#pragma omp parallel for
    for (int n = 1; n <= maxN; ++n)
    {
        double an_local = 0.0;
        double bn_local = 0.0;
```

```
      for (int i = 0; i < numPoints; ++i)
      {
         double x = -PI + i * step;
         an_local += signal[i] * cos(n * x);
         bn_local += signal[i] * sin(n * x);
      }
      an[n] = (2.0 / numPoints) * an_local;
      bn[n] = (2.0 / numPoints) * bn_local;
   }
}
```

2.4 Parallelized Version Using MPI Library

Parallelization with using the Message Passing Interface (MPI), a framework for distributed computing across multiple processes or nodes has been implemented. The *computeFourierCoefficientsMPI* function distributes the computation of a_n and b_n across processes, with results gathered at the root process (rank 0). The code snippet is given below:

```
void computeFourierCoefficientsMPI(const std::vector<double> &signal, int maxN, std::vector<double> &an, std::vector<double> &bn) {
   int numPoints = signal.size();
   double step = 2 * PI / numPoints;
   int rank, size;
   MPI_Comm_rank(MPI_COMM_WORLD, &rank);
   MPI_Comm_size(MPI_COMM_WORLD, &size);
   if (rank == 0) {
      an[0] = 0.0;
      for (int i = 0; i < numPoints; ++i) {
         an[0] += signal[i];
      }
      an[0] *= step / (2 * PI);
   }
   int terms_per_process = maxN / size;
   int remainder = maxN % size;
   int start_n = rank * terms_per_process + (rank < remainder ? rank : remainder);
   int extra = (rank < remainder ? 1 : 0);
   int local_maxN = terms_per_process + extra;
   int end_n = std::min(start_n + local_maxN, maxN + 1);
   start_n = std::max(1, start_n);
   std::vector<double> local_an(maxN + 1, 0.0), local_bn(maxN + 1, 0.0);
   for (int n = start_n; n < end_n; ++n) {
      double an_local = 0.0, bn_local = 0.0;
      for (int i = 0; i < numPoints; ++i) {
         double x = -PI + i * step;
         an_local += signal[i] * cos(n * x);
```

```
            bn_local += signal[i] * sin(n * x);
        }
        local_an[n] = (2.0 / numPoints) * an_local;
        local_bn[n] = (2.0 / numPoints) * bn_local;
    }
    MPI_Reduce(local_an.data(), an.data(), maxN + 1, MPI_DOUBLE, MPI_SUM,
0, MPI_COMM_WORLD);
    MPI_Reduce(local_bn.data(), bn.data(), maxN + 1, MPI_DOUBLE, MPI_SUM,
0, MPI_COMM_WORLD);
}
```

In this implementation, each process computes a subset of n values based on its rank and the total number of processes (size). The *MPI_Reduce* function combines local results into the global a_n and b_n arrays, introducing communication overhead which is absent in OpenMP.

2.5 Performance Evaluation

Measurement of the execution performance of different methods achieved by using the *std::chrono* library [19]. Calculation of the execution times is determined by subtraction of the start and end time of function. High-resolution clocks are used to record precise timings. The computational complexity for the sequential approach is expressed as:

$$O(maxN \cdot numPoints) \tag{9}$$

The parallelized version has a complexity of:

$$O((maxN \cdot numPoints)/T) \tag{10}$$

where T represents the number of threads used. This method demonstrates how each variant performs as data sizes increase and highlights the effectiveness of parallelism in decreasing computation time, especially when dealing with the large signals.

3 Parallelization Block Diagram

Parallelization block diagram (Fig. 1) represents how tasks are divided and executed in parallel to optimize performance performed during function execution, which is applicable to both OpenMP and MPI implementations. The computation of a_0, the mean value, is performed sequentially because it does not depend on frequency terms, and calculated by the sum of all sample points and does not benefit so much from parallelization due to its simplicity and potential overhead. In OpenMP variant this part is performed once by a single thread, whereas in MPI version it happens in the root process.

Main parallelization happens during the computation of the a_n and b_n coefficients for n ranging from 1 to *maxN*. In this process, the workload, represented by the outer loop iterating over the n values, is segmented into smaller, autonomous tasks. Each of these tasks calculates the sums of the signal multiplied by the corresponding cosine and sine components for a designated range of n. Subsequently, these tasks are performed simultaneously:

1. In the OpenMP variant, the tasks are distributed across multiple threads running on a shared-memory multi-core processor. Each thread calculates its assigned range of n values independently, via updating the shared a_n and b_n arrays without additional communication.

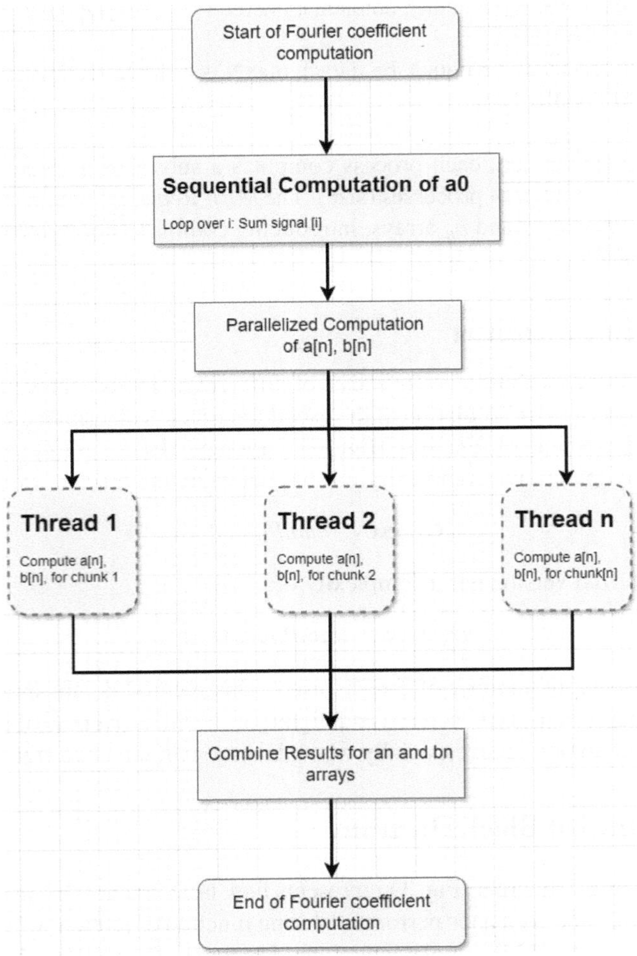

Fig. 1. Parallelization block diagram.

2. In the MPI variant, the tasks are assigned to separate processes, which may run on the same node. Each process computes its subset of n values locally, keeping results in temporary arrays. After computation, the results are combined through a reduction operation, aggregating the local calculations into the final a_n and b_n arrays on the root process.

In both implementations, the parallel tasks work without dependencies, which guarantees efficient use of resources. The key difference is in the coordination: OpenMP relies on shared memory for immediate result access, while MPI requires explicit communication to gather results. This diagram (Fig. 1) represents the task division and execution flow, showing how parallelism reduces processing time by distributing the computational load, regardless of the framework used.

4 Tests and Results Analysis

After executing the provided code, various results of calculations for the sequential, OpenMP, and MPI implementations (Table 2) have been obtained. This table shows the correlation between number of Fourier terms and computation times (in milliseconds) for all three approaches, tested on the HP ProLiant DL 360 Gen9 server with 10, 100, 200, 300, 400, 500 and 1000 *numPoints* relatively.

Table 2. Computation times for sequential, OpenMP, and MPI implementations.

Number of Fourier terms	Sequential	Parallel (OpenMP)	Parallel (MPI)
10	0.8183	0.5169	1.5944
100	6.9809	2.293	2.2934
200	13.9411	3.9712	3.4069
300	21.1175	6.644	3.9286
400	27.8889	7.2111	4.5289
500	34.8119	9.2266	6.2997
1000	71.1401	19.4607	8.5128

Correlation between Number of Fourier terms for both parallel implementations and simple approach is shown in Fig. 2.

Several conclusions regarding the effectiveness of each method can be made from the obtained results. In the sequential version it is noticeable that there is a consistent increase in execution time as the number of Fourier terms grows. For instance, it takes 0.8183 ms with 10 terms but increases significantly to 71.1401 ms with 1000 terms. Given that its computational cost is *O (maxN * numPoints)*, this behavior is to be expected. Here every calculation is performed sequentially, which causes a large computational load as *maxN* increases.

Compared to the sequential approach, the OpenMP parallel implementation has a significantly shorter execution time. As a number of terms grow, performance improvement becomes more apparent. For example, it reaches 0.5169 ms, at 10 terms, which is a slight improvement over 0.8183 ms in the sequential method. This shows that the overhead of thread management limits the benefit for small workloads. At 1000 terms, the execution time reduces to 19.4607 ms, with a speedup of about 3.65 times. Even though the maximum possible speedup of 8x is not achieved due to the coordination overhead and memory limitations of this method, it can be said that slightly more efficient use of the 8-core Intel Xeon processor was achieved.

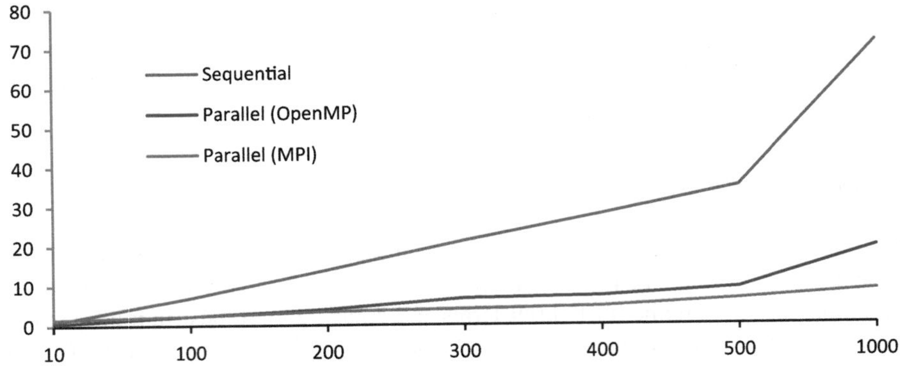

Fig. 2. Number of Fourier terms vs time for both parallel and simple variants

The performance characteristics of the MPI implementation, tested with 8 cores, show considerable variation. With 10 terms, it takes as much as 1.5944ms, which is slower than both the sequential version (0.8183 ms) and OpenMP version (0.5169 ms). This indicates that for small datasets, the overhead from process initialization and communication overhead in *MPI_Reduce* becomes more significant. While MPI implementation with 2.2934 ms and OpenMP with 2.2930 ms are approximately the same at 100 terms, MPI continuously outperforms OpenMP after 200 terms. For example, at 200 terms, MPI takes 3.4069 ms compared to OpenMP's 3.9712 ms, and at 1000 terms, MPI achieves 8.5128 ms against OpenMP's 19.4607 ms. This results in a speedup of almost 8.36 times over sequential version, which is significantly faster than OpenMP's 3.65x. This suggests that MPI scales remarkably well on this configuration for greater *maxN* values.

When comparing the parallel methods, OpenMP shows an advantage with smaller term counts because of its shared-memory architecture. With 10 terms, its time of 0.5169 ms significantly outperforms MPI's 1.5944 ms, which indicates reduced overhead. Nevertheless, MPI outperforms OpenMP starting from 200 terms and the difference increases as *maxN* increases, especially at 1000 terms (8.5128 ms compared to 19.4607 ms). This shift takes place because MPI uses separate processes to deal with bigger workloads when computation demands exceed communication costs. OpenMP's performance stabilizes due to limitations in thread scheduling and memory bandwidth, whereas MPI's process-oriented method continues to scale effectively.

These results show that choosing the optimal method depends on the number of terms. The sequential method for small *maxN* (with 10 terms) is still acceptable, and OpenMP offers a slight advantage. For medium sizes (with 100 terms), both parallel methods perform the same, but after 200 terms, MPI outperforms all of them. In fact, it achieves nearly the theoretical maximum speed at 1000 terms. For huge workloads, parallelism without a doubt increments productivity; in any case, maintaining a from overhead is still necessary for little workloads.

5 Conclusion

The results of this study confirm the efficiency of parallel Fourier coefficient computations. It is more notable in cases with large number of terms. With its *O (maxN * numPoints)* complexity, the sequential method struggles as *maxN* increases. With 10 terms it takes 0.8183 ms but increases significantly to 71.1401 ms with 1000 terms. By splitting the calculations across multiple cores, parallelism removes this barrier, but their efficiency varies depending on the problem's complexity and structure.

At 1000 terms with approximately a 3.65x speedup (19.4607 ms), the OpenMP implementation has a significantly shorter execution time. Nevertheless, due to the overhead of thread management, its performance on smaller datasets, such as 0.5169 ms with 10 terms, shows limited gains compared to the sequential algorithm with 0.8183 ms. This suggests OpenMP is viable for medium-to-large workloads but has scalability limits as coordination costs increase.

The MPI implementation outperforms both alternatives at higher term counts, with the record 8.5128 ms at 1000 terms. It has a speedup of 8.36x over sequential method, and much better than OpenMP's 19.4607 ms. Its poor performance at 10 terms shows the overhead from process initialization and communication, which makes it not recommended for small datasets. However, for large *maxN*, MPI is better among these methods and can bring greater advantages in distributed multi-node environments where computation can further outweigh communication costs.

These results show that parallel computing is important not only for efficiency but also provides a solution for dealing with the demands imposed by modern signal processing, but the choice of method depends on the task. OpenMP suits moderate workloads on shared-memory systems, while MPI shines for larger computations. The obtained results can be applied to optimize calculations for signal analysis and spectral processing of images. The developed methods are planned to be applied both in control and management systems in the oil industry and in the navigation of unmanned aerial vehicles.

References

1. Edwards, R.E.: Fourier Series: A Modern Introduction Volume 1. Institute for Advanced Studies, The Australian National University, Canberra, Second edition, pp. 14–43, December 2012
2. Zygmund, A.: Trigonometric Series, pp. 1–4. Cambridge University Press, February 2015
3. Pinsky, M.A.: Introduction to Fourier Analysis and Wavelets, pp. 13–34. Northwestern University (2008)
4. Jackson, D.: Fourier series and orthogonal polynomials. Am. Math. Soc. 1–42 (1941)
5. Olson, T.: Applied Fourier Analysis, pp. 1–3, 19–30, 45–80. Birkhäuser, New York (2017)
6. Kammler, D.W.: A First Course in Fourier Analysis, pp. 1–40. Cambridge University Press (2010)
7. Libretexts: Fourier Trigonometric Series. https://math.libretexts.org/Bookshelves/Differential_Equations/Introduction_to_Partial_Differential_Equations_(Herman)/03%3A_Trigonometric_Fourier_Series/3.02%3A_Fourier_Trigonometric_Series
8. University of North Carolina: Trigonometric Fourier Series. https://people.uncw.edu/hermanr/pde1/pdebook/Fourier.pdf

9. Wikipedia: Fourier Series. https://en.wikipedia.org/wiki/Fourier_series
10. Tutorialspoint: Trigonometric Fourier Series – Definition and Explanation. https://www.tutorialspoint.com/trigonometric-fourier-series-definition-and-explanation
11. Hewlett Packard: Cray Compiler Environment. https://cpe.ext.hpe.com/docs/24.03/cce/index.html#overview
12. TechPowerUP: Intel Xeon E5-2660. https://www.techpowerup.com/cpu-specs/xeon-e5-2660.c976
13. Cooley, J.W., Tukey, J.W.: An algorithm for the machine calculation of complex Fourier series. Math. Comput. 297–301 (1965)
14. C++ reference: Standard Containers. https://cplusplus.com/reference/stl
15. CsInParallel: Parallel Computing in the Computer Science Curriculum. https://csinparallel.org/csinparallel/ppps/openmp.html
16. Microsoft: Enable OpenMP Support. https://learn.microsoft.com/en-us/cpp/build/reference/openmp-enable-openmp-2-0-support?view=msvc-170
17. OpenMP Documentation: Guide to parallelizing computations in C++ for multi-core processors. https://www.openmp.org
18. OpenMP Examples: OpenMP Application Programming Interface Examples. https://www.openmp.org/wp-content/uploads/openmp-examples-5.2.2-final.pdf
19. C++ reference: Date and time utilities (2024). https://en.cppreference.com/w/cpp/chrono

The Impact of River Transport and Tourism on the Wetlands in the Bulgarian Section of the Danube River Basin

Asen Asenov[1](✉), Velizara Pencheva[1], Ekaterina Batchvarova[2], Boian Koulov[2], Zoya Mateeva[2], Mladen Kulev[1], Valeri Geogriev[1], and Kalina Tilko[2]

[1] Department of Transport, University of Ruse, Ruse, Bulgaria
asasenov@uni-ruse.bg
[2] Climate, Atmosphere and Water Research Institute at Bulgarian Academy of Sciences, Sofia, Bulgaria

Abstract. The Danube River stands as the largest international transport artery within the European continent, underscoring its critical role as a conduit connecting more than 19 nations, numerous socio-economic regions, and diverse ecosystems. This study aims to analyze the specific development of transport and tourism-related economic activities within the Bulgarian segment of the Danube and to evaluate their impact on the sustainable development of wetlands in its basin. The research employs innovative methodologies and derives insights from the scientific project "Danube Wetlands and Floodplains Restoration through Systemic, Community-Engaged, and Sustainable Innovative Actions (DaWetRest)," which is part of the European Union's "Horizon Europe" program under the "Restoration of Oceans, Seas, and Waters" mission. The study proposes solutions and policy recommendations for mitigating environmental risks and promoting the sustainable management of the Danube's wetlands, as well as its riparian economy and social communities. Also the results indicate that, despite the threats from the unpredictable variations in water levels, it is possible to achieve a balance between the economic utilization of the river and the conservation of its wetlands through the implementation of innovative and sustainable solutions.

Keywords: Wetlands · Environmental Risks · Sustainable Management · River Transport · Biodiversity

1 Introduction

The Danube River is one of Europe's most significant waterways, both ecologically and economically. Spanning approximately 2,857 km, it traverses ten countries and integrates diverse ecosystems ranging from mountain streams to extensive wetlands and deltas [1]. Owing to its strategic geographical position, the Danube has long functioned as a vital transport corridor linking Central and Eastern Europe with the Black Sea [2]. In contemporary times, it is an integral part of the Trans-European Transport Network (TEN-T), with its navigation development playing a crucial role in the economies of the riparian states [3].

A. Abbasov et al. (Eds.): PLMO 2025, CCIS 2767, pp. 45–57, 2026.
https://doi.org/10.1007/978-3-032-13672-5_5

Despite its economic benefits, the expansion and modernization of Danube navigation present formidable challenges to river ecosystems. The construction of hydrotechnical structures such as locks and dikes, and dredging activities alter the river's natural hydrodynamics, exacerbate bank erosion, and leads to the loss of crucial habitats [4]. Additionally, shipping contributes to chemical and noise pollution, while the transfer of invasive species via ballast water poses a significant threat to native ecosystems [5]. Species such as the zebra mussel (Dreissena polymorpha) and the Chinese mitten crab (Eriocheir sinensis) have been introduced in this manner and are already exerting substantial influence on the Danube's biodiversity [6].

To ensure the sustainable development of navigation on the Danube, the implementation of environmentally conscious policies and measures is imperative. The International Commission for the Protection of the Danube River (ICPDR) and other organizations advocate for an integrated approach that incorporates eco-friendly technologies, enhanced management of river ecosystems, and strengthened cooperation among regional states [1]. Programs such as "Danube Navigation and Environment" seek to minimize the adverse impact of navigation through the promotion of best practices and technological innovations [7]. Intensive river transport and its associated infrastructure projects induce changes in wetland ecosystems along the Danube, which are vital for both biodiversity conservation and the well-being of local communities.

This research seeks to analyze the intricate relationship between navigation and biodiversity in the Danube, examining the primary threats, existing conservation measures, and opportunities for sustainable water transport development in the region. It outlines the objectives, scope, and methodologies employed within the DaWetRest project—an initiative funded by the European Commission under the "Horizon Europe" program—dedicated to the restoration and conservation of wetlands and floodplains in the Danube Basin.

2 River Transport Along the Danube

To As part of the TEN-T network, the Danube serves as one of Europe's busiest inland waterways [8]. With its strategic 2,857 km length and connectivity to major European ports, the river plays a pivotal role in the economic development of the region.

Within the TEN-T framework (Fig. 1), the Danube is a component of the "Rhine-Danube Corridor," one of the nine principal transport corridors facilitating the movement of goods and services across Europe (Fig. 2).

Key characteristics of the Danube River transport include high freight volumes, port infrastructure development, and the influence of hydrotechnical structures on water regimes and navigation. The river accommodates a substantial volume of commercial shipments, with the primary cargo including bulk commodities (coal, grain, and mineral resources), liquid fuels, and containers [9]. In recent years, containerized transport has witnessed a notable increase. Waterborne transport along the Danube provides an economically viable and environmentally friendlier alternative to road and rail transport, particularly for heavy and voluminous cargo [10].

Throughout its course, the Danube hosts significant ports that function as crucial hubs for international trade and logistics. Among the most prominent are Vienna (Austria)—a highly automated logistics center; Budapest (Hungary)—a key hub for container and industrial cargo; Belgrade (Serbia)—a gateway with growing importance, linking Western Europe and the Balkans; and Ruse (Bulgaria)—a strategic port connecting Bulgaria to international transport corridors and the Black Sea region [11]. The expansion and modernization of these ports form part of the European Union's long-term strategies for reinforcing river transport in the region.

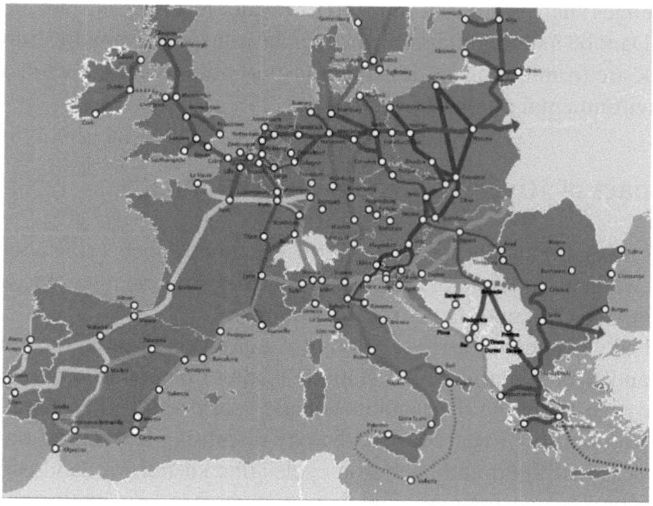

Fig. 1. Principal transport corridors in the TEN-T.

Fig. 2. Rhine-Danube corridor network.

Numerous hydrotechnical structures constructed along the Danube influence river transport. Locks and hydroelectric plants regulate water levels, facilitating navigation while simultaneously altering natural ecosystems [12]. One of the most significant installations is the "Iron Gates" dam system between Serbia and Romania, which ensures navigability yet restricts fish migration and affects sedimentary processes [4]. Water fluctuations, particularly those driven by climate change, further complicate navigation, creating challenges such as drought-induced low water levels or extreme floodings [13].

Given the Danube's strategic significance for the transport sector, the European Union and the ICPDR are formulating sustainable transport initiatives that reconcile economic needs with environmental conservation efforts.

3 The Impact of River Transport on Wetlands

Intensive river transport and its associated infrastructure projects bring about significant alterations to wetland ecosystems, including hydrological changes, biodiversity loss, water pollution, and climate-related transformations.

Hydrological Changes – The regulation of water levels through the construction of dams, locks, and hydroelectric power stations leads to profound modifications in the natural hydrodynamics of the river and its aquatic ecosystems. These structures diminish the natural variability of water levels, thereby disrupting fish migration patterns and impeding the seasonal flood-and-recession cycles that sustain wetland ecosystems. As a result, the habitat range for numerous aquatic species - especially those reliant on seasonal fluctuations—is significantly reduced. Notable examples of such hydrotechnical structures along the Danube include the "Iron Gates" dam system and a network of locks, which have fundamentally altered hydrological conditions [12]. These changes have also disrupted ecological functions such as sediment redistribution, which is crucial for biodiversity in the river's lower stretches.

Biodiversity Loss – Hydrological modifications and habitat destruction contribute to a decline in populations of rare and endangered species residing in wetland and river ecosystems [13]. Reduced biological resilience in the riverine environment accelerates ecosystem degradation, ultimately impairing essential ecological functions such as water filtration and climate regulation.

Water Pollution – Increased vessel traffic and the heightened use of inland waterways contribute to rising pollution levels in the Danube. Among the most pressing concerns are sediment disturbances, chemical discharges, and petroleum-based contaminants, which enter the water either through accidental spills or as a byproduct of routine ship operations. Such pollution not only degrades water quality but also disrupts aquatic flora and fauna by interfering with their life cycles. Contaminated water presents risks not only for local ecosystems but also for human populations relying on the river for drinking water and industrial purposes.

Climate Change - The interplay between climate change and river transport intensifies pressure on wetland ecosystems, both directly - by altering hydrological cycles - and indirectly, through increased pollution and ecosystem stress. Climate change can cause a decline in Danube water levels, creating navigation challenges that necessitate additional dredging, thereby exacerbating ecological pressures on wetlands [9]. Lower water levels also reduce port capacity, leading to demands for additional infrastructure and new hydrotechnical engineering projects [8]. Moreover, rising temperatures and diminished water levels result in higher pollutant concentrations in aquatic environments, a situation worsened by increased shipping activities [14]. Economic growth-driven intensification of river transport further burdens wetland ecosystems, reducing their resilience to climate-related shifts [12].

Mitigating the adverse effects of river transport on the Danube's wetlands necessitates an integrated approach encompassing transport, hydrological, and ecological considerations. Developing a model to quantitatively assess and manage these impacts—while minimizing the effects of river transport on sensitive ecosystems—is a complex yet essential endeavor. This model can be structured around three primary components, as illustrated in Fig. 3. Sustainable solutions aimed at reducing the negative impacts of river transport on wetlands and aquatic ecosystems along the Danube require the application of an integrated framework that incorporates transport, hydrological, and ecological elements.

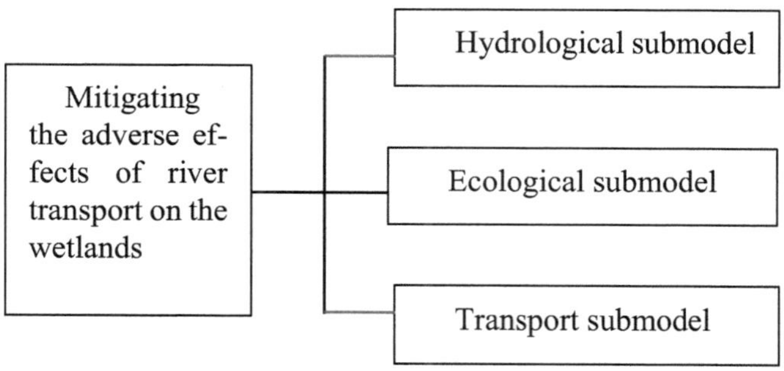

Fig. 3. Main components of the model for limiting the negative impact of river transport on wetlands.

The transport submodel [15, 16] aims to analyze the influence of river transport, including vessel routes, navigation intensity, and vessel types, on hydrology and ecology. The model parameters include vessel passage frequency, cargo capacity, speed, emissions, and wave impact.

The wave impact of a vessel can be estimated using the wave height formula:

$$H_s = \alpha \frac{B}{T} v^2, \tag{1}$$

where H_s is wave height generated by the vessel;

α- empirical coefficient;

B- vessel width;

T- vessel draft;

v- vessel speed.

The rate of bank erosion is given by:

$$E = k_e H_s^m \tau^{n2}, \tag{2}$$

where E is erosion rate;

k_e- erosion coefficient dependent on soil type;

H_s- wave height;

m, n - empirical coefficients.

The hydrological submodel [17] aims to simulate the river's hydrodynamics, including currents, water levels, and interactions with wetlands. Model parameters include river discharge, riverbed topography, meteorological data, infiltration, and evaporation.

The continuity equation (mass conservation equation) is expressed as:

$$\frac{\partial A}{\partial t} + \frac{\partial (Av)}{\partial x} = 0, \tag{3}$$

where A is cross-sectional area of the flow;

v- average velocity of the flow;

t - time;

x - spatial coordinate along the river.

The momentum equation (Saint-Venant equations) is given by:

$$\frac{\partial v}{\partial t} + v\frac{\partial v}{\partial x} + g\frac{\partial h}{\partial x} + \frac{gn^2 v|v|}{R^{\left(\frac{3}{4}\right)}} = 0, \tag{4}$$

where g is gravitational acceleration;

h- water depth;

n - roughness coefficient of the riverbed (Manning's coefficient);

R- hydraulic radius.

The Saint-Venant equations are widely used for modeling unsteady flows in rivers and canals, forecasting floods, analyzing tidal waves, and assessing the impacts of hydrotechnical structures such as dams and locks; for analyzing the interaction between river transport and aquatic ecosystems, etc. These equations serve as the foundation for many modern hydrodynamic models and software applications used in water resource engineering and research.

The ecological submodel [18, 19] evaluates the condition of wetlands and aquatic ecosystems, considering biodiversity and ecosystem services. The model parameters include species diversity and density, water quality, and habitat availability.

The spread of pollutants in a fluid medium is assessed using the advection-diffusion equation:

$$\frac{\partial C}{\partial t} + v\frac{\partial C}{\partial x} = D\frac{\partial^2 C}{\partial x^2} - kC, \tag{5}$$

where C is pollutant concentration;

D - molecular diffusion coefficient;

k - pollutant decay coefficient (e.g., due to chemical reaction or biological degradation);

v- water velocity;

x - spatial coordinate describing pollutant dispersion direction;

t - time.

Biodiversity assessment (population dynamics of a given species over time, considering natural growth, environmental constraints, and additional mortality due to external factors like pollution) follows the equation:

$$\frac{\partial N}{\partial t} = rN\left(1 - \frac{N}{k}\right) - nm, \tag{6}$$

where N is population of a given species;

r - natural growth rate;

k - environmental carrying capacity;

m - mortality rate due to external factors such as pollution, etc.

The integration of these three submodels allows for the evaluation of river transport's impact on hydrological conditions and the ecological state of wetlands. For instance, increased traffic may lead to larger waves (H_s), which enhance bank erosion (E), subsequently affecting habitats and biodiversity (N).

By employing mathematical methods, such as linear programming techniques, the composite model of these three submodels can propose strategies for managing river transport to minimize its negative ecological impact. Potential mitigation strategies include:

- Restricting vessel speeds in ecologically sensitive areas;
- Establishing alternative routes bypassing high-value ecological zones;
- Implementing time-based restrictions for passage through specific river segments.

4 Tourism Development in the Danube Tourism Region of Bulgaria and Its Impact on Wetlands

The Danube River defines the characteristics of the Danube Tourism Region, which is the largest in Bulgaria in terms of area but remains one of the least developed. According to the 2015 Tourism Zoning Concept of Bulgaria, adopted by the Ministry of Tourism [20], the country is divided into nine tourism regions: Danube, Stara Planina, Sofia, Thrace, Rose Valley, Rila-Pirin, Rhodopes, Varna Black Sea Coast, and Burgas Black Sea Coast. Among these, the Danube Region leads in the number of municipalities (67) and covers 21% of the country's territory; however, in terms of population, it ranks lower. In contrast, key tourism development indicators - such as the number of accommodation facilities, overnight stays, and tourism revenues - position the Danube Region among the least developed in Bulgaria.

The zoning document recommends that the region specialize primarily in cultural and cruise tourism, while its extended specialization should include cultural-historical tourism, river cruises, adventure and eco-tourism, urban entertainment and shopping tourism, wine and culinary tourism, as well as religious and pilgrimage tourism. Following the official adoption of the concept, management organizations for tourism regions have gradually been established, with a primary focus on marketing functions.

The Danube River itself and other natural attractions are the main draws for tourists to Bulgaria's Danube Tourism Region. However, there is a significant deficit in the availability of additional tourism services related to the river, such as water sports, fishing, river cruises, and sightseeing boat trips [21]. The overall development of tourism in the region faces numerous challenges. The average length of tourist stays remains short, highlighting the need for infrastructure and attraction improvements. Additional shortcomings include environmental pollution, limited recreational facilities, and a lack of diverse tourism offerings.

Despite the region's generally favorable conditions for the development of cycling tourism - such as its predominantly flat terrain - the existing road infrastructure is largely inadequate and not well-adapted to the needs of cyclists [22].

Based on the findings thus far, the low level of tourism development in the Danube Tourism Region of Bulgaria has, in effect, contributed to the preservation of wetlands along the Danube River, as its environmental impact has remained minimal. However, should this trend shift in the future, tourism must not be overlooked as a potential factor contributing to wetland degradation. The analysis thus far identifies river transport as the most significant factor exerting negative pressure on wetland ecosystems.

5 Sustainable Solutions and Policies

To mitigate the negative impact of river transport on wetlands and aquatic ecosystems along the Danube, it is essential to implement sustainable solutions and policies that balance economic needs with ecological requirements. Key measures that can be undertaken include: Development of environmentally friendly port technologies and alternative fuels; Integration of nature-based approaches in infrastructure construction and maintenance; Utilization of more efficient, low-emission vessels powered by alternative fuels; Enhancement of river ecosystem monitoring and management through international cooperation; Advancement of scientific research and innovation.

Development of Environmentally Friendly Port Technologies and Alternative Fuels [9] - With increasing traffic along the Danube, modernizing ports to minimize environmental harm is crucial. Sustainable technologies include intelligent navigation management systems, automated cargo-handling equipment that reduces energy consumption, and the integration of renewable energy sources such as solar and wind power into port infrastructure. Additionally, transitioning to alternative fuels such as biofuels or hydrogen can significantly reduce carbon emissions and toxic pollution, which is vital for the protection of water resources and ecosystems [3]. These measures not only reduce the environmental footprint of shipping but also generate economic benefits by fostering new technologies and job opportunities.

Integration of Nature-Based Approaches in Infrastructure Construction and Maintenance [12] - When constructing new hydrotechnical structures and modernizing existing infrastructure, sustainable development principles must be adhered to. This includes the application of ecological criteria in the design of locks, dams, and ports to minimize their impact on aquatic ecosystems and fish migration. For instance, incorporating fish passage systems in locks or using eco-friendly water level management techniques can improve migration conditions for aquatic species. Additionally, during infrastructure maintenance, efforts should focus on minimizing pollution and the release of harmful chemicals into the river, which often occur during construction and repair activities [1]. These steps are vital for maintaining ecological balance in river and wetland ecosystems.

Reduction of Dredging Activities and Implementation of Nature-Based Hydraulic Solutions – Establishing natural buffer zones along riverbanks [23] is another sustainable approach that helps mitigate erosion and sediment displacement.

Utilization of More Efficient, Low-Emission Vessels Powered by Alternative Fuels – The adoption of electric propulsion, hydrogen fuel cells, and liquefied natural gas (LNG) [8] can significantly contribute to the sustainability of river transport while reducing air and water pollution.

Enhancement of River Ecosystem Monitoring and Management through International Cooperation [13] – Sustainable management of the Danube requires an integrated approach that unites the efforts of all riparian states. International cooperation is key to effective water quality monitoring, establishing common environmental standards, and identifying threats that can only be addressed through coordinated actions. Programs such as the Danube Water Quality and Monitoring Program aim to integrate environmental and economic goals through joint scientific research and information exchange. Furthermore, efficient monitoring mechanisms can facilitate timely responses to pollution incidents, invasive species invasions, and other critical threats to the river's biodiversity [1]. International organizations, such as the International Commission for the Protection of the Danube River (ICPDR) and the European Commission, play a vital role in coordinating these efforts and implementing transboundary policies for sustainable water management.

Scientific Research and Innovation – Research and innovation are fundamental tools for sustainable development in the shipping industry, providing a scientific foundation for improved policies, technologies, and best practices. The introduction of smart and eco-friendly solutions will facilitate the advancement of transport along the Danube and other inland waterways while preserving the river's ecosystem functions.

6 Dawetrest Project: Research Methods

The DaWetRest Project (Danube Wetlands and Floodplains Restoration through Systemic, Community-Engaged, and Sustainable Innovative Actions) (https://dawetrest.eu/) focuses on wetland restoration through innovative habitat rehabilitation methods and sustainable water resource management. It aims to develop strategies for climate change adaptation while minimizing the environmental impact of river navigation. DaWetRest is funded under the Horizon Europe program, Mission Ocean (HORIZON-MISS-2022-OCEAN-01-02).

Scientific research and innovation play a crucial role in the successful implementation of wetland restoration and conservation projects. Within the DaWetRest project, these efforts contribute in several key areas:

Enhancement of Wetland Restoration Methods – Research on wetland ecosystem services (e.g., water filtration, carbon storage, flood mitigation) will serve as a foundation for the application of proven restoration techniques. The use of innovative monitoring technologies such as satellite imaging, drones, and sensors will enable rapid and precise observation of changes in wetland ecosystems. This will lead to more effective restoration management and timely responses to emerging issues.

Development of Sustainable and Innovative Management Practices – Scientific studies on interactions between vegetation, water, and soil will support the creation of innovative techniques for restoring the hydrological balance of wetlands. For instance, the use of natural barriers, such as wetland buffer strips and water storage areas, may be based on new scientific discoveries. Innovations in plant genetics and microbiology can facilitate the development of new plant species that are more resistant to climate change or pollution, making them suitable for restoration initiatives.

Optimization of Monitoring and Ecosystem Assessment – Research on biodiversity within wetland habitats will provide new insights into species composition, behavior, and adaptation to environmental conditions. This will aid in the better planning and adaptation of restoration projects according to ecosystem needs. Innovations in artificial intelligence (AI) and machine learning will allow the processing of vast datasets collected via sensors and satellites, predicting long-term changes in wetland health. These tools will improve ecosystem management and provide reliable forecasts for restoration efforts.

Creation of New Solutions for Sustainable Agriculture and Economic Integration – Research into sustainable agricultural practices suitable for wetland-adjacent areas will provide economic justification for restoration projects. Studies on agricultural techniques that minimize environmental damage will lead to new strategies that harmonize farming activities with conservation efforts. Innovations in sustainable tourism and ecological business models will offer new approaches to utilizing wetland resources while simultaneously supporting the local economy and ensuring long-term financial sustainability for conservation initiatives.

Education and Community Awareness – Research on community engagement and public perception will help develop effective educational programs aimed at raising awareness about the importance of wetlands. Innovative learning tools, such as virtual reality simulations or mobile applications for ecosystem monitoring, will enable local residents and stakeholders to actively participate in restoration projects while learning how to preserve their natural heritage.

DaWetRest aims to develop and demonstrate specific solutions applicable to the Danube River and the Black Sea to address challenges affecting inland and coastal wetlands.

The project is structured into three key phases:

- Development and demonstration of specific solutions in the Danube River basin;
- Validation of solutions by local communities and stakeholders across Europe;
- Planning and scaling of implementation to ensure long-term adoption.

DaWetRest seeks to translate European policies into innovative local actions, which will be tested and validated in three main demonstration sites, paving the way for future large-scale implementation. The three pilot locations focus on coastal wetland conservation: Middle Danube (Croatia), Lower Danube (Bulgaria), Danube Delta (Romania) (Fig. 4).

By integrating scientific research and innovation, the DaWetRest project will not only develop effective and adaptable solutions for wetland restoration but also enhance the long-term resilience of these ecosystems. These efforts will yield scientific discoveries

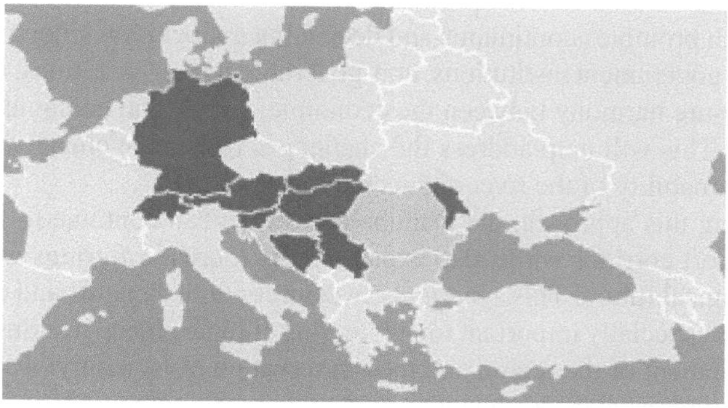

Fig. 4. Geographical location of the three demonstrators and associated regions.

with global applications, ensuring the sustainability of wetlands and the biodiversity they support.

7 Conclusion

River transport along the Danube and tourism in the adjacent tourism region are among the key economic drivers that play a vital role in the economy, logistics, and well-being of numerous European nations. However, the intensive exploitation of the river has significant negative consequences for its ecosystems, particularly its wetlands, and affects both the quantity and quality of water resources. Alterations in the river's morphostructure, loss of biodiversity, and water pollution are just some of the challenges that endanger the natural heritage and sustainability of these valuable ecosystems.

Climate change further exacerbates the situation. Rising temperatures, shifting precipitation patterns, and an increased frequency of extreme climatic events such as floods and droughts are exerting a growing influence on the hydrological regime of the Danube and its associated ecosystems. These climatic changes often lead to unpredictable variations in water levels, which worsen navigation conditions, increase the risk of bank erosion, and disrupt the natural balance of wetlands. This, in turn, poses serious risks to ecosystem services, biodiversity, and the regulation of local climate conditions.

The findings of this study indicate that, despite these threats, it is possible to achieve a balance between the economic utilization of the river and the conservation of its wetlands through the implementation of innovative and sustainable solutions. The development of integrated policies that reconcile ecological, socio-economic, and climate adaptation goals is essential for the future of the Danube River and its riparian wetlands. Such policies must include modernizing port infrastructure, incorporating energy-efficient technologies and alternative fuels, and optimizing navigation efficiency, all while adhering to strict environmental standards that account for climatic fluctuations.

A critical aspect of Danube management is fostering cooperation among the countries in its basin, encouraging shared research on ecosystem services, enhancing community engagement, facilitating knowledge exchange, and strengthening joint efforts for water ecosystem monitoring and conservation. An integrated river basin management approach, which promotes continuous and deepening cooperation among all stakeholders—including government institutions, non-governmental organizations, and the private sector—can ensure harmony between the economic, social, and ecological dimensions of the Danube. This will help address the challenges of climate change and secure the long-term sustainability of the river and its natural resources.

By following this approach, the Danube ecosystem can continue to function as an essential transport corridor while also expanding its tourism offerings without jeopardizing its ecological future. This synergy between economic benefits and environmental responsibility is especially important for addressing climate objectives. Ensuring the sustainable development of the region and the conservation of its natural wealth for future generations requires a balanced and integrated strategy that safeguards ecosystems while preserving the economic potential of river transport and tourism.

Research and innovative initiatives within the DaWetRest project, funded under the Horizon Europe program and the European Commission's "Restore Our Ocean and Waters" mission, represent just one of many approaches that contribute to the sustainable development of the Danube region, particularly its wetlands and floodplains.

Acknowledgement. This work is co-funded by the European Union Horizon Europe programme (HORIZON-MISS-2022-OCEAN-01) under Grant Agreement № 101113015 (DaWetRest).

References

1. ICPDR: Danube River Basin Management Plan – Update 2021, Vienna (2021)
2. Jungwirth, M., Schinegger, R., Muhar, S.: Ecological integrity of river systems. Hydrobiologia **729**(1), 1–5 (2014)
3. European Commission: Sustainable and Smart Mobility Strategy, Brussels (2020). https://eur-lex.europa.eu/legal-content/EN/TXT/HTML/?uri=CELEX:52020DC0789. Accessed 10 Mar 2025
4. Schmutz, S., Moog, O.: Dams, hydrological alterations and fragmentation. In: Rivers of Europe, pp. 71–86. Academic Press (2018)
5. Nehring, S.: Aquatic invasive species in European waters: distribution, impacts, and management. Aquat. Conserv. Mar. Freshwat. Ecosyst. **15**(3), 279–288 (2005)
6. Leuven, R.S., et al.: The river Rhine: a global highway for dispersal of aquatic invasive species. Biol. Invasions **11**(9), 1989–2008 (2009)
7. WWF: Guidelines for environmentally sustainable inland navigation on the Danube River (2019)
8. European Union: Transport Policy Report 2023. Annual Report on Transport in the European Union. European Commission, Directorate-General for Mobility and Transport, p. 45 (2024). https://commission.europa.eu/publications/annual-activity-report-2023-mobility-and-transport_en. Accessed 10 Mar 2025
9. European Commission: Inland Waterway Transport in Europe: A Key to Sustainable Mobility, Brussels, pp. 1–5 (2022). https://www.europarl.europa.eu/RegData/etudes/BRIE/2022/698918/EPRS_BRI(2022)698918_EN.pdf. Accessed 10 Mar 2025
10. Organization for Economic Co-operation and Development: The Role of Inland Waterways in Sustainable Transport. OECD Publishing (2021)
11. Danube Commission: Annual Report 2021: Waterway Traffic and Infrastructure Developments on the Danube, Budapest, p. 136 (2021), https://www.ccnr.eu/files/documents/om/om21_II_en.pdf. Accessed 10 Mar 2025

12. International Commission for the Protection of the Danube River: Danube River Basin Management Plan – Update 2021, Vienna, p. 290 (2022). https://www.icpdr.org/sites/default/files/nodes/documents/danube_river_basin_managament_plan_-_update_2021_full_text.pdf. Accessed 10 Mar 2025
13. World Wide Fund for Nature: Danube: A River in Crisis – The Impact of Climate Change and Human Activity on the Danube Ecosystem, WWF International (2021)
14. European Environment Agency: State of the Environment Report: Water Quality in European Rivers, Copenhagen (2023)
15. Bühler, B., Mühlich, L.: Ship-induced waves and their impact on river morphology. J. Hydrol. **314**(1–4), 192–206 (2005)
16. Fenton, J., Lovell, P.: Hydrodynamic effects of ship traffic on the environment. Environ. Impact Assess. Rev. **16**(4), 291–314 (1996). https://doi.org/10.1016/S0195-9255(96)00017-3
17. Chow, V., Maidment, D., Mays, L.: Applied Hydrology, p. 294. McGraw-Hill (1988)
18. Mitsch, W.J., Gosselink, J.G.: Wetlands, p. 736. Wiley, Hoboken (2015). ISBN-10 1118676823
19. Jørgensen, S.E., Fath, B.D.: Fundamentals of Ecological Modelling. Elsevier, Amsterdam (2004). ISBN 978-0444815729
20. Ministry of Tourism: Concept for Tourism Zoning in Bulgaria, Sofia, p. 66 (2015). [In Bulgarian: Министерство на туризма, Концепция за туристическо райониране на България, София, с. 66 (2015)]. https://www.tourism.government.bg/sites/tourism.government.bg/files/uploads/raionirane/koncepcia.pdf. Accessed 10 Mar 2025
21. Ministry of Tourism (n.d.): Marketing Strategy for the Danube Tourism Region 2021–2024, Sofia, p. 298 (2024), [In Bulgarian: Министерство на туризма, Маркетингова стратегия на Дунавски туристически район 2021–2024, София, с. 298 (2024)]. https://outr.bulgariatravel.org/sites/default/files/documents/2024-04/04.%20Дунавски%20туристически%20район.pdf. Accessed 10 Mar 2025
22. Kaloyanov, K.: Research and Development of Bicycle Tourism along the Bulgarian Danube Corridor. St. Kliment Ohridski University Press, p. 234 (2019). [In Bulgarian: Калоянов, К. Проучване и развитие на велосипедния туризъм по българското поречие на р. Дунав. София, с. 234 (2019)]. https://www.baatbg.org/docs/Danube.cycling.research.BG.pdf. Accessed 10 Mar 2025
23. Wetlands International: The State of Wetlands in Europe: Challenges and Opportunities (2022)

Basic Approaches to Digitalization of National Segments of International Transport Corridors Crossing the Territory of Azerbaijan

Tofig Babayev(✉) and Valery Virkovski

Institute of Control Systems, Ministry of Science and Education of the Republic of Azerbaijan, 68, B. Vahabzada, Baku AZ1141, Azerbaijan
babayev.tofig@gmail.com

Abstract. The article examines the conceptual and practical foundations for the digitalization of national segments of international transport corridors (ITCs) in Azerbaijan. It analyzes international experience and the evolution of approaches to the creation of digital transport corridors (DTCs) in the EU, Eurasian Economic Union, and Asia-Pacific region. The multilevel architecture of DTCs and principles for their construction—such as digital sovereignty, interoperability, and multimodality—are described in detail. Special attention is paid to the development of national eLogistics systems (NELS) as integration platforms for multimodal transport. The article presents Azerbaijan's current strategies and initiatives, including legal frameworks and infrastructure development plans for key corridors such as the Trans-Caspian International Transport Route, the North-South Corridor, and the Zangezur Corridor. Technological solutions for the digitalization of these corridors, including blockchain-based platforms and data pipeline concepts, are also proposed to ensure secure cross-border information exchange and improve the efficiency of logistics operations.

Keywords: Digital Transport Corridor (DTC) · eLogistics · International Transport Corridor (ITC) · Digital Sovereignty · Blockchain · Data Pipeline · Cross-border Logistics · Zangezur Corridor · Multimodal First Section

1 Introduction - State of the Art

Conceptual development of approaches and projects on digitalization of transport and logistics sector and transport corridors in the Eastern Partnership (EaP) countries, including Azerbaijan, was launched in 2015, when the topic of electronic logistics (eLogistics) and digital transport corridors (DTC) was recognized as a priority and included in the EU and EaP Ministerial Declaration on the Digital Economy [1]. This declaration highlighted the importance of cross-border connectivity between transport infrastructures and transport corridors of partner countries and the EU, as well as solving the problem of interoperability of multimodal eLogistics platforms. At the same time, the European Commission established the Digital Transport and Logistics Forum (DTLF) [2]. Within DTLF a special expert group was set up to develop interoperable information systems for the EU transport corridor network (TEN-T).

A. Abbasov et al. (Eds.): PLMO 2025, CCIS 2767, pp. 58–69, 2026.
https://doi.org/10.1007/978-3-032-13672-5_6

In 2016, the United Nations Economic Commission for Asia and the Pacific (UNESCAP) published the report on its regional study "The use of logistics information systems for increased efficiency and effectiveness" [3]. The main objectives of the UNESCAP study were to review the technical aspects of existing national and transnational logistics information systems (such as LOGINK in China, NEAL-NET network connecting national logistics information systems of the PRC, Japan and South Korea, etc.), identify best practices and provide recommendations on the functional architecture and technological approaches to the creation and use of such systems. UNESCAP recommendations were to create national eLogistics systems for digitization of business processes in all modes of transport with their subsequent integration into supranational systems/platforms for transcontinental DTC management.

In 2017–2019, the countries of the Eurasian Economic Union (EAEU) declared digital transport corridors as one of the strategic priorities of the EAEU's digital agenda and implemented a research project to develop the concept of the EAEU DTC ecosystem. As a result of this research project, the program for building DTC ecosystem was formed in 2020–2022 and projects were initiated to develop a set of priority services and digital platforms for national segments of EAEU transport corridors.

In 2019–2022, two large-scale projects, FEDeRATED and FENIX, were implemented in the EU countries to create organizational and technological approaches to the digitalization of TEN-T corridors and to build a European information exchange network in the transport and logistics sector. In the course of these projects, a number of TEN-T corridors were certified for pilot digitalization. In 2020, the European Commission adopted a large-scale regulatory directive for the exchange of information in the transport and logistics sector, eFTI (electronic Freight Transport Information) [4], and started to implement a 7-year plan for the introduction of relevant regulations, standards, technological norms, as well as eFTI certified platforms in the EU countries.

In 2021–2022, an expert team led by China's LOGINK National Logistics Information Platform developed a draft ISO23355 standard on formats and exchange of structured data between logistics information service providers, and in 2023, LOGINK announced the International Logistics Trusted Information Sharing initiative to ensure the effective development and digitalization of One Belt-One Road transport corridors.

2 Multilevel Architecture and Principles of DTC Construction

In 2017–2018, studies were conducted in the Eastern Partnership countries on the topics of eCommerce, eLogistics and DTC [5]. In the course of those studies the following extended DTC definition was developed and adopted: Digital Transport Corridor is a federated network (chain) of interconnected digital platforms that integrate information resources of the participants of the international transport corridor (ITC) and form a trusted information space around it in the form of a "data pipeline" for the purpose of digitalization and increasing the efficiency of end-to-end business processes in transcontinental supply chains, optimization of data flow and the use of electronic (digital) logistics. In this regard, the concept of electronic (digital) logistics was also explained, which deals with the analysis, optimization and management of information flows in supply chains, as well as the formation and provision of digital services on this basis. The main functions of eLogistics platforms were considered to be as follows:

- Collection and analysis of data (data capture & mining) in supply chains for their subsequent collective use (data sharing) and exchange in order to improve the efficiency of interaction and synergetic cooperation of all participants of logistics processes, as well as managerial decision-making;
- Ensuring interoperability of processes and systems used by different modes of transport (multimodality);
- Unification of standards for logistics data exchange based on structured electronic messages and/or standardized electronic documents.

The following levels were distinguished in the architecture of interaction between the information systems of DTC participants as a heterogeneous interregional information network (Fig. 1):

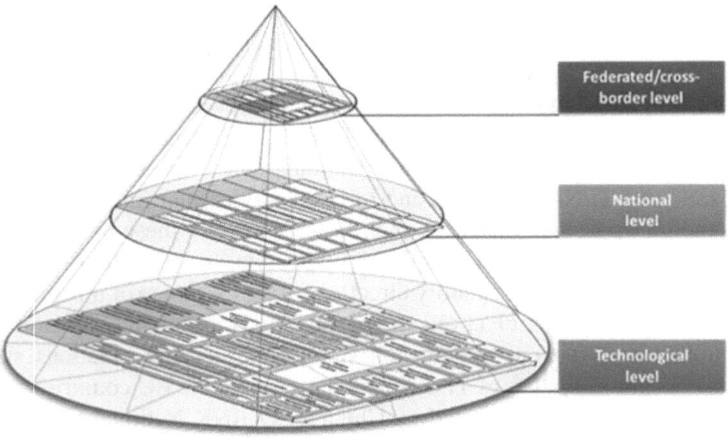

Fig. 1. Levels of information interaction between DTC participants.

The first (basic/technological) DTC level consists of information systems of transport corridor participants: cargo owners, trade organizations, carriers, owners of transport and logistics infrastructure and vehicles, national regulatory and supervisory authorities, financial institutions, freight forwarders, insurance companies, cargo security companies, etc.

The second level of national DTC segments are national eLogistics systems (**NELS**) created on the basis of integration platforms.

The third supranational DTC level is interregional information and service platforms with a federated structure, built on the principle of "Single Window", form data pipelines that integrate NELSs of the countries participating in a particular corridor and can be created on the basis of balanced business models and joint ventures of key players in the transport and logistics sector of the countries involved.

A common characteristic of the federated approach to building a DTC architecture is the principle of maintaining the digital sovereignty of each participating country, while working towards a common business outcome through the use of their infrastructure and resources. As a structural and organizational principle, federalization equalizes the rights of DTC actors and gives them a sufficient degree of freedom to operate and provide services at their national level. Therefore, for the supranational level of the DTC architecture, federalism and integration of national segments are effective principles for harmonizing the market interests of DTC member countries, allowing them to join their efforts on mutually beneficial terms to provide a joint package of transport, logistics and digital services on the global market. Compliance with this principle of DTC building can become an effective tool for the coordinated development of digital and transport infrastructures of the countries participating in a particular corridor and contribute to the effective realization of its transit potential and increase competitiveness.

In addition, the following basic requirements for the above functional levels and elements should be taken into account in the course of DTC projects:

- The federated level platform should not replace the information systems of transport corridor participants (the first level of DTC) or national eLogistics systems of the countries involved (the second level of DTC), but should create synergy effects from the interaction of these systems within the integral DTC architecture and ensure information security of cross-border transactions.
- DTC should be created through seamless integration of national segments (NELS) capable of serving multimodal cargo transportation by sea, rail, road and air. To implement this principle, it is advisable to build NELS using interoperable digital eLogistics platforms. Such platforms are considered to become "building blocks" of digital infrastructure, from which DTCs of any configuration can be built by composing the member countries of a transport corridor into a transit chain.
- Seamless integration of national systems requires addressing regulatory, organizational, semantic (documentary) and technical interoperability. In each country, the national platform is designed to act as the information flows integrator that processes data from the main participants and controllers of multimodal transportation as well as converts them into standardized formats of international electronic documents used to accompany transit cargo. Thus, NELS interoperable platforms, as well as standardized formats of data and electronic documents used by supply chain participants, will help to ensure interoperability of national segments of DTC as a federated and scalable information and service system.
- The DTC should provide transportation control and monitoring of cargo flows along its entire transportation route from consignor to consignee.
- During the DTC construction, it is necessary to build a unified trusted information space of the corridor participants, which can be effectively created in the form of

a data pipeline [6]. For the effective information exchange, the DTC should implement electronic document management and exchange of structured data/messages in accordance with international standards and formats.

- DTC construction requires solving the tasks of re-engineering and digitalization of end-to-end business processes in transport corridors, including transit and export-import transportation.
- For the development and optimization of DTC elements it is advisable to use digital models of infrastructure objects and vehicles, which can be created on the basis of relevant data transmitted from the first DTC level of technological systems or from the second level of NELS digital platforms.
- DTCs should enable the provision of a developed package of value-added digital services to key ITC and supply chain participants.

Taking into account these requirements, the experts of the interregional working group on eLogistics and DTC of the EaP and SPECA countries have developed the following principles for building digital corridors:

1. The principle of preserving the digital sovereignty of ITC member countries, implemented through the creation of DTC national segments, which can be integrated into transport corridors of various configurations.
2. The principle of interoperability of national segments, information systems and digital platforms of DTC participants.
3. The principle of federated approach to the formation of a supranational DTC platform.
4. The principle of multimodality, which implies the creation of systems and digital platforms serving transportation by all major modes of transport.
5. The principle of visualization: cargo transportation monitoring and traceability.
6. The principle of digital trust and information security, based on the creation of a trusted information space in the DTC, modern methods of identification of participants and objects, as well as ensuring a high level of information security in data and documents exchange.
7. The principle of seamless cross-border information exchange using standardized data formats and electronic documents, ensuring their legal significance.

The above principles have been effectively used and confirmed in assessing the level and parameters of DTC projects currently being developed in the countries of the Eurasian continent [7].

3 Approaches to Digitalization of National ITC Segments in Azerbaijan

The main tasks on digitalization of the transport and logistics sector of the country were included in the strategy of socio-economic development of Azerbaijan 2026 [8]. In particular, this document stipulates the implementation of a unified transport and logistics strategy aimed at the development of transit transportation, taking into account the potential role of Azerbaijan in international transport corridors, as well as the expansion of the use of digital technologies to improve transit transportation and logistics, including:

- Creation of a system ensuring integration of international transportation and logistics participants on a single digital platform;
- Joining and implementation of the provisions of the electronic CMR and eSMGS protocols;
- Cargo tracking and tracing services along the entire route;
- Integration of transportation operations into a national digital platform for 24/7 prompt implementation.

These tasks were detailed in the Decree of the President of the Republic of Azerbaijan No. 4179 dated November 23, 2023, on international transport passing through the territory of the country and increasing the transit potential of corridors and transportation of transit cargoes for 2024–2026 [9]. This decree approved a plan of practical actions for the development and digitalization of international transport corridors crossing the territory of the Republic of Azerbaijan, as well as the creation of an electronic portal and a national digital transport and logistics platform. The core technological solution developed by eLogistics and DTC Working Group of the Eastern Partnership countries for the DTC between Baltic and Black Seas can be used as a basic approach to the creation of such a platform [10]. The functional flow diagram of such an integration platform is presented in Fig. 2.

The functional architecture of the platform includes an integration level with modules providing NELS connection to technological systems of different transport modalities, as well as verification, storage and processing of data received from them. Such integration platform also provides NELS interaction and connectivity with transport and logistics platforms of other DTC member countries.

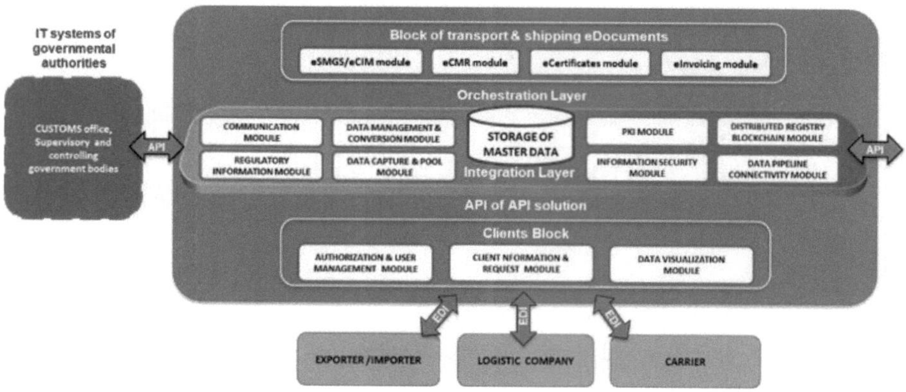

Fig. 2. Functional architecture of a typical NELS integration platform.

The orchestration layer should ensure digitalization of the main multimodal business processes and include the main NELS service modules, as well as implement the exchange of various data sets and electronic documents for all modes of transport, including eCMR, eSMGS/CIM, eCertificate of Origin and eTIR. The client block of modules provides authorization and management of NELS users, as well as processing their requests for access to data and documents, transfer of requested information and its visualization. To implement this functionality in Azerbaijan the following technical tasks shall be accomplished:

a. Development and implementation of a NELS integration platform to ensure connectivity with IT systems of government agencies and TLS participants at the national level;
b. Secure information exchange in TLS, as well as in cross-border exchange of data and electronic documents with DTC member countries based on data pipeline technology;
c. Formation of trusted information space in TLS of Azerbaijan;
d. Selection of a technological approach for monitoring the transportation of cargo and goods (tracking and tracing).

The considered approaches were used to develop schemes for digitalization of the national segments of the main ITCs crossing the territory of Azerbaijan: Trans-Caspian International Transport Route (TITR), the western branch of the North-South Corridor, Baku-Tbilisi-Kars and the Zangezur Corridor, the corresponding ITC configurations are shown in Figs. 3, 4 and 5.

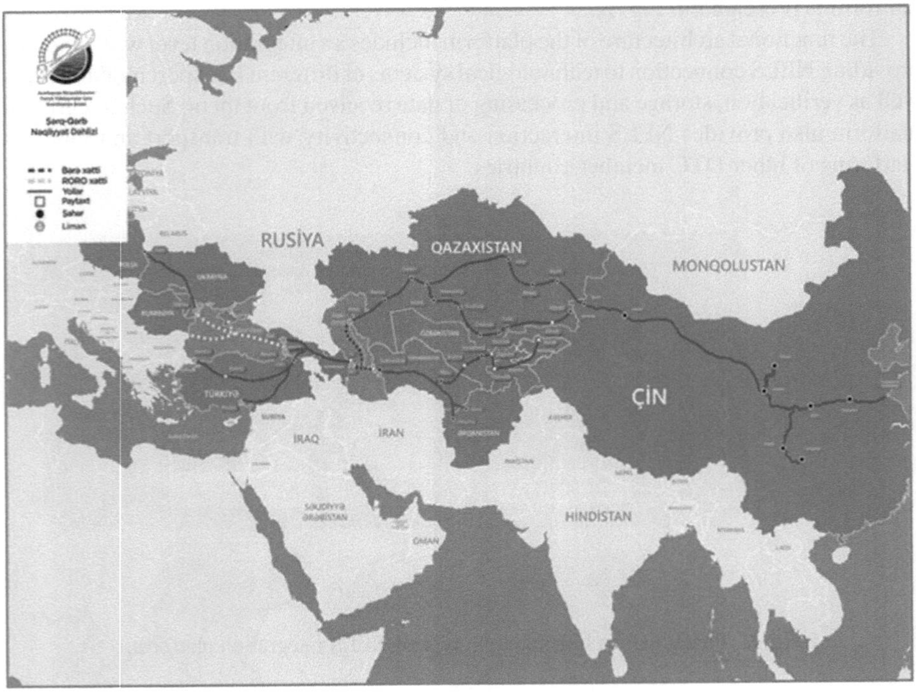

Fig. 3. Trans-Caspian International Transport Route (TITR).

Fig. 4. North-South International Transport Corridor.

The digitalization schemes for the TMTM and the North-South corridor are shown in Figs. 6 and 7.

The approaches to digitalization of the TITR and North-South ITC have been previously discussed at the previous PLMO conference in 2024. In this paper, we will consider in more detail the proposed solutions for the digitalization of the Zangezur corridor. It's known, that Azerbaijan has successfully completed the construction of the national segment of the Baku-Tbilisi-Kars railroad corridor, modernization of the Baku International Port of Alyat and the Astara (Azerbaijan)—Astara (Iran) section of the railroad. Thus, Azerbaijan, as the core country located at the crossroads of the key East-West and North-South transport corridors, is currently positioned as an important regional logistics and trade hub. After the liberation of the occupied territories in 2020, a new geopolitical situation has emerged in the region and a new Zangezur corridor became open for the development, which significantly expands the possibilities of effective use of the mentioned transport corridors TITR and North-South. In this regard, the construction of transportation infrastructure of the Zangezur corridor was activated, see Fig. 8.

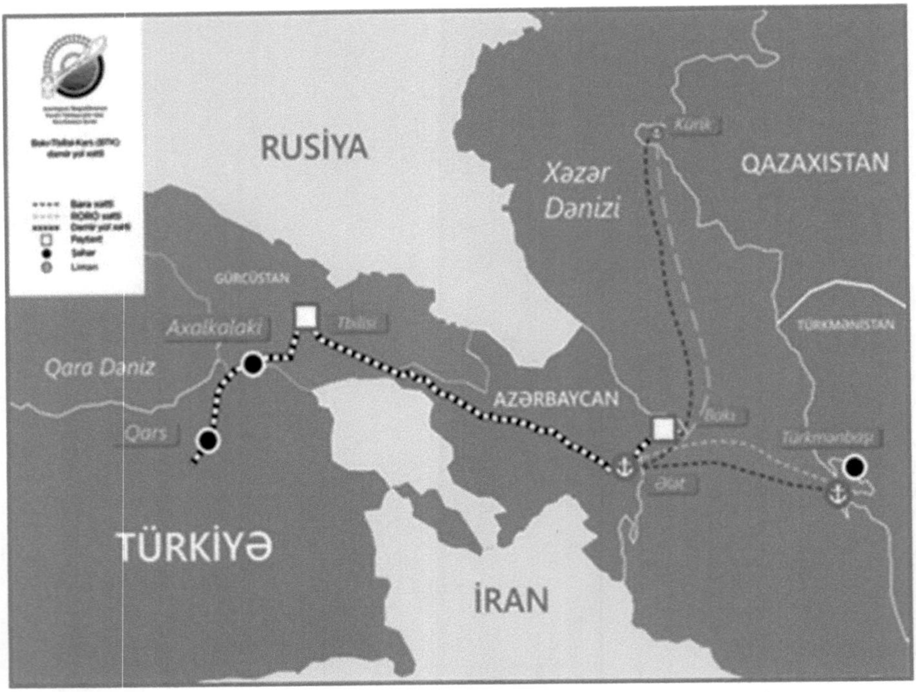

Fig. 5. Baku-Tbilisi-Kars international transport corridor.

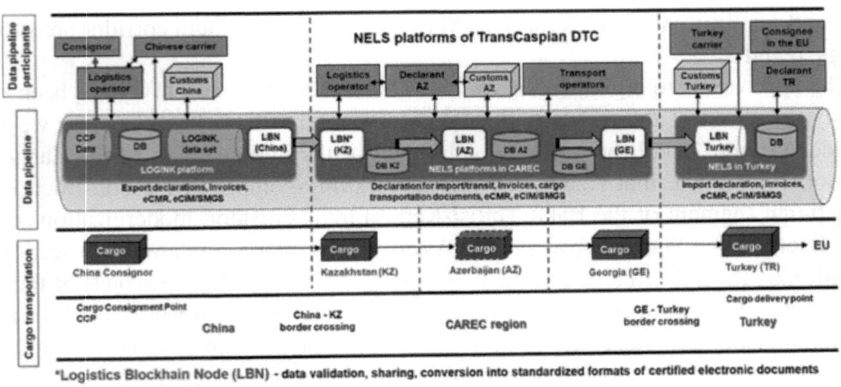

Fig. 6. Digitalization scheme for the TITR corridor.

Using Zangezur corridor, the main part of Azerbaijan's territory can be connected to the Nakhichevan Autonomous Republic, thus opening up a completely new transport corridor to Türkiye, and making possible to serve the growing number of requests to transport cargoes from the Central Asia to the EU through Azerbaijan. As a result, the Zangezur corridor, being linked to the port of Alyat and the international airport under construction in Zangilan, will create additional multimodal opportunities for the

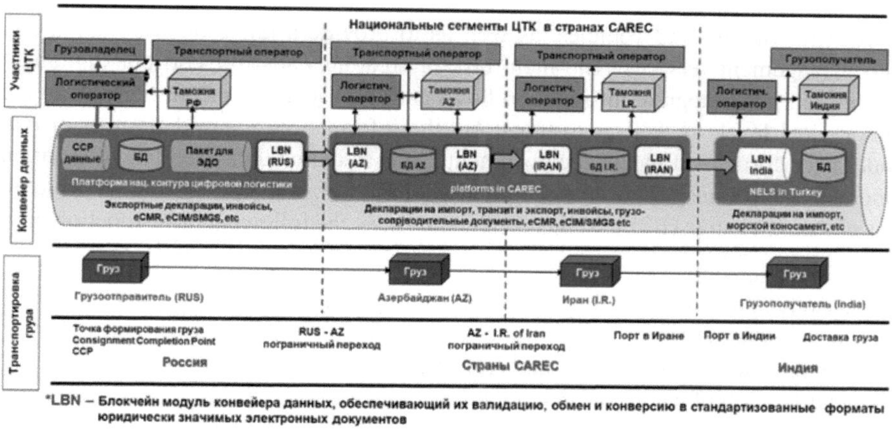

Fig. 7. Digitalization scheme for the North-South corridor.

Fig. 8. Zangezur Corridor Development and Digitalization Scheme.

development of trade and logistics routes through Central Asian countries. Therefore, in addition to developing Azerbaijan's transport infrastructure and secure its role as a key international trade and logistics hub, appropriate initiatives should also be undertaken to digitalize transport and logistics processes as well as to create the necessary digital infrastructures for Zangezur Corridor.

The developed technical solution for the information and service system of the Zangezur corridor is shown schematically on Fig. 8. It was designed to combine information resources of the corridor participants in order to digitalize and improve the efficiency of end-to-end business processes in international supply chains, optimize the use of infrastructure and vehicles, as well as to provide a range of information and cargo management services. The main task in creating Zangezur corridor digitalization solution is to integrate information flows and IT systems of the participants at the technological level, as well as to transform the information received from them into standardized formats of electronic documents and structured data used for information support of cargo transportation at the international level. The system shall provide all types of data exchange (B2B, B2G and G2G) and have the following basic functionality:

- User Management;
- Data exchange with technological systems integrated;
- Information requests;
- Information service, regulatory and reference information;
- Standardization of electronic documents and messages;
- Data integrity, security and privacy;
- Monitoring and tracking of shipments.

The integration platform of Zangezur DTC is supposed to be implemented using the PaaS (Platform-as-a-Service) ideology. PaaS is to host logistics block chain nodes (LBN) to ensure the maintenance of decentralized ledgers (blockchain) of DTC architecture, including LBNs of national and regional levels. Technical solutions will be built on the basis of the developed logistics blockchain platform implemented on industrial open-source technologies.

To solve the problem of cross-border information exchange the cryptographic information protection tools in distributed registry technologies (blockchain) can be used, which will allow to use the advantages of a distributed ledger (decentralized databases) in cross-border exchange of transport and logistics data. A successful technical solution of this problem will allow to implement "smart contracts" based on distributed ledger transactions as legally significative electronic documents. The blockchain is supposed to be used with the following basic functionality:

- electronic legally significative document flow in the transport corridor when executing shipping documents (including multimodal transportation);
- decentralized storage of structured data in the form of an electronic document;
- contractual and other mutual obligations of DTC participants (in the form of executable "smart contracts") to organize transit transportation in cross-border cargo transportation, certified by electronic digital signatures of officials from different countries.

Preliminary list of services to be provided as a result of digitalization of Zangezur corridor may include:

- Support of electronic documents flow for DTC transportation on all transport modes;
- Transportation contracts (including smart contracts) online;
- Monitoring and tracking of cargo (cargo tracking system);
- Analysis of the state of the DTC infrastructure;
- Processing of commercial, transportation and customs electronic documents at the stages of cargo cross-border transportation.

This project initiative has been prepared with the participation of experts from eLogistics and DTC Working Group coordinated by the Institute of Control Systems of the Ministry of Science and Education of the Republic of Azerbaijan.

References

1. https://digital-strategy.ec.europa.eu/en/news/first-eastern-partnership-ministerial-meeting-digital-economy
2. https://transport.ec.europa.eu/transport-themes/digital-transport-and-logistics-forum-dtlf_en
3. https://www.unescap.org/resources/regional-study-use-logistics-information-systems-increased-efficiency-and-effectiveness
4. EU Regulation 2020/1056 on electronic freight transport information (eFTI). https://www.transport-community.org/wp-content/uploads/2021/12/EU-Regulation-20201056-on-electronic-freight-transport-information-eFTI.pdf
5. https://eufordigital.eu/library/study-on-the-harmonisation-of-the-digital-markets-in-the-eastern-partnership-etrade-elogistics-digital-transport-corridors/
6. White Paper on Data Pipeline Concept for Improving Data Quality in the Supply Chain. https://unece.org/trade/documents/2023/10/session-documents/white-paper-data-pipeline-concept-improving-data-quality
7. Basic Principles for the Creation of Digital Transport Corridors and project analysis in the countries of Eurasia – Proceedings of 7th International Conference "Transport Bridge Europe-Asia" (2023)
8. chromeextsion://efaidnbmnnnibpcajpcglclefindmkaj/. https://brussels.mfa.gov.az/files/shares/2022%202026%20Social%20and%20Economic%20Development%20Strategy.pdf
9. https://monitoring.gov.az/en/page/46/azerbaycan-respublikasinin-erazisinden-kecen-beynelxalq-neqliyyat-dehlizlerinin-tranzit-potensialinin-artirilmasina-ve-tranzit-yukdasimalarin-tesviqine-dair-20242026-ci-iller-ucun-fealiyyet-plani
10. Preparatory Actions to pilot a Digital Multi-modal Transport Corridor between the Baltic Sea and the Black Sea. https://eufordigital.eu/wp-content/uploads/2020/06/DTC-report-draft.pdf

Transformative Strategies in the Energy Sector for a Low-Carbon Transport Future

Piotr F. Borowski[1,2](✉)

[1] Department of Economics and Management, Khazar University, 41 Mahsati Str., AZ1096 Baku, Azerbaijan
pborowski@autograf.pl

[2] Faculty of Business and International Relations, Vistula University, 3 Stokłosy Str., 02-787 Warsaw, Poland

Abstract. This chapter examines the crucial role that innovative strategies adopted by energy companies play in the decarbonization of the transport sector. As climate change mitigation becomes an urgent global priority, and the European Union tightens its regulations and environmental policy frameworks, a coordinated and systemic approach to energy production, distribution, and consumption in the transport sector is becoming increasingly important. Energy companies are emerging as key actors in this transformation, moving beyond their traditional roles to become active drivers of low-emission mobility. Their contributions include the generation and integration of renewable energy sources, investment in energy storage technologies and smart grids, and the development of electric vehicle charging infrastructure. Furthermore, energy companies are engaging in cross-sector collaboration and digital innovation to support the efficient management of energy flows and mobility services. These initiatives not only reduce greenhouse gas emissions from the transport sector but also enhance energy security, system flexibility, and economic resilience. By implementing comprehensive and forward-looking innovation strategies, energy companies are accelerating the transition to sustainable transport, aligning business practices with climate goals, and responding proactively to market and policy changes. This study highlights the strategic importance of the energy sector's involvement in shaping a carbon-neutral future for transport, thereby contributing to a more sustainable and resilient mobility ecosystem at both national and European levels.

Keywords: Decarbonization of Transport · Energy Sector Innovation · Renewable Energy Integration · Energy Storage Technologies · Smart Grids · Electric Vehicle Charging Infrastructure

1 Introduction

To decarbonize the transport sector and make it environmentally friendly, a systemic and integrated approach is required—one that aligns closely with the broader transformation of the energy sector.

A. Abbasov et al. (Eds.): PLMO 2025, CCIS 2767, pp. 70–81, 2026.
https://doi.org/10.1007/978-3-032-13672-5_7

The first key strategy is the electrification of transport, which involves replacing internal combustion engines with electric vehicles (EVs) across private, public, and commercial fleets. However, electrification will only be as sustainable as the electricity that powers it. This underscores the need for investments in renewable energy production, smart grids, and energy storage systems that ensure the stability and availability of clean power. Fast and ultra-fast charging infrastructure, increasingly integrated with solar or wind energy sources, must also be widely deployed to support the growing demand for EVs [1].

The second strategy focuses on the deployment of green hydrogen and synthetic fuels (e-fuels). These alternative energy carriers are especially crucial for transport modes that are difficult to electrify, such as long-haul freight, maritime shipping, and aviation. Green hydrogen—produced through electrolysis using renewable electricity—can be used in fuel cells or new-generation combustion engines. E-fuels, made from captured CO_2 and green hydrogen, offer a carbon-neutral solution compatible with existing infrastructure. For both hydrogen and e-fuels, scaling production and developing refueling infrastructure are essential to ensure availability and affordability [2].

The third essential strategy is the development of smart, integrated mobility systems. Digitalization plays a critical role in managing transport and energy systems efficiently. Technologies such as artificial intelligence, big data, and Internet of Things (IoT) enable real-time monitoring, predictive maintenance, and dynamic traffic management. Smart mobility solutions optimize transport flows, promote modal shifts to low-emission options, and facilitate user access to clean transport services. Additionally, vehicle-to-grid (V2G) technology allows electric vehicles to supply energy back to the grid, enhancing energy flexibility and supporting renewable integration.

Together, these three strategies—electrification, alternative fuels, and digitalized mobility—form the foundation of a modern, resilient, and low-emission transport system. When coordinated with the decarbonization of the energy sector, they create a pathway toward achieving climate neutrality and building a more sustainable future.

2 Literature Review

Decarbonizing the transport sector has become a key topic in contemporary economic, environmental, and green energy policy discussions [3, 4]. Scientists widely recognize that transport is one of the most emitting sectors globally, particularly in industrialized countries, but increasingly also in developing and emerging economies [5–8]. The continued reliance on fossil fuels, especially in road transport, poses a significant obstacle to achieving climate neutrality [9].

In many countries, this problem is exacerbated by the widespread import of outdated internal combustion engine (ICE) vehicles, which increases both emissions and infrastructure burden [10, 11]. In recent literature, the integration of renewable energy sources (RES) into the transport system is a central theme. Driven by innovative solutions and advances in electric vehicles (EVs) and the expansion of charging infrastructure, electrification is often considered a cornerstone of sustainable transport strategies [12, 13]. Researchers emphasize that the success of this transformation largely depends on the availability of clean electricity and energy storage solutions, particularly to balance intermittent energy sources such as solar and wind [14–16].

In addition to the deployment of electric vehicles, hydrogen and synthetic fuels (e-fuels) have gained scientific attention as alternatives to traditional solutions, including heavy road transport, aviation, and maritime shipping [17, 18]. The production of green hydrogen through electrolysis using renewable energy is considered a key technological breakthrough, although barriers remain in terms of infrastructure scalability and economic viability [19, 20]. The interconnectedness of the energy and transportation sectors is also increasingly addressed in the literature [21, 22]. The concept of sectoral coupling—integrating energy systems with transportation through digital platforms and smart grid technologies—has been identified as crucial for managing energy demand and reducing emissions across systems [23–25]. The development of intelligent, data-driven mobility systems, such as smart mobility and intermodal transport planning, is seen as crucial for optimizing urban transport and adapting it to sustainable energy use [26].

Furthermore, researchers emphasize that in many developing countries, challenges such as insufficient public transport, traffic congestion, poor road conditions, and limited access to clean energy significantly hinder the implementation of decarbonization strategies [27–30]. The literature highlights the importance of local policies and international cooperation to address these imbalances, emphasizing both technology transfer and infrastructure development [31]. Current research emphasizes the need for multi-level, integrated approaches that combine technological innovation, energy policy, and transportation planning. Transforming the transportation sector is not just about replacing vehicles, but also about building an adaptive and resilient mobility ecosystem powered by sustainable energy.

3 Innovative Strategies in the Energy Sector for Decarbonizing Transport Sector

3.1 Contemporary Climate and Energy Challenges in the Transport Sector

Contemporary climate challenges are forcing countries, economic sectors, and societies to take decisive action to reduce greenhouse gas emissions. Among the sectors with a significant impact on global emissions, transport plays a particularly crucial role – it accounts for a significant portion of CO_2 emissions, especially in highly industrialized countries, but increasingly also in developing and emerging economies [32]. The continued dependence of road transport on fossil fuels remains a significant barrier to achieving climate neutrality. Decarbonizing the transport sector requires a profound and systemic transformation, closely linked to innovation and development in the energy sector. Three key strategies are emerging as the foundations of this change: increased electrification, the implementation of green hydrogen and synthetic fuels (e-fuels), and the development of intelligent, integrated mobility systems.

Road transport, the main source of emissions within the transport sector, is currently facing the need for a profound transformation. Modernizing the vehicle fleet, implementing innovative technological solutions that reduce emissions—such as electric, hybrid, or hydrogen-powered vehicles—and developing intelligent traffic and mobility management systems are becoming key elements of this transformation [21]. These actions are essential not only for climate goals but also for improving air quality and public health in cities and areas with high traffic density. With the increasing electrification of transport, the energy sector's role as a supplier of low-emission, stable, and intelligently managed energy is becoming increasingly crucial—making cooperation between both sectors one of the pillars of the green transformation.

In many cities of developing countries, there is a lack of basic transport infrastructure, which hinders efforts to improve residents' quality of life and develop effective mobility systems. Common issues include traffic congestion, poor infrastructure conditions, and limited access to affordable and efficient public transport. Additionally, weak integration between different modes of transport negatively affects daily home-to-work connections, posing a significant challenge to the development of sustainable and smart cities in the Global South [10].

In many countries of the Global South and Eastern Europe, the situation is further exacerbated by the massive import of used combustion engine vehicles. These vehicles are often not equipped with modern exhaust gas aftertreatment systems, have higher fuel consumption, and fail to meet current emission standards. Their continued use not only prolongs the life cycle of outdated technologies but also increases environmental pressure in regions already facing serious infrastructure deficits, limited public transport options, and inadequate access to clean and affordable energy sources [33, 34]. As a result, these regions face a dual challenge: modernizing both the vehicle fleet and energy systems, amidst economic and technological constraints.

At the same time, the energy sector worldwide is undergoing a dynamic transformation, marked by the accelerated development of renewable energy sources (RES), decentralization, and the increasing use of digital technologies. These changes are transforming the way energy is produced, distributed, and consumed, offering new opportunities to support low-emission transport solutions. Innovations such as smart grids, energy storage systems, and real-time data management play a key role in increasing the flexibility and efficiency of energy use in transport. The convergence of the transport and energy sectors, driven by electrification and digitalization, provides a strategic path to achieving climate goals and building more sustainable and resilient economies.

3.2 Transport Decarbonization in the Context of Systemic Transformation

Road, maritime, and air transport still rely heavily on fossil fuels, making these modes of transport among the main sources of greenhouse gas emissions [35]. In response to growing climate challenges, European Union member states and other countries are implementing increasingly stringent regulations that enforce emission reductions and promote the development of alternative, low-emission, and zero-emission propulsion systems [36]. In this context, the energy sector plays a strategic and multifaceted role – not only as an energy supplier, but also as an initiator of innovation and a partner in the creation of modern transport infrastructure.

The development of electromobility, hydrogen technologies, biofuels, and e-fuels requires not only the modernization of transport systems but, above all, ensuring access to stable and clean energy sources. Green energy – derived from renewable sources such as solar, wind, hydropower, and geothermal energy – is becoming a key factor in enabling low-emission operation of new forms of mobility. When powering electric vehicles with renewable energy, particularly energy from photovoltaic installations, the implementation of efficient energy storage becomes crucial. They allow for the storage of surplus energy during periods of high solar radiation and its use during peak demand or in conditions of limited production. This ensures the stability of the vehicle charging infrastructure and increases independence from traditional energy sources. Energy storage systems therefore play a key role in integrating electromobility with renewable energy sources and building a flexible, sustainable transport system.

The production of green hydrogen, produced through electrolysis using renewable energy, is of particular importance in the energy transformation of transport. This hydrogen is used not only in heavy-duty and rail transport but is also becoming a promising alternative for the maritime and aviation sectors, which are particularly difficult to electrify [37]. Simultaneously, concepts for using small modular reactors (SMRs) as a power source for ships are being developed, especially on long-haul routes. SMRs offer a stable, emission-free energy source, making them a potentially groundbreaking technology in the decarbonization of maritime transport [38, 39].

Implementing renewable energy solutions in transport not only reduces emissions but also increases energy independence, lowers long-term operating costs, and improves quality of life by reducing air pollution. In this context, cooperation between the energy and transport sectors is becoming the foundation for sustainable mobility in the future.

3.3 Innovative Strategies in the Energy Sector for Decarbonizing Transport Sector – Investment in Charging Infrastructure

The construction of a charging network, especially fast and ultra-fast chargers, is a key element in the development of electromobility [40]. Its availability and reliability directly influence consumers' and fleet operators' decisions to switch to electric vehicles. Companies such as Orlen, E.ON, and other infrastructure operators are actively investing in the expansion of charging networks, increasingly integrating them with renewable energy sources, such as photovoltaic installations and wind power plants. These solutions aim not only to reduce the carbon footprint of the electricity used for charging but also to increase the attractiveness of electromobility in the eyes of consumers.

Infrastructure operators focus on placing chargers in high-traffic areas – near shopping centers, fuel stations, office buildings, and residential complexes – significantly improving the accessibility of charging in everyday use. Investments are also being made in mobile applications for locating and reserving charging points and enabling cashless payments, which enhances user comfort and eliminates technological barriers. At the same time, digital platforms and systems for managing electric vehicle fleets are being developed, allowing transport and logistics companies to better plan charging schedules, routes, and operational costs.

As a result, these efforts not only support the development of technical infrastructure but also build customer trust in electromobility as a viable, efficient, and environmentally friendly alternative to combustion vehicles. Through the integration of charging networks with digital services and renewable energy sources, electromobility is gaining a sustainable and systemic character, which accelerates the decarbonization of transport [41]. This type of integration not only reduces the carbon footprint of energy supply but also strengthens energy independence and the resilience of the transport system to market energy price fluctuations.

In addition, energy companies are implementing innovative technological and organizational solutions to support the decarbonization of the transport sector [42]. These include platforms for managing electric vehicle fleets, which enable optimization of routes, charging, and energy consumption. Dynamic tariff systems that adjust energy prices to peak hours and available capacity are also becoming more common, supporting better demand management and reducing stress on power grids. Charging services based on actual energy consumption ensure cost transparency and billing efficiency, which is particularly important for fleet users.

Moreover, the integration of charging infrastructure with smart grids is gaining importance. These networks allow for bidirectional communication and energy exchange between vehicles and the grid. This enables the introduction of advanced solutions such as vehicle-to-grid (V2G), where electric vehicles function as mobile energy storage units, supporting grid stability [43]. As a result, the charging infrastructure is no longer a passive energy consumer but becomes an active component of an intelligent, decarbonized energy-transport system.

In this context, digital platforms play a crucial role in integrating all elements of this ecosystem. They enable remote infrastructure management, real-time monitoring of equipment status, charging schedule planning, and analysis of operational and energy data. Thanks to the use of cloud computing, artificial intelligence, and the Internet of Things (IoT), it is possible to create flexible, scalable systems serving both individual and fleet users [44]. Digitalization thus contributes to increased efficiency, reliability, and sustainable development of electric transport based on low-emission energy sources.

The introduction of smart meters, load management systems, sensors, and automation allows for efficient vehicle charging and their integration with power grids (vehicle-to-grid). Smart charging enables the adjustment of charging times and power to the current conditions of the electrical grid, supporting grid stability and better utilization of available energy resources. In particular, vehicle-to-grid (V2G) technology allows for two-way energy exchange between a vehicle and the grid – electric vehicles can not only draw energy to charge but also return it to the grid during peak demand periods. Such solutions support peak load management, increase the flexibility of energy systems, and enable the creation of decentralized energy resources.

Digitalization plays a key role in the transformation of the energy and transport sectors – it allows for dynamic balancing of energy supply and demand, optimization of charging infrastructure performance, and predictive energy flow management [45].

The digitalization of fleet management has significantly enhanced the ability of fleet owners to efficiently oversee diverse vehicle operations. Today, most fleet operators utilize advanced digital platforms and applications that integrate GPS tracking, real-time fuel consumption monitoring, driver performance analytics, and automated reporting of fleet operations, transactions, and compliance data. These digital tools enable smarter, data-driven decision-making and streamline daily operations. A schematic diagram regarding the application of digital fleet management of transport vehicles is presented in Fig. 1.

In the rapidly evolving landscape of mobility, it is essential for vehicle agencies and transport companies to invest in digital fleet management solutions that support the

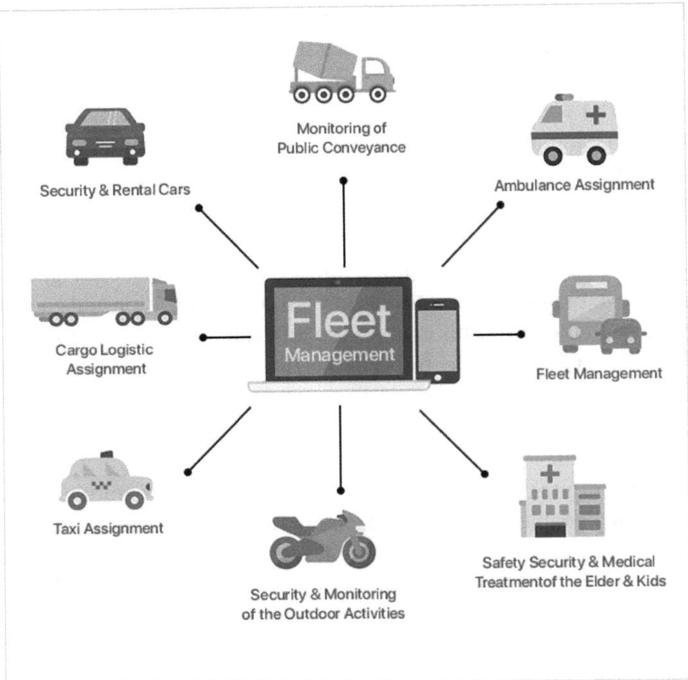

Fig. 1. Schematic diagram of the application of digital management of the most important elements of the transport vehicle fleet [46].

acquisition, operation, and maintenance of vehicles through intelligent automation and analytics.

The core objective of implementing digital fleet management systems is to minimize operational risks, boost vehicle productivity, optimize energy and fuel efficiency, and ensure compliance with regulatory standards—all through integrated, intelligent digital infrastructure.

Digital solutions such as big data systems, artificial intelligence, blockchain, and digital twins are being implemented by energy companies to increase system flexibility and resilience [47]. In transportation, digitalization enables not only real-time monitoring and management of electric vehicle fleets but also integration with intelligent traffic management, route planning, and urban logistics systems. This facilitates reduced traffic congestion, better infrastructure utilization, and reduced emissions. Furthermore, the development of digital platforms enables consumers to more consciously use transportation and energy services, supporting the development of new mobility models, such as car sharing, mobility-as-a-service (MaaS), and dynamic charging tariffs. Thanks to these solutions, digitalization is becoming the foundation of modern, integrated, and sustainable energy and transportation ecosystems.

3.4 Green Hydrogen in Energy and Transport: The Potential to Reduce CO_2 Emissions

The production of green hydrogen in the energy sector also has direct applications in transportation, constituting a key link in the transition towards zero-emission mobility [48]. Produced through electrolysis using renewable energy sources (such as solar or wind power), green hydrogen is a completely ecological fuel – its use does not emit carbon dioxide or other pollutants, contributing to a significant reduction in the carbon footprint of transportation.

Green hydrogen is particularly important for the decarbonization of sectors such as heavy transport, rail, maritime, and aviation [49]. Using hydrogen as a fuel in the transportation sector is a key strategy towards decarbonization. Its CO_2 emission reduction potential varies depending on the mode of transport and the hydrogen production method. Green hydrogen – produced using renewable energy sources – enables the near-complete elimination of emissions in certain transport segments, and its use is becoming increasingly feasible thanks to technological developments and infrastructure investments.

In road transport, particularly in the truck and fleet sectors, the use of hydrogen fuel cells can lead to a 50–70% reduction in CO_2 emissions compared to diesel engines, provided that green hydrogen is used. In rail transport – where electrified infrastructure is lacking – hydrogen-powered trains can almost completely eliminate emissions, becoming an alternative to diesel traction units.

The maritime sector, responsible for approximately 3% of global emissions, also has significant reduction potential – thanks to hydrogen fuels and derivatives (such as green ammonia or methanol), emissions could be reduced by approximately 50%. In air transport, where electrification is technically limited, hydrogen is used both in the form of synthetic fuels (e-fuels) and in hydrogen-hybrid systems. Depending on the solution, emissions can be reduced by 50–80% [50, 51].

The table below summarizes the estimated CO_2 emission reductions in individual transport sectors after using hydrogen as an energy carrier (Table 1).

Table 1. Estimated CO_2 emission reductions by transport mode

Transport Sector	Estimated CO_2 Emission Reduction
Road transport (trucks)	50–70%
Rail transport	100% (on non-electrified lines)
Maritime transport	50%
Air transport	50–80% (synthetic or hybrid fuels)

It's worth noting that the actual scale of reduction depends largely on the type of hydrogen used. Only green hydrogen, produced through electrolysis from renewable energy sources, provides full environmental benefits. Other forms, such as gray, blue, pink, or turquoise hydrogen, have varying impacts on emissions – from moderate reductions (in the case of blue hydrogen, with CO_2 capture) to no significant environmental benefits (gray hydrogen produced from natural gas).

Implementing hydrogen in the transport sector, although it requires significant investments in infrastructure and technology development, is one of the most promising tools for achieving climate goals in the medium and long term.

Besides green hydrogen, other "colors" of hydrogen are also gaining importance, differing in production technology and environmental impact. Blue hydrogen is produced from natural gas while simultaneously capturing and storing CO_2, which reduces its emissions but still involves the use of fossil fuels. Turquoise hydrogen, on the other hand, is produced through the pyrolysis of methane, where the byproduct is solid carbon, and its decarbonization impact depends on the energy source used in the process. Pink hydrogen is produced using nuclear energy and provides a stable power source independent of atmospheric conditions [52, 53]. Although only green hydrogen is completely zero-emission, the diversity of hydrogen technologies contributes to the construction of a diversified and flexible energy system that can support the decarbonization of transportation in its various forms. In the long term, the development of these technologies enables increased energy independence and accelerates the transition towards a low-emission economy.

4 Conclusion

The analyses presented in this chapter clearly demonstrate that the transport sector is at the intersection of the urgent need to adapt to the demands of climate change and technological opportunities. Faced with growing climate challenges and the urgent need to reduce greenhouse gas emissions, transport must undergo a fundamental, systemic transformation—one that cannot occur in isolation from the development of the energy sector.

Green energy, and in particular electricity generated from renewable sources and green hydrogen, is emerging as a cornerstone of a low-emission future for transport. Its integration with mobility systems—from road and rail to maritime and air transport—opens new paths to significant emission reductions, improved air quality, and long-term energy independence. It is estimated that the use of green hydrogen could reduce CO_2 emissions by approximately 50–70% in truck transport, nearly 100% in rail (on non-electrified lines), approximately 50% in maritime transport, and 50–80% in aviation—depending on the technology adopted and the type of synthetic fuel. These data confirm that a green energy-driven transformation has a real impact on reducing the global carbon footprint.

Achieving these goals, however, requires not only clean energy but also intelligent and innovative systems for managing its production, distribution, and use. Implementing advanced technologies—such as smart grids, vehicle-to-grid (V2G) solutions, AI-based fleet management, and digital charging infrastructure—is the second pillar of this transformation. These innovations enable optimization of energy consumption, improved system flexibility, and enhanced user experiences, ultimately accelerating the transformation towards sustainable transport.

In summary, decarbonizing transport relies on synergies between clean energy and digital innovation. Only through coordinated efforts across the transport and energy sectors—supported by a robust regulatory framework, cross-sectoral investments, and research-based solutions—can we ensure a fair and effective transition towards climate-neutral mobility.

References

1. Pereirinha, P.G., González, M., Carrilero, I., Anseán, D., Alonso, J., Viera, J.C.: Main trends and challenges in road transportation electrification. Transp. Res. Proc. **33**, 235–242 (2018)
2. Yuan, M., Thellufsen, J.Z., Lund, H., Liang, Y.: The electrification of transportation in energy transition. Energy **236**, 121564 (2021)
3. Zhang, R., Zhang, J.: Long-term pathways to deep decarbonization of the transport sector in the post-COVID world. Transp. Policy **110**, 28–36 (2021)
4. Dai, J., Alvarado, R., Ali, S., Ahmed, Z., Meo, M.S.: Transport infrastructure, economic growth, and transport CO2 emissions nexus: does green energy consumption in the transport sector matter? Environ. Sci. Pollut. Res. **30**(14), 40094–40106 (2023)
5. IEA, Road transport Net Zero Emissions Guide. https://www.iea.org/reports/road-transport. Accessed 21 July 2025
6. IPCC, Sixth Assessment Report. https://www.ipcc.ch/report/ar6/wg3/chapter/summary-for-policymakers/. Accessed 21 July 2025
7. ITF, Transport Outlook 2023. https://www.itf-oecd.org/itf-transport-outlook-2023. Accessed 21 July 2025
8. Sun, Y.F., Zhang, Y.J., Su, B.: How does global transport sector improve the emissions reduction performance? A demand-side analysis? Appl. Energy **311**, 118648 (2022)
9. Agarwal, O.P., Mohan, I., Sansanwal, K.: Beyond fossil fuels: revolutionizing transportation for a sustainable world. J. Resour. Energy Dev. **21**(1 and 2), 1–17 (2024)
10. Aderibigbe, O.-O., Fadare, S.O., Gumbo, T.: Transport situation in the global south: insights from Nigeria, South Africa and India. In: Aderibigbe, O.-O., Fadare, S.O., Gumbo, T. (eds.) Emerging Technologies for Smart Cities: Sustainable Transport Planning in the Global North and Global South, pp. 43–77. Springer, Cham (2024). https://doi.org/10.1007/978-3-031-66943-9_3
11. UNEP, Emissions Gap Report 2024. https://www.unep.org/resources/emissions-gap-report-2024
12. Baumgarte, F., Kaiser, M., Keller, R.: Policy support measures for widespread expansion of fast charging infrastructure for electric vehicles. Energy Policy **156**, 112372 (2021)
13. Halder, P., et al.: Performance, emissions and economic analyses of hydrogen fuel cell vehicles. Renew. Sustain. Energy Rev. **199**, 114543 (2024)
14. Victoria, M., Zhu, K., Brown, T., Andresen, G.B., Greiner, M.: The role of storage technologies throughout the decarbonisation of the sector-coupled European energy system. Energy Convers. Manag. **201**, 111977 (2019)
15. Czepło, F., Borowski, P.F.: Innovation solution in photovoltaic sector. Energies **17**(1), 265 (2024)
16. Di Somma, M., Graditi, G.: Challenges and opportunities of the energy transition and the added value of energy systems integration. In: Technologies for Integrated Energy Systems and Networks, pp. 1–14 (2022)
17. Gunkel, P.A., Bergaentzlé, C., Jensen, I.G., Scheller, F.: From passive to active: flexibility from electric vehicles in the context of transmission system development. Appl. Energy **277**, 115526 (2020)

18. Mehlig, D., Staffell, I., Stettler, M., ApSimon, H.: Accelerating electric vehicle uptake favours greenhouse gas over air pollutant emissions. Transp. Res. Part D: Transp. Environ. **124**, 103954 (2023)
19. Zainal, B.S., et al.: Recent advancement and assessment of green hydrogen production technologies. Renew. Sustain. Energy Rev. **189**, 113941 (2024)
20. Borowski, P.F., Karlikowska, B.: Clean hydrogen is a challenge for enterprises in the era of low-emission and zero-emission economy. Energies **16**(3), 1171 (2023)
21. Borowski, P.F.: Innovation management in transport – an economic perspective in the era of climate transformation. Transp. Probl. **2**(20) (2025)
22. Ahmed, Z., Rasheed, M.Q., Pinzon, S.: Analyzing the effects of wind energy and transportation on the ecological footprint: a pathway to sustainable development in leading economies. Environ. Dev. Sustain. 1–27 (2025)
23. Borowski, P.F.: Digital transformation and prosumers activities in the energy sector. In: Kahraman, C., Haktanir, E. (eds.) Intelligent Systems in Digital Transformation: Theory and Applications. LNNS, vol. 549, pp. 129–150. Springer, Cham (2022). https://doi.org/10.1007/978-3-031-16598-6_6
24. Ramsebner, J., Haas, R., Ajanovic, A., Wietschel, M.: The sector coupling concept: a critical review. Wiley Interdiscip. Rev.: Energy Environ. **10**(4), e396 (2021)
25. Brown, T., Schlachtberger, D., Kies, A., Schramm, S., Greiner, M.: Synergies of sector coupling and transmission reinforcement in a cost-optimised, highly renewable European energy system. Energy **160**, 720–739 (2018)
26. Shaheen, S., Cohen, A.: Next generation mobility systems. In: Energy Efficiency: Innovations: Driving Prosperity, Slashing Emissions, pp. 155–175 (2021)
27. Alves, B.B., Mjahed, L.M., Moody, J.: Decarbonizing Urban Transport for Development. World Bank (2023)
28. Ho, C.Q., Tirachini, A.: Mobility-as-a-Service and the role of multimodality in the sustainability of urban mobility in developing and developed countries. Transp. Policy **145**, 161–176 (2024)
29. Pojani, D., Stead, D.: Sustainable urban transport in the developing world: beyond megacities. Sustainability **7**(6), 7784–7805 (2015)
30. Dahiya, B., Rajendran, L.P., Dashora, L.K., Chatterjee, U. (eds.) Urban Planning and Design for Megacities in the Global South: Smart and Sustainable Development. Springer, Singapore (2025). https://doi.org/10.1007/978-981-97-8370-0
31. Sachs, J.D., Schmidt-Traub, G., Mazzucato, M., Messner, D., Nakicenovic, N., Rockström, J.: Six transformations to achieve the sustainable development goals. Nat. Sustain. **2**(9), 805–814 (2019)
32. Borowski, P.F.: Efforts of the transport and energy sectors toward renewable energy for climate neutrality. Transp. Probl. **19**(2), 177–190 (2024). https://doi.org/10.20858/tp.2023.19.2.14
33. Akloweg, Y., Hayshi, Y., Kato, H.: The effect of used cars on African road traffic accidents: a case study of Addis Ababa, Ethiopia. Int. J. Urban Sci. **15**(1), 61–69 (2011)
34. Green-Simms, L.B.: Postcolonial Automobility: Car Culture in West Africa. University of Minnesota Press (2017)
35. Borowski, P.F.: Mitigating climate change and the development of green energy versus a return to fossil fuels due to the energy crisis in 2022. Energies **15**(24), 9289 (2022)
36. Salvi, B.L., Subramanian, K.A., Panwar, N.L.: Alternative fuels for transportation vehicles: a technical review. Renew. Sustain. Energy Rev. **25**, 404–419 (2013)
37. Bhuiyan, M.M.H., Siddique, Z.: Hydrogen as an alternative fuel: a comprehensive review of challenges and opportunities in production, storage, and transportation. Int. J. Hydrog. Energy **102**, 1026–1044 (2025)
38. Alavi-Borazjani, S.A., Adeel, S., Chkoniya, V.: Hydrogen as a sustainable fuel: transforming maritime logistics. Energies **18**(5), 1231 (2025)

39. Senemmar, S., et al.: Navigating the future: exploring small modular reactors in the maritime sector. IEEE Electrif. Mag. **12**(4), 30–42 (2024)
40. Yuvaraj, T., Devabalaji, K.R., Kumar, J.A., Thanikanti, S.B., Nwulu, N.I.: A comprehensive review and analysis of the allocation of electric vehicle charging stations in distribution networks. IEEE Access **12**, 5404–5461 (2024)
41. Barman, P., et al.: Renewable energy integration with electric vehicle technology: a review of the existing smart charging approaches. Renew. Sustain. Energy Rev. **183**, 113518 (2023)
42. Dall-Orsoletta, A., Romero, F., Ferreira, P.: Open and collaborative innovation for the energy transition: an exploratory study. Technol. Soc. **69**, 101955 (2022)
43. Mojumder, M.R.H., Ahmed Antara, F., Hasanuzzaman, M., Alamri, B., Alsharef, M.: Electric vehicle-to-grid (V2G) technologies: impact on the power grid and battery. Sustainability **14**(21), 13856 (2022)
44. Farahpoor, M., Esparza, O., Soriano, M.: Comprehensive IoT-driven fleet management system for industrial vehicles. IEEE Access **12** (2023)
45. Yigitcanlar, T., et al.: Digital technologies of transportation-related communication: review and the state-of-the-art. Transp. Res. Interdiscip. Perspect. **23**, 100987 (2024)
46. Miller, S.R.: The Best 7 Free and Open Source Fleet Management Software Solutions. https://www.goodfirms.co/fleet-management-software/blog/best-free-open-source-fleet-management-software-solutions. Accessed 23 July 2025
47. Borowski, P.F.: Digitization, digital twins, blockchain, and industry 4.0 as elements of management process in enterprises in the energy sector. Energies **14**(7), 1885 (2021)
48. Paraschiv, S., Paraschiv, L.S., Serban, A.: Global hydrogen production capacity for sustainable decarbonization and green transition in transport applications to mitigate climate change: a comprehensive overview. Manag. Environ. Qual.: Int. J. (2025)
49. Jayachandran, M., et al.: Challenges and opportunities in green hydrogen adoption for decarbonizing hard-to-abate industries: a comprehensive review. IEEE Access **12**, 23363–23388 (2024)
50. O'Connell, A., Pavlenko, N., Bieker, G., Searle, S.: A comparison of the life-cycle greenhouse gas emissions of European heavy-duty vehicles and fuels. In: International Council on Clean Transportation, Washington, DC, USA, pp. 1–36 (2023)
51. Din, T., Hillmansen, S.: Energy consumption and carbon dioxide emissions analysis for a concept design of a hydrogen hybrid railway vehicle. IET Electr. Syst. Transp. **8**(2), 112–121 (2018)
52. Singla, M.K., Gupta, J., Beryozkina, S., Safaraliev, M., Singh, M.: The colorful economics of hydrogen: Assessing the costs and viability of different hydrogen production methods-a review. Int. J. Hydrog. Energy **61**, 664–677 (2024)
53. Borowski, P.F.: Hydrogen as an energy source and as a form of energy storage. Econ. Environ. **93**(2), 941 (2025)

Participant-Level Injury Outcome Prediction in Road Traffic Incidents Using Machine Learning: A Case Study in Poland

Artur Budzyński[1(✉)] and Aleksander Sładkowski[2]

[1] Krakow University of Economics, Rakowiecka 27, 31-510 Kraków, Poland
abudzyns@uek.krakow.pl
[2] Silesian University of Technology, Krasiński 8, Katowice, Poland

Abstract. This study investigates the application of supervised machine learning methods for predicting injury outcomes among participants involved in road traffic incidents. The analysis is based on detailed participant-level data collected in Poland between 2015 and 2022, covering over six million records. The dataset includes individual and incident-related characteristics, such as participant role, gender, driving license status, legal responsibility, and area type. A multi-class classification framework was developed to predict the injury status of participants, categorized as no injury, light injury, severe injury, or fatality. Three machine learning models - Random Forest, XGBoost, and LightGBM - were implemented and evaluated in terms of predictive performance. In addition, an analysis of feature importance was conducted to identify the most influential factors contributing to injury severity. The results demonstrated that ensemble learning models, particularly XGBoost, achieved the highest predictive performance. Participant role and legal responsibility were identified as the most critical factors influencing injury outcomes. The findings confirm the potential of machine learning techniques to improve the understanding of individual-level determinants of injury severity and to support data-driven road safety policies.

Keywords: Road Traffic Incidents · Injury Severity Prediction · Participant-Level Data · Supervised Machine Learning · Ensemble Learning · Feature Importance · Predictive Modelling · Road Safety · Poland

1 Introduction

Road traffic incidents are a major public safety concern, often resulting in injuries or fatalities and generating significant social and economic costs. Numerous studies have examined the factors influencing the severity of road traffic incidents, primarily focusing on incident-level characteristics such as roadway conditions, weather, and vehicle attributes. Early research in this area predominantly employed statistical modelling techniques. For example, Abdel-Aty and Keller applied logistic regression models to analyse crash severity levels at signalized intersections [1], while Yamamoto and Shankar used bivariate ordered probit models to investigate injury severity outcomes in fixed-object collisions [2]. Xie et al. further extended this approach by employing Bayesian ordered probit models to account for uncertainty in injury severity analysis [3].

A. Abbasov et al. (Eds.): PLMO 2025, CCIS 2767, pp. 82–93, 2026.
https://doi.org/10.1007/978-3-032-13672-5_8

In recent years, data-driven approaches based on machine learning techniques have gained increasing attention in road safety research. These methods offer greater flexibility in capturing complex, non-linear relationships between variables and do not require the strict statistical assumptions associated with traditional models. Chang and Chen demonstrated the effectiveness of tree-based models in analysing freeway accident severity [4]. Similarly, Zhang et al. applied various machine learning algorithms to investigate risk factors associated with traffic violations and injury severity in China [5]. Despite the growing popularity of such approaches, most prior studies have primarily focused on incident-level characteristics or environmental conditions, rather than on individual attributes of participants involved in traffic incidents.

While previous research has provided valuable insights into the environmental and incident-related determinants of injury severity, relatively little attention has been devoted to the analysis of participant-level characteristics. Factors such as the role of the participant, driving experience, gender, or legal responsibility may have a significant impact on the severity of injuries sustained in road traffic incidents. However, limited research has explicitly examined these participant-level factors in injury severity analysis, highlighting the need for further investigation in this area.

2 Problem Statement

The primary objective of this study is to investigate the relationship between participant-level characteristics and injury severity in road traffic incidents using machine learning techniques. Recent literature has demonstrated the effectiveness of various machine learning algorithms in predicting crash injury severity and highlighted their potential to improve road safety analysis [6]. The research presented in this paper focuses on analysing a dataset of incidents that occurred in Poland between 2015 and 2022, containing detailed information about the participants involved. The specific research problems addressed in this study are formulated as follows:

1) Can machine learning classification models accurately predict the injury status of participants based on individual and incident-related features?
2) Which participant-level and incident-related factors are the most influential in determining injury severity?
3) To what extent does the role of a participant (e.g., driver, passenger, pedestrian) affect the likelihood of sustaining different levels of injury?
4) How does the predictive performance differ across selected machine learning algorithms?

To answer these questions, the study applies supervised machine learning classification models and evaluates their predictive performance using appropriate metrics. Furthermore, the analysis includes an assessment of feature importance and additional exploratory analyses to better understand the relationship between participants' roles and injury outcomes.

3 Methods

The primary data source for this study is a dataset provided by the Polish Police. It contains detailed information on participants involved in road traffic incidents that occurred in Poland between 2015 and 2022. The dataset was obtained directly from the internal databases of the Polish Police and is not publicly available. Access to the data was granted exclusively for the purpose of this research. In total, the dataset includes over six million records, covering incidents reported across all administrative regions of Poland during the specified period.

The dataset consists of separate CSV files for each year between 2015 and 2022. Each annual file contains data exclusively about the participants involved in road traffic incidents reported in that particular year. All files share a consistent structure, enabling efficient consolidation and subsequent analysis across the entire study period. The CSV format was selected due to its simplicity, wide adoption, and suitability for systematic data analysis [7].

All annual CSV files were consolidated into a single dataset, resulting in over six million records in total. For efficient storage, faster loading times, and optimal performance during data analysis, the combined dataset was saved in the Apache Parquet format, which provides columnar storage and built-in compression. The selection of the Parquet format was motivated by its superior performance characteristics and optimized analytical query capabilities, especially when handling large datasets [8].

The data preparation stage involved transforming two original features, **Killed** and **Injured**, into a single categorical feature named **Injury_status**. Initially, the **Killed** feature included three unique values: "Killed at scene", "Killed within 30 days", and "Unspecified". The **Injured** feature contained values: "Severely injured", "Lightly injured", and "Unspecified". A custom Python function named **determine_injury_status()** was developed and applied conditional logic to each record, merging these two features into one with five mutually exclusive categories: "Killed at scene", "Killed within 30 days", "Severely injured", "Lightly injured", and "No injury". The transformation was executed across the entire dataset using the **apply()** method, facilitated by the Pandas library, which provides efficient data manipulation capabilities for structured datasets [9, 10].

Data visualization methods were employed to facilitate exploratory analysis and clearly illustrate key patterns in the dataset. Specifically, categorical data distribution was visualized using bar plots. These visualizations were created utilizing the Python libraries Matplotlib and Seaborn. Matplotlib provides extensive functionality for generating publication-quality graphics in Python, supporting detailed customization of visual outputs [11]. Seaborn, built on top of Matplotlib, was employed due to its intuitive functions tailored specifically for statistical data visualization, enabling concise and informative graphical summaries [12].

Before building the predictive model, the dataset underwent further preprocessing. The feature **Accident_type** was excluded from the analysis to prevent data leakage, as this feature directly describes the nature of the incident (collision or accident), and therefore strongly correlates with participant injury. All remaining categorical features were encoded using Label Encoding, transforming text-based categories into numerical values suitable for modelling [13]. The target variable, **Injury_status**, was also numerically encoded. Subsequently, the dataset was randomly partitioned into training (70%) and testing (30%) subsets. Stratified sampling was used to ensure proportional representation of each injury category in both subsets, following best practices recommended in machine learning literature [14]. This preprocessing stage provided a robust basis for evaluating the predictive performance and generalization capability of the classification model.

A Random Forest classifier [15] was selected for predictive modelling due to its ability to handle large datasets, manage nonlinear relationships, and provide robustness against overfitting. The model was initialized with 100 decision trees (**n_estimators**=100), each limited to a maximum depth of 15 (**max_depth**=15) to control complexity and computational efficiency. The parameter **class_weight**='balanced' was applied to address class imbalance by automatically adjusting the weights of each class inversely proportional to their frequencies. Additionally, the model was trained using all available processor cores (**n_jobs**=−1) for computational efficiency, and the random state parameter (**random_state**=42) was fixed to ensure reproducibility of results. The trained model was subsequently evaluated on the independent test set, and performance metrics including accuracy, precision, recall, and F1-score, were computed and summarized using a classification report and confusion matrix [14].

The predictive performance of the classification model was evaluated using a confusion matrix. A confusion matrix is a widely used visualization tool in classification problems, summarizing prediction outcomes by displaying the number of correct and incorrect predictions for each class in the dataset. The confusion matrix was computed by comparing the model's predicted labels (**y_pred**) to the actual labels (**y_test**) from the test dataset. The resulting matrix was visualized as a heatmap using the **heatmap()** function from the Seaborn library, with explicitly defined class labels to clearly identify each injury category on both axes. This visualization approach facilitates the intuitive interpretation of the classifier's accuracy and helps identify specific classes that the model finds challenging to distinguish correctly [16].

To select the optimal predictive model, three widely-used classification algorithms were compared: Random Forest, XGBoost, and LightGBM. The Random Forest classifier was previously described. XGBoost [17] and LightGBM [18] are both ensemble-based algorithms utilizing gradient boosting techniques, which iteratively build decision trees to minimize prediction error by focusing on misclassified instances from previous iterations. Each model was initialized with consistent parameters: 100 decision trees (**n_estimators**=100) and a maximum depth of 15 (**max_depth**=15). Random states were fixed (**random_state**=42) to ensure reproducibility, and class imbalance was addressed by setting the **class_weight**='balanced' parameter in Random Forest and LightGBM.

Model performance was evaluated using three metrics: accuracy, macro-average F1-score, and weighted-average F1-score. Accuracy measures the overall proportion of correctly classified observations but can be misleading in datasets with significant class imbalance, as previously discussed. Therefore, the F1-score, defined as the harmonic mean of precision and recall, was also used to obtain a balanced measure of model performance. Specifically, the macro-average F1-score calculates the metric independently for each class and then averages these values equally, giving more importance to minority classes. In contrast, the weighted-average F1-score computes class-specific F1-scores and averages them weighted by class frequency, thus emphasizing the dominant classes in imbalanced datasets [19]. Finally, the results of the comparative analysis were visualized using Matplotlib and Seaborn libraries, facilitating clear interpretation of performance differences across evaluated models.

The relative importance of individual features was determined using the feature importance functionality implemented in the XGBoost algorithm. The importance score for each feature was calculated based on the gain criterion, which measures the average improvement in the model's predictive accuracy brought by a feature when used to split a decision node. Specifically, the gain reflects the reduction in the loss function achieved by including the feature in the tree-building process. The overall importance score assigned to each feature is the sum of gain values across all trees in the ensemble, normalized so that the total importance across all features equals one (gain-based feature importance). This approach enables the identification of variables that most significantly contribute to the predictive performance of the model.

To investigate the relationship between participants' roles and injury severity, a bivariate analysis was performed using cross-tabulation. Two contingency tables were constructed: the first captured the distribution of injury status within each participant type, while the second reflected the distribution of participant types within each injury severity category. Both tables were normalized to express the results as relative frequencies, facilitating interpretation of proportional differences. This analytical approach is commonly used in categorical data analysis to explore potential associations between variables [20]. The normalized tables were subsequently visualized using heatmaps to provide a clear and interpretable graphical representation of the observed patterns.

All data preprocessing, exploratory analysis, feature engineering, model training, and evaluation were conducted using the Python programming language within a JupyterLab environment. JupyterLab is an interactive development environment designed for reproducible computational workflows, integrating code, narrative text, and visual outputs in a single document [21].

To ensure full transparency and reproducibility of the analytical process, the complete Jupyter notebook used in this study has been made publicly available on GitHub. GitHub is a widely adopted platform that facilitates collaborative development, version control, and open dissemination of scientific code [22]. The notebook includes all steps of data processing, model implementation, and visualization described in this paper. Due to data privacy restrictions, the dataset itself is not included in the repository. The notebook is available at [23].

4 Results

Figure 1 illustrates the distribution of participants' injury status based on road traffic incidents reported in Poland between 2015 and 2022. The vast majority of participants (over 6 million) did not sustain any injury. Among the injured, the number of lightly injured participants was significantly higher than severely injured ones. Fatalities were notably fewer, with participants killed at the scene slightly more numerous than those who succumbed to their injuries within 30 days after the incident.

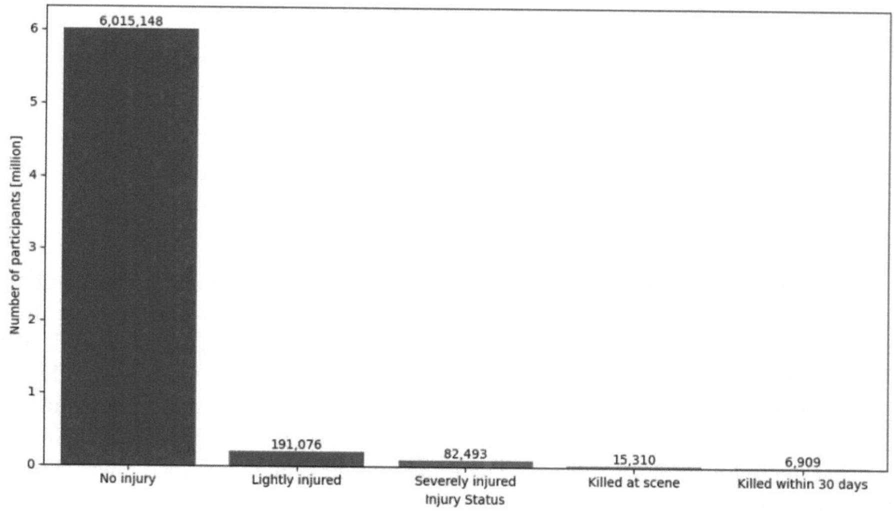

Fig. 1. Distribution of injury status among participants (2015–2022)

Figure 2 presents the confusion matrix illustrating the performance of the Random Forest classifier in predicting participants' injury status. The diagonal values indicate correctly classified observations, while off-diagonal values represent misclassifications. The model demonstrated exceptional accuracy in predicting the No injury category, correctly classifying a vast majority of these instances. However, the classifier faced significant challenges in accurately predicting minority classes, particularly those involving fatalities (Killed at scene, Killed within 30 days) and severe injuries (Severely injured). The relatively high number of misclassifications among these critical categories highlights the inherent difficulty of accurately predicting rare yet significant injury outcomes. This imbalance suggests further exploration into more specialized modeling techniques or additional balancing strategies to improve predictive performance for minority classes.

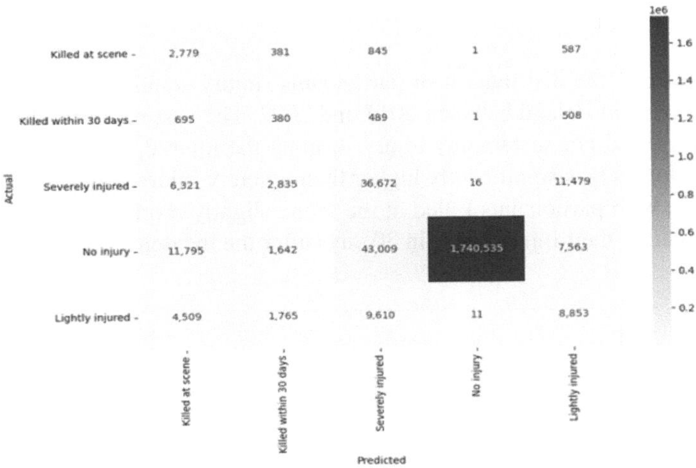

Fig. 2. Confusion matrix for injury status prediction

Figure 3 presents a comparative analysis of the classification models: Random Forest, XGBoost, and LightGBM. The evaluation was based on three performance metrics: accuracy, macro-average F1-score, and weighted-average F1-score. The XGBoost classifier achieved the highest accuracy (0.96) and weighted F1-score (0.96), clearly outperforming the other models. Additionally, XGBoost obtained the highest macro-average F1-score (0.40), indicating better classification performance across all injury categories, including minority classes. The Random Forest model yielded lower scores, with an accuracy of 0.91 and macro-average F1-score of 0.34, while the LightGBM model demonstrated the weakest performance among the three classifiers. These results confirm the superior predictive capacity of XGBoost in the analysed dataset.

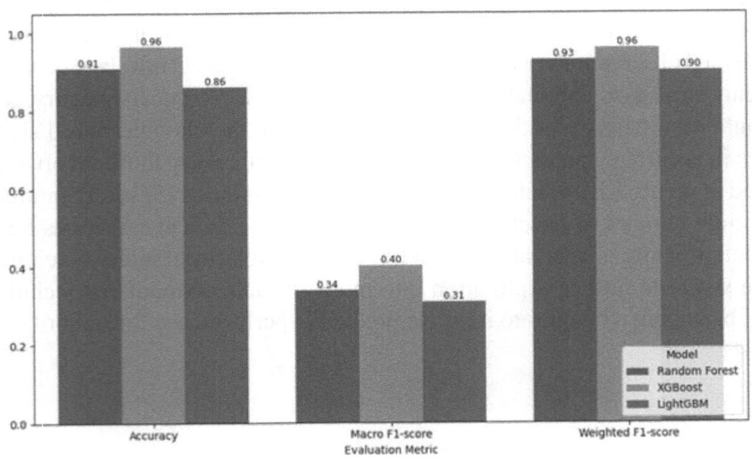

Fig. 3. Comparison of classification models

Figure 4 presents the ranking of the fifteen most important features identified by the XGBoost classifier. The feature importance was determined based on the contribution of each variable to the model's predictive performance. The analysis revealed that the variable **Participant_type** had by far the highest importance score (0.70), indicating its dominant role in predicting participants' injury status. Other features, such as **Driving_license_status** (0.06) and **Legal_decision** (0.03), also demonstrated some predictive relevance, albeit substantially lower. The remaining features contributed marginally to the model's decisions. These results suggest that the type of participant involved in the incident is the most influential factor in determining injury severity, while the predictive value of other attributes is comparatively limited.

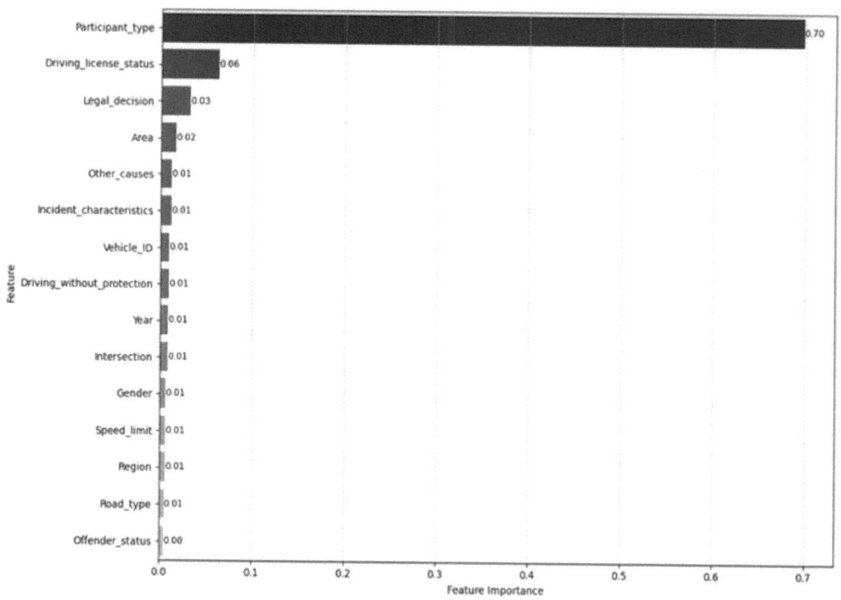

Fig. 4. Top 15 most important features (XGBoost)

A clear association was observed between participants' roles in road traffic incidents and the severity of their injuries. The distribution of injury outcomes, presented in Fig. 5, indicates that drivers and individuals with an unknown participant type were the least affected, with the vast majority (97% and 100%, respectively) classified as uninjured. In contrast, passengers and pedestrians exhibited a substantially higher risk of injury. Among passengers, 66% sustained light injuries and 22% were severely injured. Pedestrians demonstrated the most unfavorable distribution, with nearly half (49%) of cases involving injuries, including 17% classified as severe. Although fatalities were relatively rare, they were more likely to occur among pedestrians and passengers. These findings confirm the strong relationship between participant type and injury severity, consistent with the results of the feature importance analysis.

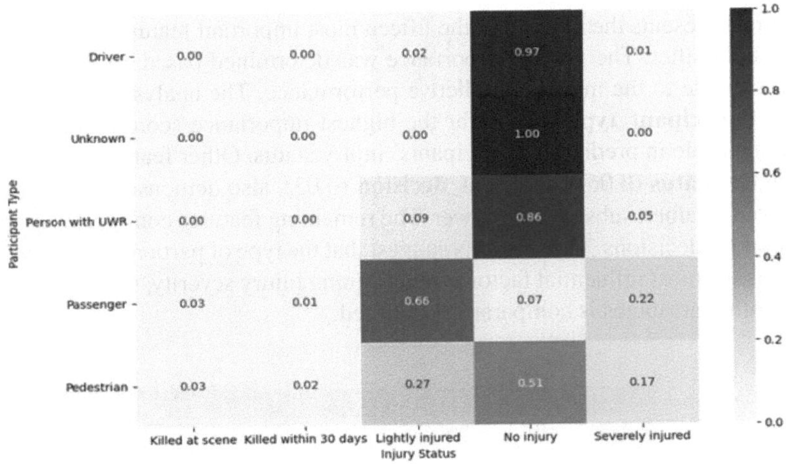

Fig. 5. Distribution of injury status by participant type

An additional analysis was conducted to examine the composition of participant types within each injury severity category. The results, Fig. 6, reveal substantial differences in the distribution of participant roles across injury outcomes. Uninjured participants were predominantly drivers, who accounted for 86% of cases in this category. Conversely, the majority of fatalities occurred among pedestrians and passengers. Specifically, pedestrians represented 51% of participants killed at the scene and 43% of those who died within 30 days of the incident. Passengers also constituted a considerable proportion of fatalities and severe injuries. The category of light injuries was dominated by passengers, who accounted for 67% of cases, followed by pedestrians. These findings further emphasize the disproportionate vulnerability of pedestrians and passengers in road traffic incidents compared to drivers.

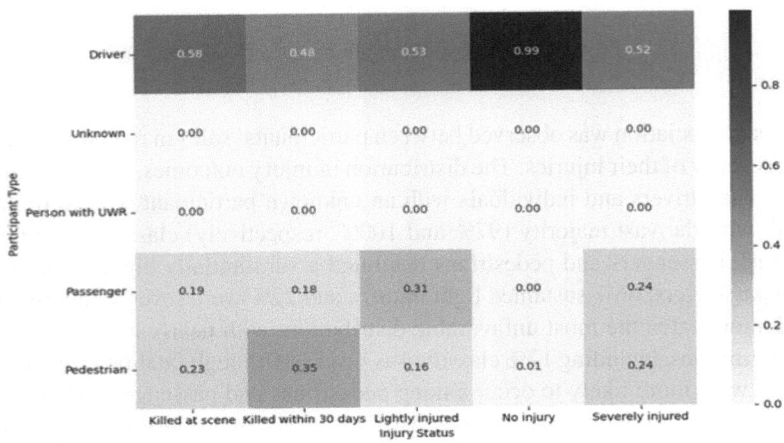

Fig. 6. Distribution of participant type by injury status

5 Discussion and Conclusions

The results of this study demonstrate the effectiveness of machine learning methods in predicting injury severity among participants involved in road traffic incidents. Among the evaluated models, XGBoost achieved the highest predictive performance across all considered metrics, including accuracy, macro-average F1-score, and weighted-average F1-score. This finding aligns with recent research indicating the superior performance of XGBoost in traffic crash severity prediction tasks. For instance, a study by Jiang et al. developed an improved XGBoost model to predict injury severity, achieving notable accuracy improvements over traditional models [24]. Such models are capable of handling complex, non-linear relationships between variables and addressing the challenges posed by imbalanced datasets, which are common in injury severity analysis.

The analysis of feature importance revealed that the role of the participant was the most influential factor in determining injury severity. This observation is consistent with the exploratory analyses conducted in this study, which demonstrated substantial differences in injury outcomes depending on whether the participant was a driver, passenger, or pedestrian. Participants classified as pedestrians were particularly vulnerable, with a significantly higher likelihood of sustaining severe injuries or fatalities. Passengers also exhibited an increased risk of injury compared to drivers, reflecting their passive role in the incident and limited ability to react or avoid danger. Previous studies have highlighted this increased vulnerability among passengers in various traffic scenarios [13]. In addition to participant roles, other individual-level and incident-related variables, such as legal responsibility, driving license status, and area type, were found to moderately influence injury outcomes. These findings confirm the relevance of participant-specific information in injury severity prediction and highlight the importance of considering individual characteristics in road safety analyses.

Despite the overall high predictive accuracy of the developed models, the analysis identified persistent challenges in correctly classifying minority classes, particularly fatalities and severe injuries. The confusion matrix revealed that most misclassifications occurred in these categories, primarily due to the class imbalance inherent in the dataset. This limitation is commonly observed in classification tasks involving rare but critical outcomes and reflects the well-known difficulties associated with learning from imbalanced data. Further research should explore advanced resampling techniques, alternative modelling approaches, or the inclusion of additional explanatory variables to improve the predictive performance for minority classes. Moreover, the availability of more comprehensive participant-level data, including behavioural and contextual factors, could enhance the understanding of the underlying determinants of injury severity. Previous studies have demonstrated that such variables may significantly improve the accuracy of injury severity prediction models. The findings of this study may support policymakers and road safety authorities in developing targeted preventive measures based on individual-level risk factors.

References

1. Abdel-Aty, M., Keller, J.: Exploring the overall and specific crash severity levels at signalized intersections. Accid. Anal. Prev. **37**(3), 417–425 (2005). https://doi.org/10.1016/j.aap.2004.11.002
2. Zhang, Y., Fu, C., Cheng, S.: Exploring driver injury severity at intersection: an ordered probit analysis. Adv. Mech. Eng. **7**(2), 567124 (2015). https://doi.org/10.1155/2014/567124
3. Xie, Y., Zhang, Y., Liang, F.: Crash injury severity analysis using Bayesian ordered probit models. J. Transp. Eng. **135**(1), 18–25 (2009). https://doi.org/10.1061/(ASCE)0733-947X(2009)135:1(18)
4. Chang, L.-Y., Chen, W.-C.: Data mining of tree-based models to analyze freeway accident frequency. J. Saf. Res. **36**(4), 365–375 (2005). https://doi.org/10.1016/j.jsr.2005.06.013
5. Zhang, G., Yau, K.K.W., Chen, G.: Risk factors associated with traffic violations and accident severity in China. Accid. Anal. Prev. **59**, 18–25 (2013). https://doi.org/10.1016/j.aap.2013.05.004
6. Santos, K., Dias, J.P., Amado, C.: A literature review of machine learning algorithms for crash injury severity prediction. J. Saf. Res. **80**, 254–269 (2022). https://doi.org/10.1016/j.jsr.2021.12.007
7. Van Den Burg, G.J.J., Nazábal, A., Sutton, C.: Wrangling messy CSV files by detecting row and type patterns. Data Min. Knowl. Disc. **33**(6), 1799–1820 (2019). https://doi.org/10.1007/s10618-019-00646-y
8. Zeng, X., Hui, Y., Shen, J., Pavlo, A., McKinney, W., Zhang, H.: An empirical evaluation of columnar storage formats (2023). https://arxiv.org/abs/2304.05028
9. McKinney, W.: Data structures for statistical computing in Python. In: Proceedings of the Python in Science Conference, Austin, Texas, pp. 56–61 (2010). https://doi.org/10.25080/Majora-92bf1922-00a
10. Hunter, J.D.: Matplotlib: a 2D graphics environment. Comput. Sci. Eng. **9**(3), 90–95 (2007). https://doi.org/10.1109/MCSE.2007.55
11. Waskom, M.: Seaborn: statistical data visualization. J. Open Source Softw. **6**(60), 3021 (2021). https://doi.org/10.21105/joss.03021
12. Géron, A.: Hands-on Machine Learning with Scikit-Learn, Keras, and TensorFlow, 2nd edn. O'Reilly Media, Sebastopol (2019)
13. Kuhn, M., Johnson, K.: Applied Predictive Modeling. Springer, New York (2013). https://doi.org/10.1007/978-1-4614-6849-3
14. Breiman, L.: Random forests. Mach. Learn. **45**(1), 5–32 (2001). https://doi.org/10.1023/A:1010933404324
15. Chen, T., Guestrin, C.: XGBoost: a scalable tree boosting system. In: Proceedings of the 22nd ACM SIGKDD International Conference on Knowledge Discovery and Data Mining, pp. 785–794. ACM, San Francisco (2016). https://doi.org/10.1145/2939672.2939785
16. Ke, G., et al.: LightGBM: a highly efficient gradient boosting decision tree. In: Advances in Neural Information Processing Systems, pp. 3146–3154 (2017)
17. Sokolova, M., Lapalme, G.: A systematic analysis of performance measures for classification tasks. Inf. Process. Manag. **45**(4), 427–437 (2009). https://doi.org/10.1016/j.ipm.2009.03.002
18. Agresti, A.: Categorical Data Analysis. Wiley, Hoboken (2002). https://doi.org/10.1002/0471249688
19. Kluyver, T., et al.: Jupyter Notebooks - a publishing format for reproducible computational workflows. In: International Conference on Electronic Publishing, Göttingen (2016). https://api.semanticscholar.org/CorpusID:36928206

20. Tsay, J., Dabbish, L., Herbsleb, J.: Influence of social and technical factors for evaluating contribution in GitHub. In: Proceedings of the 36th International Conference on Software Engineering, pp. 356–366. ACM, Hyderabad (2014). https://doi.org/10.1145/2568225.2568315
21. Budzyński, A.: Injury Severity Analysis. https://github.com/BudzynskiA/injury-severity-analysis. Accessed 20 July 2025
22. Vadhwani, D., Thakor, D.: An improved XGBoost model to predict the injury severity of person in road crash. Int. J. Crashworthiness **30**(2), 115–124 (2025). https://doi.org/10.1080/13588265.2024.2366567
23. Yang, T., Fan, W.D., Song, L.: Modeling pedestrian injury severity in pedestrian-vehicle crashes considering different land use patterns: mixed logit approach. Traffic Inj. Prev. **24**(2), 114–120 (2023). https://doi.org/10.1080/15389588.2022.2156789
24. Lee, C., Abdel-Aty, M.: Comprehensive analysis of vehicle–pedestrian crashes at intersections in Florida. Accid. Anal. Prev. **37**(4), 775–786 (2005). https://doi.org/10.1016/j.aap.2005.03.019

Transport Corridors and Trade Barriers

Vasyl Gorbachuk(✉), Tamara Bardadym, Maksym Dunaievskyi, Seit-Bekir Suleimanov, Victor Godliuk, and Dmytro Rybachok

V.M.Glushkov Institute of Cybernetics of NAS of Ukraine, Kyiv, Ukraine
VGorbachuk@nas.gov.ua

Abstract. A transport corridor has the interrelated dimensions: infrastructure (prioritization, border, cross-border interconnectivity, investment, seaport, mode interface, economic cluster, consolidation, clearing, forwarding, dry port, inland container depot); operational services (shipping, national transit, international transit, cross-border integration, customs and border management, road and rail transport services, interoperability, change of vehicles, air transport, third-party access to the port, storage, clearing, forwarding); institutions and regulations to coordinate corridor activities (corridor management; access rights, transit regime, service contracts). Some estimates suggest that each day saved in shipping time is equivalent to about a percentage reduction in ad valorem tariffs (charged as a percentage of the product price applied to imported goods); the percentage of tariff reduction depends on the specific product. Therefore, the corridor operation should include the total time required to deliver goods from the point of origin to the destination. Any international transport impediments are essentially trade barrriers. Under perfect competition, a quota is equivalent to a tariff: a restriction on the physical volume imported will have essentially the same effect as the application of a certain level of tariff. However, this equivalence does not hold under imperfect competition.

Keywords: Tariffs · Quotas · Import Regulations · Consumer Surplus · Competition

1 Introduction

In its most common configuration, a trade and transport corridor does have international gateways (for instance. ports, airports, land borders) at the entrance to a large populated area and/or production cluster, which usually provide intramodal or inter-modal transfer. Additional gateways may be located at intermediate points along the corridor (for example, regional airports, inland river or sea ports serving coastal or inland waterway corridors).

Gateways are considered part of the corridor because of their capacity and quality of service, which can affect the cost of international travel: providing faster and more reliable traffic for international transport will stimulate trade growth and attract larger and more efficient transport [1, 2]. Moreover, some corridors are being developed to increase traffic volumes at the gateways.

A. Abbasov et al. (Eds.): PLMO 2025, CCIS 2767, pp. 94–106, 2026.
https://doi.org/10.1007/978-3-032-13672-5_9

An example is the development road from Namibia's largest port, Walvis Bay (founded by the (world's first joint-stock) Dutch East India Company (1602–1798) in the late 18-th century) via Ndola (Zambia) to Lubumbashi (Democratic Republic of the Congo), which is 2,700 km long. Another example is the Maputo (the capital and largest port of Mozambique) Development Corridor, which began in 1895 with a 567 km railway to Pretoria, South Africa, built by the Netherlands–South African Railway Company (1887 – 1902). Maritime transport should be explicitly modelled in corridor designs. Improving port infrastructure is also important because it is part of the river-sea corridors for the general international movement of goods [3]. In most cases, sea transport time accounts for a significant portion of the total time for inter-national goods transport [4].

Although the possibilities for improving international shipping may be limited in one way or another, the choice of port and its connections with foreign ports can be a decisive factor in the commercial value of the corridor [5]. Since multimodal operations are common on most corridors, modular approaches can be used to assess them, considering the sequential operations between different modes of transport, which have different productivity and efficiency, which are revealed when switching from one mode of transport to another (for example, in dry port interfaces).

A corridor can perform various functions: to help prioritize infrastructure investments, trade and economic policy reform, and service development; to promote network effects, promoting the consolidation of trade and transport volumes across several links and nodes, which in turn can improve the quality of services; to influence spatial planning and development in the subregions and countries served; to help enterprises optimize their production networks [6].

Historically, towns and industrial and economic clusters have been located near convenient harbors or other transport network nodes to enable access to food, production components, and markets.

While the development of transport and communication technologies facilitates the inclusion of remote areas and peripheral countries in supply chains, the geographical clustering of economic activity is also developing: an obvious example is the European Union (EU). Although transport, communication and other trade costs are decreasing, trade volumes are increasing, and overall trade costs affect the organization and location of production: for example, according to the World Bank, in 2023 the share of part-time workers in Ukraine (2021) and neighboring Belarus, Bulgaria (EU), Georgia (2020), Moldova, Poland (EU), Romania (EU), the RF, Slovakia (EU), Turkey, Hungary (EU) was 7 and 14, 13, 20, 12, 21, 11, 7, 30, 24, 27%, respectively. Firms are increasing their transport costs to save on the prices of inputs and inventories. Aggregates and classifications are used and developed to account for supply chains. For example, the US Bureau of Labor Statistics (BLS; the main agency of the US Federal Statistical System; founded in 1884; a division of the US Department of Labor), performing a government fact-finding function in the broad field of labor economics and statistics, conducts a monthly survey under the Current Employment Statistics (CES) Program, which provides estimates of employment, hours worked, and earnings based on payroll reports in enterprises.

Since 1997, North American countries (Canada, Mexico, the United States) have been using the North American Industry Classification System (NAICS) – a classification of enterprises by type of economic activity (production process), which has largely replaced the previous Standard Industrial Classification (SIC) system. NAICS offered expanded coverage of the service sector compared to SIC.

The 2002 version of NAICS made significant changes to the Information sector. Starting in 2012, NAICS has been updated every 5 years. BLS has grouped NAICS sectors into groups called Supersectors:

06 Goods-Producing Industries (Sectors 10 Natural Resources and Mining, 20 Construction, 30 Manufacturing);

07 Service-Providing Industries (Sectors 40 Trade, Transportation, and Utilities, 50 Information, 55 Financial Activities, 60 Professional and Business Services, 65 Edu-cation and Health Services, 70 Leisure and Hospitality, 80 Other Services, 90 Government).

Thus, manufacturers increasingly outsource non-core activities to external suppliers, who are often expected to deliver their goods or services several times a day, with a delay of no more than minutes per delivery.

In addition, peripheral areas are becoming economically more remote compared to central areas, where infrastructure and logistics are improving: better roads will encourage investment in larger trucks that cannot economically serve remote areas; better ports will encourage investment in larger and faster ships that cannot be technically serviced in smaller ports, and so on.

Therefore, for many developing countries, integration into world markets requires qualitative changes in terms of the availability and quality of logistics services.

Another factor holding back peripheral countries is the spread of just-in-time (JIT) production systems aimed at reducing inventory costs. This principle, introduced in 1962, at Toyota's car factories (founded in 1937), has spread to retail and complex supply chains. An example of the application of the JIT principle is the supply of new (seasonal) versions and models developed on the basis of observed consumer behavior. The application of the JIT principle usually requires the location of suppliers close to the sales market, where production costs may be relatively high. The seasonal high prices of the latest models are often more important than the scale of production.

2 Consumer and Producer Surplus, Social Welfare

Import tariffs, quotas and subsidies are widely used in trade policy. Let us focus on import quotas and export subsidies and examine whether these forms of policy de-pend on the type of competition in the market.

Under perfect competition, a quota is equivalent to a tariff [7]: a restriction on the physical volume imported will have, in essence, the same effect as the application of a certain level of tariff. However, this equivalence does not hold under imperfect competition. The situation of a domestic import monopoly [7] has been generalized to a duopoly between domestic and foreign firms [8, 9]. It can be shown that a quota and a tariff have comparable effects on the level of imports, but quite different effects on the import price and hence on the welfare of an importing country.

Another reason for the difference in the effects of tariffs and quotas is that foreign firms can choose the quality of the goods they export. Then the effect of a (quota) restriction on the physical volume of exports will be different from the effect of an (ad valorem) tariff on the value of exports (the ad valorem tariff is defined as a fixed percentage of the declared value of the imported good). The importance of this difference became apparent in the 1980s, when Japan applied quotas on car exports to the United States, choosing expensive, high-quality models.

The result that trade strategies have different effects depending on the market structure is carried over to the case of export subsidies. In the conventional two-sector model, there is no reason to use export subsidies, because they would lead to irreversible losses (similar to a tariff) for a small country and would have additional terms-of-trade losses (unlike a tariff) for a large country. Since many countries use export subsidies to support their industries for some time, it is necessary to go beyond the two-sector model with perfect competition. The transition to a multi-sector model highlights the potential role of targeted export subsidies.

The transition from perfect competition to a duopoly of domestic and foreign firms, operating in a third market, also changes the picture. The question is whether the domestic government can provide its firm with a strategic advantage by providing it with subsidies. Such a subsidy is in the national interest when the increase in exports is greater than the subsidy. This advantage would hold at least under Cournot–Nash competition, but under Bertrand competition there is a disadvantage instead of an advantage [10, 11, 12]: export subsidies are in the national interest only under some forms of market competition. The effects of subsidies on the prices and profits of commercial aircraft production by Airbus (Europe) and Boeing (America) are studied.

The graphical analysis of perfect competition starts from the (linear) demand and supply curves of a small country, measuring price vertically and yield horizontally. If the world price is lower than the domestic equilibrium price, then under free trade domestic demand and supply are and respectively, and imports are.

The analysis of the import market starts from the import demand and export supply curves, measuring price vertically and imports horizontally. If the government of a small country imposes an import quota, then the volume of imports cannot exceed, which effectively establishes a vertical export supply that intersects with import demand at. The price increases supply to and decreases demand to.

In terms of its impact on price, consumption, and production, the quota mentioned is equivalent to a tariff. Indeed, a quota reduces consumer surplus (the area above the market price and under the demand curve) by

$$c_1(p_1 - p^*) + \frac{(p_1 - p^*)(c_0 - c_1)}{2} = (p_1 - p^*)\left(c_1 + \frac{c_0 - c_1}{2}\right) = \frac{(p_1 - p^*)(c_1 + c_0)}{2}$$

and increases producer surplus (the area below the market price and above the supply curve) by

$$y_1(p_1 - p^*) - \frac{(y_1 - y_0)(p_1 - p^*)}{2} = (p_1 - p^*)\left(y_1 - \frac{y_1 - y_0}{2}\right) = \frac{(p_1 - p^*)(y_1 + y_0)}{2}, \tag{1}$$

changing the sum of these surpluses by

$$\frac{(p_1 - p^*)(y_1 + y_0)}{2} - \frac{(p_1 - p^*)(c_1 + c_0)}{2} = \frac{(p_1 - p^*)[(y_1 - c_1) + (y_0 - c_0)]}{2}$$

$$= \frac{(p_1 - p^*)[S(p_1) - D(p_1) - m_0]}{2} = -\frac{(p_1 - p^*)(m_1 + m_0)}{2} < 0. \quad (2)$$

When a quota is introduced, the importer receives a net profit (net quota rent) $m_1(p_1 - p^*)$, then the change in domestic social welfare is

$$m_1(p_1 - p^*) - \frac{(p_1 - p^*)(m_1 + m_0)}{2} = \frac{(p_1 - p^*)(m_1 - m_0)}{2} < 0. \quad (3)$$

This change is equal to the area between the world price, the import demand curve, and the export supply. Quota rent is distributed in various ways.

3 Quota Rent

First, quota licenses can be granted to domestic firms, which will then be able to import at the world price p^* and sell on the domestic market at the price p_1, receiving quota rent. In the U.S. dairy industry, cheese producers obtain import licenses from abroad, with quota rents accruing to both importers and exporters. Domestic firms obtain rents $m_1(p_1 - p^*)$, consumers lose surplus $\frac{(p_1-p^*)(c_1+c_0)}{2}$, and producers gain surplus $\frac{(p_1-p^*)(y_1+y_0)}{2}$, changing domestic social welfare (as defined by Eq. (2)) to

$$m_1(p_1 - p^*) - \frac{(p_1 - p^*)(c_1 + c_0)}{2} + \frac{(p_1 - p^*)(y_1 + y_0)}{2}$$

$$= m_1(p_1 - p^*) - \frac{(p_1 - p^*)(m_1 + m_0)}{2} = \frac{(p_1 - p^*)(m_1 - m_0)}{2} < 0.$$

Second, when quota licenses are granted to domestic firms, they may engage in some inefficient activities to obtain these licenses. For example, if licenses for some imported products are allocated in proportion to production of the final good in the previous year, firms will produce more of the final product than they can sell, regardless of the quality of that good. Such activities are called rent seeking and may include lobbying and other resource-intensive behaviors. It has been suggested that the waste of resources directed to rent-seeking activities can reach the amount of quota rent $m_1(p_1 - p^*)$ at the expense of domestic firms. Consumers lose a surplus $\frac{(p_1-p^*)(c_1+c_0)}{2}$, and producers gain a surplus

$$m_1(p_1 - p^*) + \frac{(p_1 - p^*)(y_1 - y_0)}{2} + \frac{(p_1 - p^*)(c_0 - c_1)}{2}$$

$$= (p_1 - p^*)\left[m_1 + \frac{(c_0 - y_0) - (c_1 - y_1)}{2}\right] = \frac{(p_1 - p^*)(m_1 + m_0)}{2},$$

which is greater than the surplus (1) if that imports exceed domestic production:

$$\frac{(p_1 - p^*)(m_1 + m_0)}{2} - \frac{(p_1 - p^*)(y_1 + y_0)}{2} = \frac{(p_1 - p^*)[(m_1 - y_1) + (m_0 - y_0)]}{2} > 0.$$

Therefore, rent-seeking activities can also be directed to tariff revenue.

Third, quota licenses can be granted by the government of the importing country through auctions. This is the case, for example, in New Zealand. In a well-organized auction, one can hope that the revenue collected will equal the value of the rent, and the amount $m_1(p_1 - p^*)$ will be credited to the domestic government. Then consumers lose a surplus $\frac{(p_1-p^*)(c_1+c_0)}{2}$, producers gain a surplus $\frac{(p_1-p^*)(y_1+y_0)}{2}$, the government receives a rent $m_1(p_1 - p^*)$, changing social welfare (taking into account Eq. (2)) to

$$m_1(p_1 - p^*) - \frac{(p_1 - p^*)(c_1 + c_0)}{2} + \frac{(p_1 - p^*)(y_1 + y_0)}{2} = \frac{(p_1 - p^*)(m_1 - m_0)}{2}.$$

Finally, the government of the importing country can authorize the government of the exporting country to enforce the quota by giving quota rents to foreign producers. The fact that the exporting country distributes the quota among its own producers is sometimes called a «voluntary» export restraint (VER) or a voluntary restraint agreement (VRA). Such an arrangement is in place for the quotas that the United States has used for automobiles, steel, textiles, and other industries. For example, after 1981, Japan's Ministry of International Trade and Industry (MITI) told each Japanese automobile manufacturer how much it would export to the United States. Consumers then lose surplus $\frac{(p_1-p^*)(c_1+c_0)}{2}$ and producers gain surplus $\frac{(p_1-p^*)(y_1+y_0)}{2}$, changing public welfare to volume (2).

The country uses VER by giving quota rents to foreigners to prevent adverse responses from foreign countries. Rent transfer to foreigners serves as a means of incentive compatibility, and therefore an importing country will use VER only when its relevant industry is in a difficult shape.

Extending the graphical analysis to a large country, the import demand and export supply curves intersect at the price $p_0 < p_1$: $m_0 = M(p_0) = X(p_0)$. Then the quota rent is $m_1(p_1 - p^*)$ or $m_1(p_1 - p_0)$. At VER, this rent is accrued to foreign producers. Similarly to the relation (3), the irreversible losses of the importing country are

$$m_1(p_1 - p_0) - \frac{(p_1 - p_0)(m_1 + m_0)}{2} = \frac{(p_1 - p_0)(m_1 - m_0)}{2} < 0$$

and the irreversible losses of the exporting country are.

$$\frac{(p_0 - p^*)(m_1 - m_0)}{2} < 0$$

Annual losses of US import protection were estimated at hundreds billion dollars. In the dairy product group, the quota rent is distributed between US importers, foreign exporters, and the US government. In the remaining product groups, the quota rents belong to foreign exporters. In the textiles and clothing product group, the large quota rent and irreversible losses of the US are due to the global quota system known as the Multi-Fiber Arrangement (MFA) (the WTO Agreement on Textiles and Clothing (ATC) since 2005). As a result of the MFA (ATC), the irreversible losses of foreign countries are becoming greater. The quota on automobiles ceased to be a deterrent, and during the Uruguay Round of the World Trade Organization (WTO), a withdrawal from the MFA was agreed. Since these changes were postponed until 2005, new trade actions have taken place. For example, in the 1990s, the trade dispute between Japan and the United States over automobiles escalated. For steel, quotas were replaced by tariffs in the 1990s. Reported average conventional tariffs do not include additional costs due to US anti-dumping duties. In general, US quotas, tariffs, and duties continue to impose significant costs on both the United States and its foreign trading partners. Tariffs and quotas are equivalent in the sense that the same level of imports resulting from a tariff or quota means the same price. However, this equivalence does not hold in imperfect competition in the domestic market: the quota creates a protected market for the domestic firm, which will lead to a higher price and lower sales volume than the tariff at the same level of imports.

4 Monopoly

For a fixed world price p^*, the domestic monopolist has horizontal demand, and therefore its marginal revenue $MR\,(y)$ is horizontal and intersects its marginal cost $MC\,(y)$ at output y_0, which maximizes its profit: $MR\,(y_0)= MC\,(y_0)$ [7]. Since the competitive firm (industry) also chooses y_0 when it has the same function $MC\,(y)$, free trade eliminates the monopolist's market power, that is, its ability to limit supply and raise price. Therefore, free trade is a potential additional source of gains from trade. If a tariff t is applied to imports, the domestic monopolist charges a price $p^* + t$, has horizontal demand, and marginal revenue $MR_t(y)$, which intersects its marginal cost $MC\,(y)$ at output $y_1 = c_1 - m_1 > y_0$: $MR_t(y_1)= MC\,(y_1)$.

Suppose that instead of a tariff t, a quota $m_1 = c_1 - y_1$ is applied to imports, that is, at an arbitrary price above p^*, the volume imported is m_1, and the monopolist has demand $D\,(p) - m_1$, where $D\,(p)$ is the domestic demand without a quota: $D\,(p^*) = c_0$; $D\,(p^* + t) = c_1$. Unlike the situation with a tariff, with a quota the monopolist retains the ability to influence the domestic price by choosing such price p and output y that $D\,(p) - m_1 = y$. The monopolist maximizes its profit at some price $p_2 > p^* + t$ and output $y_2 = D\,(p_2) - m_1 = c_2 - m_1$, where marginal revenue $MR_m(y)$ intersects marginal costs $MC\,(y)$: $MR_m(y_2)= MC\,(y_2)$. Since $p_2 > p^* + t$, with the same volume of imports m_1, the quota leads to a higher domestic price than the tariff. Here, the quota and the tariff are not equivalent: the quota allows the monopolist to use market power, and therefore has greater welfare losses than the tariff.

A quota can lead to both a situation $y_2 < y_0$ (a decline in domestic production compared to free trade) and a situation (a decline in domestic production compared to free trade) $y_2 > y_0$. The situation $y_2 < y_0$ means that the quota will reduce employment in the domestic industry and protection of the domestic labor market. Thus, under imperfect competition, a quota loses out to a tariff as an instrument of economic policy [7]. However, the assumption that a domestic monopoly does not interact with foreign firms is not satisfactory: a domestic firm will certainly compete with foreign firms according to Cournot or Bertrand [10, 11].

Under Cournot competition (in the domestic market), an import quota has a fairly predictable effect: if foreign firms' sales are lower than those under free trade, then domestic firms' sales are higher than those under the reaction curves without quota. If a VER is negotiated with a foreign firm, where the firm agrees to sell below the free trade level, then such a VER will affect the equilibrium. If a VER is negotiated with a foreign firm, where the firm agrees to sell no higher than the free trade level, then the VER will not affect the equilibrium.

5 Imperfect Competition

Suppose that under Bertrand competition (when both the foreign and domestic firms perceive the price (strategic variable) of the competitor as given), the foreign and domestic products are imperfect substitutes (if they are perfect substitutes, then pricing is based on marginal costs) [8, 9]. Let us denote p the price of the imported product and q the price of the domestic product. Let the foreign firm export the volume x of its product, and the domestic firm sell the volume y of its product. If the elasticity of demand for each product is increasing relative to the price of this product, then the response curves $p = r^*(q)$ and $q = r(p)$ are increasing in q and p, respectively. When the relative price of the imported (domestic) product increases, the elasticity of the domestic (imported) product decreases, and both firms will charge a higher price for their product. There is also a dumping response of price p to price q, as well as price q to price p.

When there is no additively separable basic (numeraire) product that absorbs all income effects, then the demand for the foreign and domestic products is $x = d^*(p, q, I)$ and $y = d(p, q, I)$, respectively, where I are the costs of both products. Both of these demand functions must be homogeneous of degree 1 in prices and costs. At the ad valorem import tariff τ, the domestic price is

$$p = p^*(1+\tau). \tag{4}$$

Then the profit of the foreign firm is $\pi^* = \frac{p d^*(p,q,I)}{1+\tau} - C^*[d^*(p, q, I)]$, and that of the domestic firm is $\pi = q d(p, q, I) - C[d(p, q, I)]$, where C^* and C are the cost functions of the foreign and domestic firms, respectively.

Maximization of π^* in p gives

$$0 = \frac{\partial \pi^*}{\partial p} = \frac{d^*(p, q, I)}{1+\tau} + \frac{p}{1+\tau}\frac{\partial d^*(p, q, I)}{\partial p} - \frac{d\, C^*[d^*(p, q, I)]}{d\, d^*}\frac{\partial d^*(p, q, I)}{\partial p},$$

$$(1+\tau)\frac{d\,{}^*[d^*(p, q, I)]}{d\, d^*} = p\left[1 + \frac{d^*(p, q, I)}{p}\right] = p\left(1 - \frac{1}{\eta^*}\right), \tag{5}$$

where $\eta^* = -\frac{p}{d^*}\frac{\partial d^*(p,q,I)}{\partial p}$ is the positive elasticity of imports.

Maximization of π in q gives

$$0 = \frac{\partial \pi}{\partial q} = d(p, q, I) + q\frac{\partial d(p, q, I)}{\partial q} - \frac{d\, C[d(p, q, I)]}{d\, d}\frac{\partial d(p, q, I)}{\partial q},$$

$$\frac{d\,[d(p, q, I)]}{d\, d} = q\left[1 + \frac{d(p, q, I)}{q}\right] = p\left(1 - \frac{1}{\eta}\right), \tag{6}$$

where $\eta = -\frac{q}{d}\frac{\partial\, d\,(p,q,I)}{\partial\, q}$ is the positive elasticity of domestic demand.

The second-order condition for maximization of π^* in p is

$$0 > \frac{\partial^2 \pi^*}{\partial^2 p} = \frac{1}{1+\tau}\left[2\frac{\partial\, d^*(p,q,I)}{\partial\, p} + \frac{\partial^2 d^*(p,q,I)}{\partial^2 p}\right] - \frac{d\, C^*[d^*(p,q,I)]}{d\, d^*}\frac{\partial^2 d^*(p,q,I)}{\partial^2 p}, \tag{7}$$

and the second-order condition for maximization of π in q is

$$0 > \frac{\partial^2 \pi}{\partial^2 q} = 2\frac{\partial\, d\,(p,q,I)}{\partial\, q} + \frac{\partial^2 d\,(p,q,I)}{\partial^2 q} - \frac{d\, C\,[d\,(p,q,I)]}{d\, d}\frac{\partial^2 d\,(p,q,I)}{\partial^2 q}.$$

The Bertrand equilibrium (solution of system (5), (6)) is stable under the condition

$$0 < \frac{\partial^2 \pi^*}{\partial^2 p}\frac{\partial^2 \pi}{\partial^2 q} - \frac{\partial^2 \pi^*}{\partial\, p\,\partial\, q}\frac{\partial^2 \pi}{\partial\, q\,\partial\, p}.$$

For fixed costs I, the Eq. (5) yields the reaction curve of the import price $p = r^*(q,\tau)$, which takes into account the tariff τ, and Eq. (6) yields the reaction curve $q = r\,(p)$. Profit π increases with the increase of p, and π^* – with the increase of q. If the function $f\,(v)$ is homogeneous of the degree α ($f\,(\lambda\, v) = \lambda^\alpha f\,(v)\ \forall\, \lambda > 0$), then its first derivative $\frac{d f}{d v}$ is homogeneous of the degree $(\alpha - 1)$. Therefore, if demand $d\,(p,q,I)$ is homogeneous of the degree 0 in (p,q,I), then the function $\frac{\partial\, d\,(p,q,I)}{\partial\, q}$ is homogeneous of the degree -1. Then $\eta = -\frac{q}{d}\frac{\partial\, d\,(p,q,I)}{\partial\, q}$ is homogeneous of the degree 0 in (p,q,I):

$$\eta\,(\lambda\, p, \lambda\, q, \lambda\, I) = -\frac{\lambda\, q}{\lambda\, d}\frac{\partial\, d\,(\lambda\, p, \lambda\, q, \lambda\, I)}{\partial\,(\lambda\, q)} = -\frac{q}{d}\frac{\partial\, d\,(p,q,I)}{\partial\, q} = \lambda^0 \eta\,(p,q,I).$$

If the demand function d has an elasticity with respect to costs I, equal to 1, then $d\,(p,q,I) = I\,\psi\,(p,q)$, and the elasticity η does not depend on I:

$$\eta = -\frac{q}{d}\frac{\partial\, d(p,q,I)}{\partial\, q} = -\frac{q}{I\,\psi\,(p,q)} I \frac{\partial\,\psi\,(p,q)}{\partial\, q} = -\frac{q}{\psi\,(p,q)}\frac{\partial\,\psi\,(p,q)}{\partial\, q}.$$

Then the change of I does not affect the elasticity and the reaction curve, and the elasticity $\eta = \eta\,(p,q)$ is a function of the ratio $\frac{q}{p}$. Similarly, $\eta^* = \eta^*(p,q)$ is a function of $\frac{p}{q}$. The assumption of a decrease in the elasticity of demand with increasing volume showed that the ad valorem tariff leads to a decrease in the import price p^*, that is a gain in terms of trade. Moving from elasticities $\eta = \eta\,(p,q)$, $\eta^* = \eta^*(p,q)$ to elasticities $\eta\left(\frac{q}{p}\right)$, $\eta\left(\frac{q}{p}\right)$, we similarly assume that $\eta\left(\frac{q}{p}\right)$ and $\eta^*\left(\frac{p}{q}\right)$ increase with increasing $\frac{q}{p}$ and $\frac{p}{q}$, respectively.

Then, assuming constant foreign and domestic marginal costs $\frac{d\, C^*}{d\, d^*}$ and $\frac{d\, C}{d\, d}$, respectively, the Eqs. (5) and (6) imply that the reaction functions $p = r^*(q,\tau)$ and $q = r\,(p)$ are increasing in q and p, respectively: when the relative price of competing product increases, the elasticity decreases, and each firm will charge a higher price for its own product. Moreover, there is a dumping response of each price to the price of the competing product:

under the above assumptions, differentiation of the equation $p = r^*(q, \tau)$ gives

$$\frac{dp}{dq} = \frac{d\,r^*(q,\tau)}{dq},\ 1 > \frac{q}{p}\frac{dp}{dq} = \frac{q}{p}\frac{d\,r^*(q,\tau)}{dq};$$

under the above assumptions, differentiation of the equation $q = r(p)$ gives

$$\frac{dq}{dp} = \frac{d\,r(p)}{dp},\ 1 > \frac{p}{q}\frac{dq}{dp} = \frac{p}{q}\frac{d\,r(p)}{dp}.$$

When the ad valorem tariff τ increases, the condition (7) implies that the import price $p = r^*(q, \tau)$ increases as well. This leads to an induced increase in the domestic price q and a further increase in the import price p until a new Bertrand equilibrium with a higher ratio $\frac{p}{q}$ is reached. From the equality (4) we have

$$\frac{dp}{d\tau} = p^* + (1+\tau)\frac{dp^*}{d\tau} = \frac{p}{1+\tau} + (1+\tau)\frac{dp^*}{d\tau}, \tag{8}$$

$$\frac{(1+\tau)}{p}\frac{dp}{d\tau} = 1 + \frac{(1+\tau)^2}{p}\frac{dp^*}{d\tau} = 1 + \frac{(1+\tau)}{p^*}\frac{dp^*}{d\tau},$$

$$\frac{dp^*}{d\tau} = \frac{p^*}{p}\frac{dp}{d\tau} - \frac{p^*}{1+\tau} = \frac{1}{(1+\tau)}\frac{dp}{d\tau} - \frac{p^*}{1+\tau} = \frac{1}{1+\tau}\left(\frac{dp}{d\tau} - \frac{p}{1+\tau}\right),$$

whence $\frac{dp^*}{d\tau} < 0$ takes place at $\frac{dp}{d\tau} < \frac{p}{1+\tau} = p^*$, that is, the terms of trade gain (for the importer) takes place. In order to obtain this gain, the aforementioned assumptions about $\eta\left(\frac{q}{p}\right), \eta^*\left(\frac{p}{q}\right)$ are sufficient. Similarly, an ad valorem tariff on a foreign monopolist leads to a decrease in the import price p^* (terms of trade gain). Thus, for both a foreign monopolist and a duopoly in the import market, the key assumption for obtaining the terms of trade gain is that the elasticity of demand increases with price increase or decreases with volume increase. This assumption holds for an arbitrary demand curve that is less convex than a demand curve with constant elasticity.

From the Eqs. (4) and (5) we have

$$p^*\left(1 - \frac{1}{\eta^*}\right) = \frac{dC^*}{dd^*} = const,\ 0 = \frac{dp^*}{d\tau}\left(1 - \frac{1}{\eta^*}\right) + \frac{p}{(\eta^*)^2}\frac{d\eta^*}{d\tau},$$

$$\frac{dp^*}{d\tau} = \frac{\eta^* p}{(1-\eta^*)(\eta^*)^2}\frac{d\eta^*}{d\tau} = \frac{p}{\eta^*(1-\eta^*)}\frac{d\eta^*}{d\left(\frac{p}{q}\right)}\frac{d\left(\frac{p}{q}\right)}{d\tau}. \tag{9}$$

Then $\frac{d\left(\frac{p}{q}\right)}{d\tau} > 0$ (tariff leads to a greater increase in the price of imported goods compared to domestic) and $\frac{d\eta^*}{d\left(\frac{p}{q}\right)} > 0$ imply $\frac{dp^*}{d\tau} < 0$.

Import price $p = p^*(1+\tau)$ and domestic price q affect social welfare $W[p, q, L + \tau p^* x + qy - C(y)] = L - pD + \tau p^* x + qy - C(y)$, where

$$D = x + y, \tag{10}$$

L is given labor supply or total income of the economy:

$$\frac{dW}{d\tau} = -D\frac{dp}{d\tau} + p^*x + \tau\left(x\frac{dp^*}{d\tau} + p^*\frac{dx}{d\tau}\right) + q\frac{dy}{d\tau} + y\frac{dq}{d\tau} - \frac{dC(y)}{dy}\frac{dy}{d\tau}$$

$$= p^*\tau\frac{dx}{d\tau} + \left[q - \frac{dC(y)}{dy}\right]\frac{dy}{d\tau} - x\frac{dp^*}{d\tau},$$

where $\frac{dp}{d\tau} = \frac{dq}{d\tau}$, the Eqs. (8) and (10) are taken into account:

$$-D\frac{dp}{d\tau} + p^*x + \tau x\frac{dp^*}{d\tau} + y\frac{dq}{d\tau} = (y - D)\frac{dp}{d\tau} + p^*x + \tau x\frac{dp^*}{d\tau}$$

$$= -x\left[p^* + (1+\tau)\frac{dp^*}{d\tau}\right] + p^*x + \tau x\frac{dp^*}{d\tau} = -x\frac{dp^*}{d\tau}.$$

For small tariffs τ, the value of $p^*\tau\frac{dx}{d\tau}$ is small as well. By virtue of the relation (9), the value of $-x\frac{dp^*}{d\tau}$ is positive (with a gain in terms of trade) under the aforementioned assumptions about $\eta\left(\frac{q}{p}\right)$, $\eta^*\left(\frac{p}{q}\right)$. The sign of $\left[q - \frac{dC(y)}{dy}\right]\frac{dy}{d\tau}$ depends on the sign of $\frac{dy}{d\tau}$: a larger value of p in the new equilibrium reduces demand, and a decrease of $\frac{p}{q}$ increases demand for the domestic good.

It turns out that $\frac{dy}{d\tau} > 0$ (with a gain in terms of trade) with a small increase in q at $1 > \frac{\eta-1}{\eta} > \frac{p}{q}\frac{dq}{dp} = \frac{p}{q}\frac{dr(p)}{dp}$. If the function $y = d(p, q, I)$ is homogeneous of degree 0, then $\frac{\partial d}{\partial q}q + \frac{\partial d}{\partial p}p + \frac{\partial d}{\partial I}I = 0$; if the income elasticity of demand is equal to 1, then $\frac{p}{d}\frac{\partial d}{\partial q} = \eta - 1$. Then, if $0 < \frac{q}{p\eta}\frac{d\eta}{d\left(\frac{q}{p}\right)} < (\eta-1)^2$, then y increases with an increase in $q = r(p)$.

That domestic output can increase as a result of a tariff is based on the assumption that total costs I of imported and domestic products are constant. This will be the case if the utility function for aggregate products (d^*, d) and the rest of the economy is a Cobb–Douglas function. Total costs of domestic and imported products can fall (with a possible reduction in domestic output and loss of welfare) or rise as a result of a tariff. When the costs of a differentiated product change, the change in domestic output due to a tariff has been studied in a model of monopolistic competition. This change can be either a decline (for example, when imported goods are intermediate inputs and the tariff leads to a decrease in sales in the industry that uses these inputs) or an increase. Such a decline was found in a simulation model of the Mexican automobile industry. Therefore, profit shifting is not always an explanation for import protection in Cournot or Bertrand competition. The best indicator of whether the importing country gains or loses is the terms of trade. If the elasticity of demand increases (decreases) with price increase and decreases (increases) with volume increase, then there is a terms of trade gain for the importer, and hence the optimal tariff is positive (negative). A negative import tariff stands for a subsidy on imports. If the elasticity of demand is constant, then the optimal tariff is zero.

With a few additional constraints, the demand for the domestic product increases with $q = r(p)$ increase, and that for the imported product increases with $p = r^*(q)$ increase. Suppose a foreign firm has a VER $x(p, q) \leq \overline{x}$ for sales in the domestic market. If the quota limit $\overline{x}$ is equal to exports, which corresponds to exports in the Bertrand equilibrium under free trade, then this limit will affect the price responses of foreign and domestic firms. If this VER is known to all firms, then instead of Bertrand competition (where each firm takes the price of any other firm as given), a different behavior will occur. For example, a domestic firm will realize that an increase in its price q will create a prerequisite for the foreign firm's exports to increase and violate VER (for $x(p, q) \leq \overline{x}$), which forces the foreign firm to increase its price p to reduce $x(p, q)$ and maintain VER. Therefore, the foreign firm's reaction curve will not correspond to the Bertrand reaction. One would expect domestic firms to take advantage of VER, knowing about the forced reaction of the foreign firm. Since VER gives the domestic firm a first mover advantage in choosing its price, the domestic firm will act as a leader and the foreign firm as a Stackelberg follower.

6 Conclusion

Thus, the optimal action of the domestic firm will be to increase its price in order to maximize its profit at VER. Moreover, the effect of a discrete price increase (when the equilibrium changes) is different from the effect of a tariff: since imports are the same in both equilibria, a zero tariff will have the same effect on imports as VER, but will have no effect on prices. A quota has a much greater impact on imports and domestic prices than a tariff with the same level of imports [7].

The implication for the duopoly model is that the foreign firm also benefits from a VER: when export levels are limited by the free trade volume, the foreign firm's profits increase. Therefore, VER is indeed voluntary [8] and acts as a facilitating practice to obtain a more cooperative decision by firms [9]. Note that when the quota is smaller than the free trade export level, the foreign firm's profits will not necessarily increase. In any case, under a VER, domestic consumers lose out by paying a higher price for domestic and imported goods, without gaining in tariff revenue. The government of the exporting country applies a VER instead of a tariff to prevent an unfavorable response from the government of the importing country and to benefit from the trade restrictions. In practice, various trade restrictions generate some demand on special trade corridors, agreements, and global supply chains. In turn, such a demand creates the corresponding proposition and related employment. This research was conducted as part of the project «Development of Distributed Energy in the Context of the Ukrainian Electricity Market Using Digitalization Technologies and Systems».

References

1. Aliev, T., Musaeva, N., Suleymanova, M.: Technologies for assessing the reliability of the operational state of facilities in transport corridors. In: 2024 3rd International Conference

on Problems of Logistics, Management and Operation in the East-West Transport Corridor (PLMO), pp. 1–5. Institute of Control Systems, Baku (2024). https://doi.org/10.1109/PLMO62307.2024.10887154
2. Aliev, T.A., Musaeva, N.F., Gazizade, B.I.: Algorithm of application of high-order moments of the useful component as a diagnostic indicator of changes in the technical state. J. Autom. Inf. Sci. **11**(50), 29–43 (2018)
3. Kunaka, C., Carruthers, R.: Trade and Transport Corridor Management Toolkit. World Bank, Washington, DC (2014)
4. Hummels, D.: Time as a trade barrier. GTAP Working Paper. Lafayette, IN: Department of Agricultural Economics; Purdue University; Center for Global Trade Analysis 1152, pp. 1–40 (2001)
5. Nordas, H.K.: Time as a trade barrier. In: Waters, D. (ed.). Global Logistics: New Directions in Supply Chain Management, 6-th edn., pp. 347–364. Chartered Institute of Logistics and Transport; Kogan Page Limited; London, UK (2010)
6. Aliev, T., Babayev, T., Guluyev, G., Rzayeva, N., Gadimov, R.: Ways to improve the safety of the East-West transport corridor with the use of intelligent technologies and systems. In: 2024 3rd International Conference on Problems of Logistics, Management and Operation in the East-West Transport Corridor (PLMO), pp. 1–10. Institute of Control Systems, Baku (2024). https://doi.org/10.1109/PLMO62307.2024.10887148
7. Bhagwati, J.N.: On the equivalence of tariffs and quotas. In: Baldwin, R.E., et al. (eds.) Trade Growth and the Balance of Payments: Essays in Honor of Gottfried Haberler, pp. 53–67. Rand McNally, Chicago (1965)
8. Harris, R.: Why voluntary export restraints are «voluntary». Can. J. Econ. **18**(4), 799–809 (1985)
9. Krishna, K.: Trade restrictions as facilitating practices. J. Int. Econ. **26**, 251–270 (1989)
10. Gorbachuk, V.M.: Trade tools for development of high-tech industry. Odesa Natl. Univ. Her. Econ. **20**(1/1), 162–170 (2015). (In Ukrainian)
11. Gorbachuk, V.M.: Generalized Cournot–Stackelberg–Nash equilibrium. Cybern. Syst. Anal. **42**(1), 25–33 (2006)

Investigation of the Impact of Headwind on a Gondola Car When Disbanding from a Hill Hump

Matluba Khadzhimukhametova(✉), Makhira Usmanova, Shukhrat Saidivaliev, and Samandar Sattorov

Tashkent State Transport University, Tashkent, Uzbekistan
matluba_78@mail.ru

Abstract. This article presents a comprehensive investigation into the influence of headwind on the motion dynamics of an empty open-type gondola car during its descent from a railway sorting hump. Accurate determination of hump height is a critical aspect of marshalling yard design, directly affecting the efficiency and safety of wagon disbanding operations. Traditionally, the engineering practice has considered the empty covered wagon as the worst-case or bad runner scenario for such calculations. However, this assumption fails to reflect the aerodynamic behavior of open wagons under real-world environmental conditions. To address this gap, the motion of the open gondola car was analyzed through an integrated approach combining classical mechanical equations with computational fluid dynamics (CFD) modeling using the SOLIDWORKS Flow Simulation platform. The study characterizes the complex distribution of aerodynamic forces acting on the wagon body, including frontal impact pressure, internal turbulent recirculation, and rear-wall suction effects—factors largely neglected in standard hump design methodologies. Simulation results indicate that, for identical hump geometries and initial conditions, the terminal velocity of an open gondola is 34.6% lower than that of a covered wagon. The maximum aerodynamic pressure recorded on the frontal face was 101.602 kPa, with significant turbulent flow structures observed within the wagon's internal cavity. These findings demonstrate that the open gondola experiences not only higher overall drag but also compound resistance mechanisms that critically affect its trajectory and stopping point on the classification track. The study concludes that continued use of covered wagons as a baseline reference for hump profile calculations leads to systematic underestimation of required elevation and velocity parameters. It recommends that open-type wagons be adopted as the reference vehicle in adverse scenarios, particularly under headwind exposure. Furthermore, the integration of CFD-based methods into the design and automation of marshalling yards is strongly advocated, enabling more accurate predictions of wagon behavior, reduced manual interventions, and enhanced operational reliability.

Keywords: Sorting Hump · Headwind · Open Gondola Car · Aerodynamic Resistance · CFD Simulation · Marshalling Yard Optimization · SOLIDWORKS Flow

A. Abbasov et al. (Eds.): PLMO 2025, CCIS 2767, pp. 107–120, 2026.
https://doi.org/10.1007/978-3-032-13672-5_10

1 Introduction

The transformation of global freight transportation systems is undergoing a paradigm shift driven by digitalization, sustainability requirements, climate adaptation strategies, and increasing throughput demands. As one of the most cost-efficient and energy-saving modes of land transport, railway freight logistics is at the center of this transformation. Particular attention is being paid to the optimization of railway marshalling yards, which remain the backbone of cargo sorting and dispatching processes across major railway networks.

In Uzbekistan, these global challenges are echoed by state-led efforts to develop a resilient and competitive transport infrastructure. The Presidential Decree of December 2, 2017, "On measures to improve transport infrastructure and diversify foreign trade routes for cargo transportation for 2018–2022," outlines a national strategy that prioritizes the modernization of sorting stations, expansion of electrified railways, and deployment of intelligent control systems. These reforms align with the country's broader goals to integrate into transcontinental corridors such as the China–Central Asia–Europe transport belt and the North–South multimodal network.

A pivotal technical issue in the operation of marshalling yards is the precise determination of the hump height—the key element that governs the uncoupling, acceleration, and controlled rolling of freight wagons toward their destination tracks. The failure to accurately account for environmental and design-specific resistive forces during wagon motion can lead to inefficient operations, excessive wear, failed couplings, or even collisions.

Historically, the standard engineering assumption has been to consider an empty covered wagon as the worst-case runner when calculating the hump profile [1–5]. This assumption was established in earlier works by Obraztsov, Zemblinov, Rodimov [1–5, 8], and others in the Soviet scientific tradition, where simplified physical models did not incorporate complex environmental variables such as aerodynamic drag, crosswinds, or turbulence. However, recent research and practical experience in modernized yards have challenged this assumption, suggesting that open-type gondola cars may present even greater resistance due to their exposure to airflow and unshielded cavities.

The problem becomes more critical under headwind conditions, where airflow acts directly against the movement of the car, producing both frontal drag and internal turbulence that amplify the decelerating forces. These phenomena are often underestimated or entirely excluded in routine calculations due to the lack of accessible simulation tools and real-time weather data integration [6, 7]. Recognizing this gap, international research institutions have advanced various computational and experimental methods to study aerodynamic influences on rolling stock. Notably:

- The University of Baltimore (USA) has explored stochastic models of wind-induced delays in classification yards.
- Technische Universität Berlin (Germany) and the Swedish National Railway Administration have developed wind tunnel tests for freight wagon aerodynamics.
- -Russian and Ukrainian universities continue to refine hump yard calculation methods with limited environmental integration.

- -At the Tashkent State Transport University, a new generation of railway engineers is leveraging digital simulation tools to address Central Asia's specific topographic and meteorological challenges [9, 10, 14].

This study contributes to this global body of work by providing a comprehensive analysis of the motion dynamics of an open gondola car on a sorting slide under the influence of varying headwind velocities, using both analytical formulations and SOLIDWORKS Flow Simulation for validation. The objective is to re-evaluate the criteria for selecting a "bad runner" wagon type and to provide evidence-based recommendations for updating hump profile design methodologies in line with modern operational conditions.

2 Description of the Processing System

Over the past century, a number of prominent scientists and engineers—most notably academician Obraztsov V.N., Rodimov B.A., Zemblinov S.V., and Turanov H.T.—have developed the foundational theories for calculating the height and profile of sorting humps at railway marshalling yards. These classical models were instrumental in establishing deterministic methods for ensuring that wagons reach their destination tracks safely and efficiently after uncoupling. A central tenet of these methods was the designation of the empty covered wagon as the so-called "worst-case runner" under adverse conditions. This assumption stemmed from the idea that a lightweight closed-type freight car, when descending from the hump under headwind influence, would possess the minimum kinetic energy reserve needed to overcome all resistive forces along the way. Consequently, if such a wagon reached its target without stalling or requiring intervention, it was assumed that all other heavier or more streamlined wagons would also succeed in reaching their destinations. This assumption became widely embedded in Soviet-era hump yard design standards and continued to influence railway operations in several post-Soviet and Eastern European countries.

However, recent experimental observations and simulation studies have brought this traditional assumption into question. Contrary to the classical models, it has been found that open-type gondola cars, which are exposed to direct airflow and possess unshielded internal cavities, may actually encounter greater resistance when descending from the same hump profile. While they are marginally lighter than covered wagons, the increase in aerodynamic drag, combined with the formation of turbulent airflow inside the wagon, significantly reduces their final velocity. Empirical findings demonstrate that an empty gondola car, when released from the same hump height as an empty covered wagon, fails to reach the expected arrival point, highlighting a misalignment between theoretical assumptions and operational reality [11, 13]. These discrepancies are especially pronounced in conditions of moderate to strong headwinds, which exert pressure not only on the frontal wall but also induce vortex formations inside the car body—a factor not considered in classical equations. To formally analyze this behavior, we begin with the kinetic energy change theorem for a non-free material point over a linear displacement AB [12]. Considering the motion of the wagon under gravity, friction, and wind resistance—and assuming an initial velocity $V_{n.t}$—we obtain the following general energy balance equation:

$$\frac{G}{2g} \cdot V_A^2 + G \cdot \sin i \cdot x_{AB} = \frac{G}{2g} \cdot V_B^2 - K_f \cdot G \cdot \cos i \cdot x_{AB} - F_{vstr} \cdot x_{AB} \quad (1)$$

Considering small angles (), expression (1) takes the following form:

$$\frac{G}{2g} \cdot V_A^2 + G \cdot i \cdot x_{AB} = \frac{G}{2g} \cdot V_B^2 - K_f \cdot G \cdot x_{AB} - F_{vstr} \cdot x_{AB} \quad (2)$$

where Fvstr – the longitudinal force of the aerodynamic drag of the wind blowing against the movement of the carriage, kN

$$F_{vstr} = P_{aer1} \cdot S_1 + P_{aer2} \cdot S_2 \quad (3)$$

where Paer1, Paer2 – the aerodynamic pressure of the wind acting on the surface of the carriage, Pa;

S1, S2 – external and internal surfaces of the wagon body exposed to wind resistance, m^2 (Fig. 1).

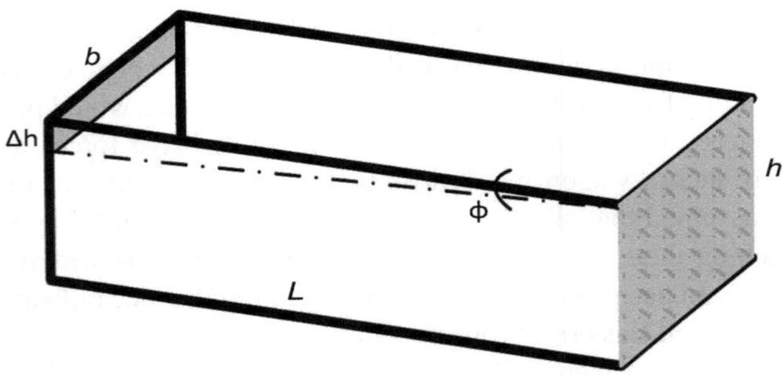

Fig. 1. Drawing of the exterior and interior surfaces of a gondola car body exposed to wind resistance

In railway marshalling operations, accurate determination of the kinematic behavior of wagons on sorting slides requires not only accounting for gravitational and rolling forces but also aerodynamic resistance—particularly under wind conditions. Figure 2 presents a spatial vector diagram of the acting airflow velocities and their resultant forces with respect to the inclined sorting slide profile.

The diagram is based on a right-handed Cartesian coordinate system OXYZ, where:

- The **X-axis** represents the direction of longitudinal wagon movement,
- The **Z-axis** is aligned with the vertical direction (gravity),
- The **Y-axis** corresponds to the transverse lateral orientation,
- The **OH axis** represents the **inclined direction of the sorting slide profile**, with slope iii, along which the wagon descends.

Multiple **wind velocity components** are shown:

- V_x—longitudinal component,
- V_y—lateral (crosswind) component,
- V_z—vertical turbulence or uplift component,
- V_r—resultant wind velocity vector acting at an angle relative to the wagon,
- V_r^{wind}—projected wind vector due to environmental wind acting obliquely toward the wagon.

By resolving these vectors along the OH axis (aligned with the slide's slope), we can more accurately compute the net retarding aerodynamic force, and subsequently integrate this into the governing kinetic energy and motion equations used for hump profile calibration.

$$\begin{cases} P_{aeri} = C_i \cdot \frac{1}{2} \cdot \rho \cdot V_i^2 \\ P_{aerx} = C_x \cdot \frac{1}{2} \cdot \rho \cdot V_x^2 \\ P_{aery} = C_y \cdot \frac{1}{2} \cdot \rho \cdot V_y^2 \\ P_{aerz} = C_z \cdot \frac{1}{2} \cdot \rho \cdot V_z^2 \\ P_{aer1} = P_{aer2} = C_x \cdot \frac{1}{2} \cdot \rho \cdot V_x^2 \end{cases} \quad (4)$$

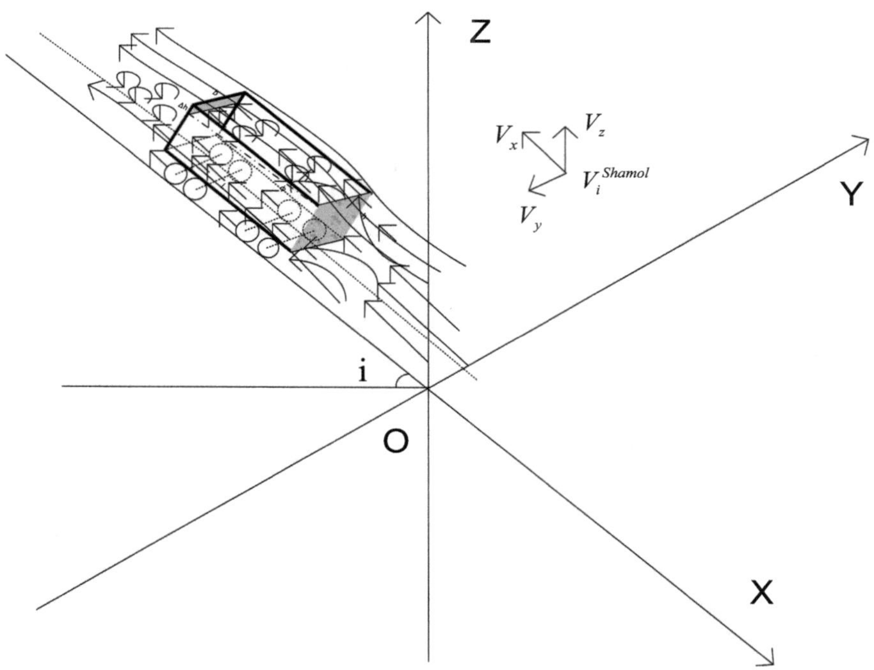

Fig. 2. The forces of the aerodynamic impact of the headwind in the direction of the axis OH

The main cross-sectional surfaces in accordance with the technical characteristics of the car are recorded in the following order:

$$S_1 = b \cdot H \quad (5)$$

$$S_2 = l \cdot b \cdot i \tag{6}$$

In accordance with expressions (4, 5, 6), substituting in expression (3) the total force of resistance to the movement of the car in the direction of the axis OH, we obtain the following equality:

$$F_{vstr} = 0,5 \cdot C_x \cdot \rho \cdot V_x^2 \cdot (b \cdot H + l \cdot b \cdot i) = 0,5 \cdot C_x \cdot \rho \cdot V_x^2 \cdot b \cdot (H + l \cdot i) \tag{7}$$

Substituting expression (7) into expression (2), we obtain the following equality:

$$\frac{G}{2g} \cdot V_A^2 + G \cdot i \cdot x_{AB} = \frac{G}{2g} \cdot V_B^2 - K_f \cdot G \cdot x_{AB} + G * \mu * x_{AB} + 0,5 \cdot C_x \cdot \rho \cdot V_x^2 \cdot b \cdot (H + l \cdot i) \cdot x_{AB} \tag{8}$$

$$V_B = \sqrt{V_A^2 + 2g \cdot i \cdot x_{AB} + 2g \cdot K_f \cdot x_{AB} + \frac{C_x \cdot g \cdot \rho \cdot V_x^2 \cdot b \cdot (H + l \cdot i) \cdot x_{AB}}{G}} \tag{9}$$

As a result of solving expression (8), it is possible to calculate the kinematic parameters of an open gondola moving along a sorting slide, as well as a universal four-axle covered wagon. And also by solving expression (10), the acceleration and kinematic characteristics of wagons moving along the sorting slide are calculated.

$$\begin{cases} a_{kti} = a_t \cdot (i - |w_{ti}|) \\ a_t = \frac{G}{M} \cdot 10^3 \\ \mathrm{l_{kti}} = V_A \cdot t_{ti} + \frac{1}{2}|a_{kti}| \cdot t_{ti}^2 \end{cases} \Rightarrow \mathrm{l_{kti}} = V_A \cdot t_{ti} + \frac{1}{2}a_t \cdot (i - |w_{ti}|) \cdot t_{ti}^2 \Rightarrow V_B = V_A + a_t \cdot (i - |w_{ti}|) \cdot t_{ti} \tag{10}$$

where a_t = const – the symbol for the linear acceleration of the car with uniformly decelerated movement in the braking zones of the braking track sections, m/s^2;

i – a dimensionless value that conditionally characterizes the slope of the slide profile, taking into account the influence of the force of the Fvx projection of the headwind according to formula (10);

$|wti|$ is a dimensionless quantity that conditionally characterizes the resistivity of various motion resistances, taking into account the longitudinal effect of the wind (and/or |wti| has a size that is not found in the system of units of measurement kgs/t) (11)

$$w_{ti} = k_{\mathrm{braking}} + k_{0i} + k_{sv} + k_{sn} \tag{11}$$

where $k_{braking} = F_{braking}/G_1$, $k_{0i} = F_{trxi}/G_1$ or $k_{0i} = F_{oi}/G_1$, $k_{sv} = F_{sv}/G_1$, $k_{sn} = F_{sn}/G_1$ are the coefficients that take into account the forces of F_{torm} when braking the retarder of the car, the forces of $F_{trx} = F_{oi}$ from the main resistances in the proportion of G_1 from the non-rotating parts of the car and the gravity of the car, F_{sv} forces from the environment and wind, F_{sn} forces from snow and frost.

3 The Results and Their Discussion

The analysis of the motion of freight wagons along the sorting slide reveals a complex interplay between gravitational acceleration, rolling resistance, braking forces, and aerodynamic drag. One of the most critical parameters in this dynamic system is the resistivity function, denoted as w_{ti}, which captures the aggregate effect of various opposing forces acting on the wagon as it moves through different zones of the hump profile—especially the braking zones, where the retardation process is both intentional and dynamic. Unlike gravitational or structural forces, the total resistivity w_{ti} is inherently nonlinear and variable. It depends on multiple operational factors including wagon type, speed, weather conditions, mechanical properties of retarders, and the presence of surface contaminants such as ice, snow, or dust. Most importantly, it is observed that w_{ti} is **not constant over time**. In fact, it exhibits **inverse correlation** with velocity—**as the wagon slows down, the relative resistivity increases**, thus further decelerating the vehicle in a self-reinforcing manner. This phenomenon presents a significant modeling challenge because it violates the assumptions of uniform resistance often used in simplified analytical calculations. To address this, the dynamic equations governing the velocity and travel time of a descending wagon must be adapted to incorporate variable resistivity and wind-dependent aerodynamic effects. Accordingly, the final speed V_B of the wagon at the end of the braking section, as well as the time t_{ti} required to traverse it, were determined using the following generalized equations derived from the conservation of mechanical energy and Newton's second law:

$$\begin{cases} V_B = \sqrt{V_A^2 + 2g \cdot i \cdot l_{\text{kti}} + 2g \cdot K_f \cdot l_{\text{kti}} - 2 * g * \mu * l_{\text{kti}} - \frac{C_x \cdot g \cdot \rho \cdot V_x^2 \cdot b \cdot (H + l \cdot i) \cdot l_{\text{kti}}}{G}} \\ t_{ti} = \frac{(V_B - V_A)}{a_t \cdot (i - |w_{ti}|)} \end{cases} \quad (12)$$

When performing the calculation, the following graph was obtained using the MATLAB programming package (Fig. 3).

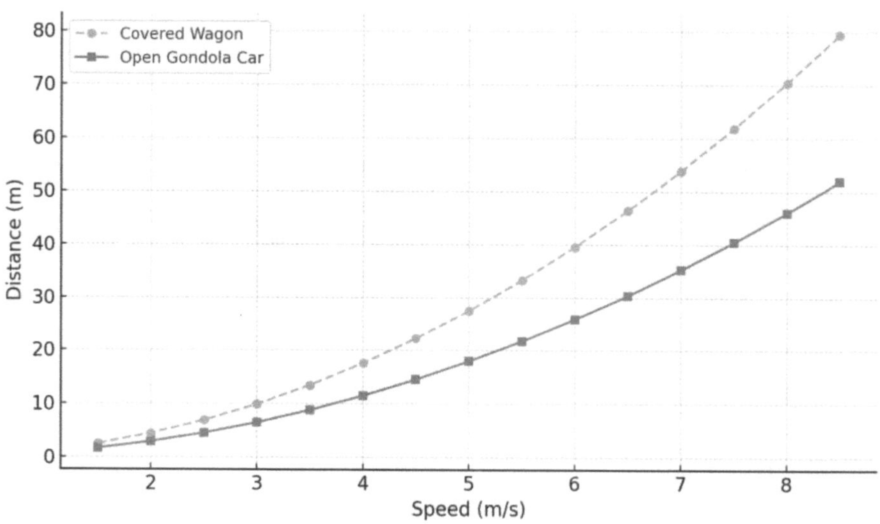

Fig. 3. Graph of the speed of covered and semi-trailers on the sorting hill

Figure 3 illustrates the relationship between wagon velocity and the distance traveled along the sorting slide, comparing two types of freight cars: a covered wagon and an open-type gondola car. The plotted data demonstrate a clear divergence in kinematic behavior as the length of the high-speed section increases from 0 to 80 m. As shown, the open gondola car consistently exhibits a lower terminal velocity than the covered wagon under the same geometric and environmental conditions. At the end of the high-speed section (80 m), the velocity of the open wagon is approximately 34.6% lower than that of its covered counterpart. This discrepancy underscores the inadequacy of using covered wagons as the reference "bad runner" in traditional engineering calculations for hump height determination. The significantly higher aerodynamic resistance experienced by the open gondola is primarily due to:

- its greater drag coefficient resulting from an unshielded frontal surface;
- the formation of internal turbulence within the car body;
- and the impact of headwind flow dynamics, which are especially pronounced at the early stages of descent.

These results provide quantitative justification for the revision of long-standing assumptions in hump profile design. Replacing the covered wagon with the open gondola as the representative worst-case runner—particularly under headwind conditions—can greatly improve the accuracy, safety, and reliability of classification yard operations. Moreover, these findings highlight the necessity of integrating CFD-based aerodynamic simulations into modern hump design workflows [14]. The following figures (Fig. 4 and Fig. 5) present computational visualization of headwind interaction with the gondola car body, enabling detailed assessment of pressure distribution and flow behavior throughout the descent trajectory.

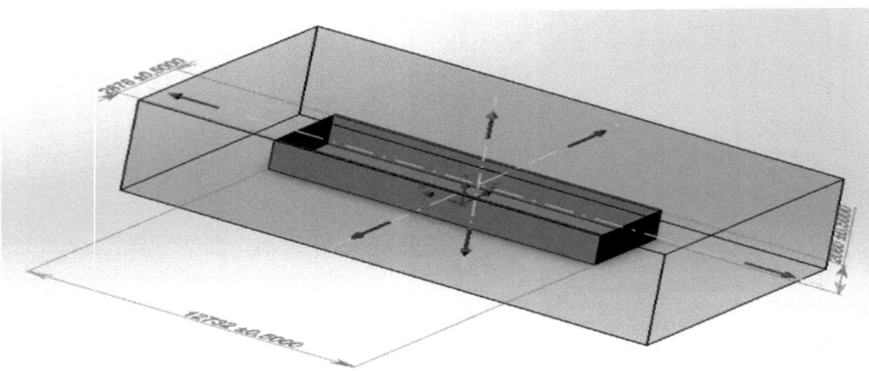

Fig. 4. Drawing of the design area of an open gondola rolling down a sorting slide

Figures 4 and 5 illustrate the setup and results of a numerical simulation performed to evaluate the aerodynamic behavior of an open gondola car subjected to frontal airflow—emulating real-world headwind conditions experienced during descent from a sorting hump.

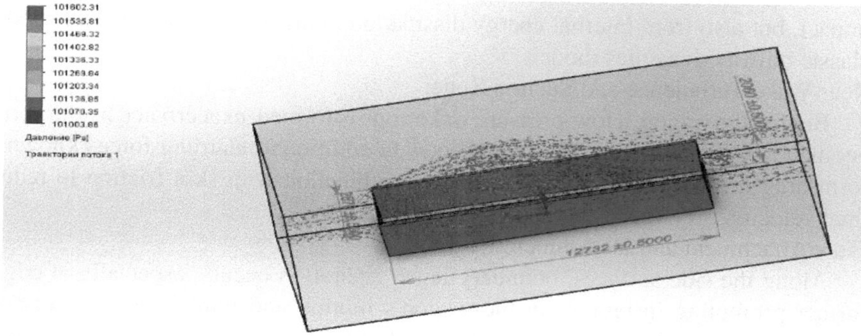

Fig. 5. Drawing of a model of the impact of oncoming air flow on a gondola car.

*Computational Domain and Boundary Conditions (*Fig. 4*).*

In Fig. 4, the computational domain is depicted as a rectangular prism extending well beyond the physical boundaries of the gondola car. This configuration ensures that airflow develops fully before reaching the model and exits without artificial interference, satisfying far-field boundary conditions essential for credible CFD analysis.

Key features of the domain include:

- Inlet and outlet zones: aligned along the longitudinal axis, through which the headwind is introduced and allowed to exit.
- Symmetry planes and wall conditions: defined to reduce computational cost while preserving flow realism.
- Mesh refinement zones: applied near the leading and trailing surfaces to capture pressure gradients and turbulence accurately.
- Wagon geometry: modeled with simplified, yet dimensionally accurate, representation of an empty gondola car with open top and flat front and rear ends.

The direction and magnitude of the imposed wind are specified as a uniform velocity field, simulating steady-state conditions typical for sorting yards located in semi-open terrain where consistent wind corridors exist.

*Aerodynamic Effects and Flow Phenomena (*Fig. 5*).*

Figure 5 presents the resulting flow field visualization with colored contours representing pressure magnitude and green streamlines indicating airflow trajectories around and through the gondola car.

Several notable phenomena are observed:

1. Frontal Stagnation Zone:

   A region of elevated pressure forms at the front face of the wagon, as the headwind collides perpendicularly with the surface. The simulation reports a maximum static pressure of 101.602 kPa at this point—substantially influencing the wagon's deceleration.
2. Internal Flow Accumulation and Vortices:

   Due to the open-top structure, part of the incoming airflow enters the interior cavity. Within the wagon's hollow body, turbulent recirculation zones emerge, generating chaotic eddy patterns. This creates aerodynamic drag not just from frontal impact, but also from internal energy dissipation, a factor traditionally neglected in classic railway dynamics models.

3. Rear-Wake Turbulence and Suction Zone:

   Behind the wagon, a low-pressure wake zone is formed, exacerbated by the abrupt geometry of the rear wall. This contributes to additional retarding forces known as form drag or pressure drag, which act in combination with skin friction to reduce final velocity.

4. Flow Attachment and Detachment Regions:

   Along the side surfaces, boundary layer separation occurs, especially at edges, further promoting instability in the wagon's motion and reinforcing the need for aerodynamic consideration in hump profile design.

Engineering and Research Significance

The results presented in Figs. 4 and 5 provide compelling evidence that the influence of headwind on open gondola cars is multifactorial and highly nonlinear. Unlike closed wagons, which mostly experience external surface drag, open wagons suffer from compound resistance mechanisms including:

- frontal pressure buildup,
- internal turbulence,
- pressure differentials between entry and exit walls.

This reinforces the idea that traditional engineering practices—which assume a covered wagon as the "worst runner"—are outdated and risk misestimating required hump height and slope profile.

The integration of CFD data into the design and operation of sorting humps enables:

- Data-driven height recalibration of the initial slope section;
- Adaptive yard control systems that factor in wind conditions in real time;
- Improved safety margins for wagon movement under unfavorable meteorological scenarios.

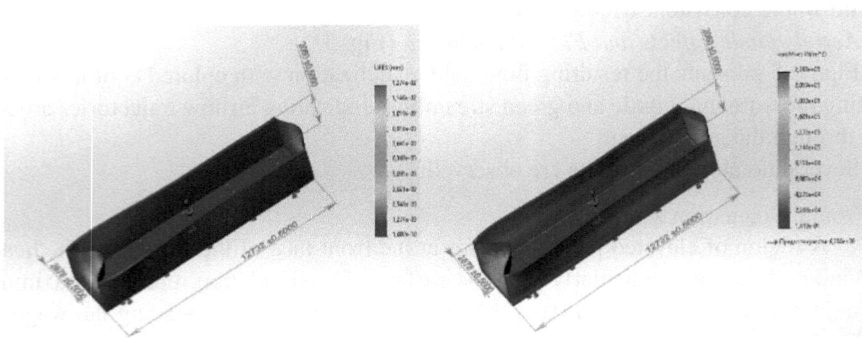

Fig. 6. Calculation of the aerodynamic pressure and sliding distance acting on the front and inner rear walls of an open gondola car under the action of oncoming air flow

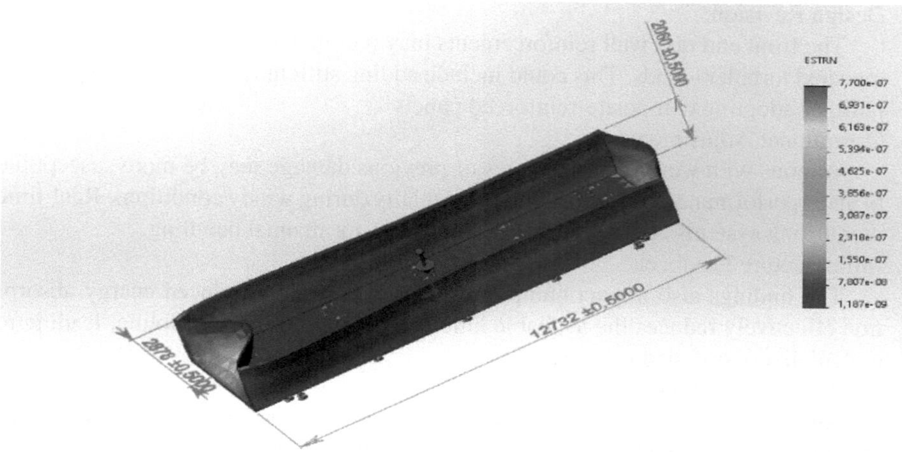

Fig. 7. Calculation of the deformation of the front and inner rear walls of an open gondola car under the action of oncoming air flow

The results presented in Figs. 6 and 7 detail the structural response of an open gondola car subjected to a frontal aerodynamic load induced by headwind. These simulations were conducted as part of a coupled CFD–FEA (Finite Element Analysis) workflow, in which aerodynamic pressure fields obtained from SOLIDWORKS Flow Simulation were transferred as surface loads to a structural mechanics module for stress-strain analysis.

During the modeling process, simplifications were applied, such as the exclusion of detailed underframe components and rigid fixing of the body to simulate worst-case constraints. As a consequence, local deformations—or “bending zones”—appear in the most exposed areas, primarily on the:

- Frontal wall, where the impact pressure is highest due to flow stagnation;
- Rear inner wall, where vortex shedding and suction effects generate tensile forces on the structure;
- Upper side walls, which experience distributed pressure and contribute to body flexing.

Figure 6 clearly shows that the pressure load is not uniformly distributed, but rather forms peak zones at the frontal edge and just behind the midpoint due to internal flow interference and resonance effects.

Figure 7 presents the resulting elastic strain distribution across the body shell. Despite the overall magnitude of strain being within the elastic range for typical wagon steel alloys, the presence of localized deformation zones suggests:

- Fatigue accumulation risks over repeated loading cycles;
- Potential failure of bolted or welded joints over time;
- Vibrational instability, particularly under higher wind velocities.

Engineering Significance and Implications

The observed structural behavior under aerodynamic loads has direct implications for both design and operation of gondola cars in sorting yards:

1. Design Revision:
   The front and rear wall reinforcements may require reconsideration to withstand repeated turbulent loads. This could include adding stiffening ribs, modifying corner radii, or adopting composite-reinforced panels.
2. Operational Adjustments:
   Wagons with weakened structures or previous damage may be more susceptible to underperformance on sorting slides, especially during windy conditions. Real-time monitoring systems could help flag such wagons for manual handling.
3. Infrastructure Feedback:
   The findings also impact hump design, as deformation-induced energy absorption effectively reduces the available kinetic energy needed for coupling, leading to underdelivery or failed roll-ins.
4. Maintenance Planning:
   Knowledge of high-strain areas supports condition-based maintenance strategies and helps prevent catastrophic failure in older rolling stock.

Scientific Contribution

These results substantiate the central hypothesis of this research: that open gondola cars exhibit not only greater aerodynamic drag compared to covered wagons, but also experience measurable structural deformation that affects their dynamic behavior on sorting slides. The coupling of fluid dynamics and structural simulation provides a more holistic understanding of wagon motion under real-world operational loads, and supports the call for revising standard engineering assumptions in marshalling yard design practices.

4 Conclusion

This study presents a comprehensive investigation into the aerodynamic effects of headwind on the motion of an open gondola car during its descent from a railway sorting slide. Through a combination of theoretical analysis, computational fluid dynamics (CFD) modeling, and structural deformation simulation, new insights have been obtained regarding the inadequacy of classical assumptions traditionally used in hump profile design.

One of the central findings of this work is that the influence of headwind—particularly in turbulent conditions—introduces substantial additional resistance, which is not uniformly distributed, but rather concentrated on the frontal and interior rear surfaces of the gondola car. This resistance is compounded by the formation of internal vortex structures within the wagon's open cavity and the emergence of pressure differentials across the car body, which do not affect closed wagons to the same degree.

It was quantitatively established that, under identical environmental and structural conditions, the final velocity of an open gondola car at the end of the high-speed section is 34.6% lower than that of a comparable covered wagon. This difference is significant and strongly suggests that open wagons should be considered the new reference 'bad runner' for engineering calculations used in sorting slide design. Moreover, the CFD simulation revealed that internal turbulence and rear-wall suction not only affect motion dynamics, but also contribute to elastic deformation of the wagon body, as confirmed by finite element analysis. While the recorded deformation remains within elastic limits, its non-uniform distribution indicates potential long-term risks for structural fatigue and operational instability.

These findings carry direct engineering implications:

- The use of covered wagons as the worst-case scenario in hump height determination may lead to systematic underestimation of required elevation, causing failed couplings, increased manual intervention, and operational delays.
- Design standards and simulation models should be updated to include aerodynamic effects for open wagon types, especially under real wind conditions.
- Digital marshalling systems, if integrated with wind sensors and aerodynamic modeling modules, could enable adaptive real-time control of hump operations, enhancing safety, energy efficiency, and throughput capacity.

In conclusion, this research advocates for a paradigm shift in the design methodology of classification yards—one that is grounded not only in traditional mechanical models but also in advanced computational simulation and aerodynamic theory. Future studies may extend this work by incorporating crosswind effects, rolling resistance variability under mixed loading, and full-scale field testing to validate simulation predictions under operational conditions.

References

1. Образцов, В.Н.: Станции и узлы. Ч. II. Трансжелдориздат, Moscow (1938). 492 с
2. Земблинов, С.В., Страковский, И.И.: Станции и узлы. Трансжелдориздат, Moscow (1963). 348 с
3. Савченко, И.Е., Земблинов, С.В., Страковский, И.И.: Железнодорожные станции и узлы: учеб. для вузов ж. – д. трансп. Под. ред. Акулиничева, В.М., Шабалина, Н.Н. Транспорт, Moscow (1980). 479 с
4. Родимов, Б.А., Павлов, В.Е., Прокинова, В.Д.: Проектирование механизированных и автоматизированных сортировочных горок. Транспорт, Moscow (1980). 96 с
5. Акулиничев, В.М., Колодий, Л.П.: Расчёт и проектирование сортировочных горок большой и средней мощности: учебн. пособ. для вузов ж. – д. трансп. МИИТ, Moscow (1981). 61с
6. Рудановский, В.М., Старшов, И.П., Кобзев, В.А.: О попытке критики теоретических положений динамики скатывания вагона по уклону сортировочной горки. Бюллетень транспортной информации **6**(252), 19–28 (2016). ISSN 2072-8115
7. Позойский, Ю.О., Кобзев, В.А., Старшов, И.П., Рудановский, В.М.: К вопросу движения вагона по уклону железнодорожного пути. Бюллетень транспортной информации **2**(272), 35–38 (2018). ISSN 2072-8115
8. Апатцев, В.И.: Железнодорожные станции и узлы: учебник. ФГБОУ «Учебно-методический центр по образованию на железнодорожном транспорте», Moscow (2014). 855 с
9. Саидивалиев, Ш.У., Джаббаров, Ш.Б., Адилов, Н.Б., Хожиев, Н.К., Бозоров, Р.Ш.: Об отсутствии теоретической основы формулы для определения высоты первого профильного участка сортировочного горба. Инновации. Наука. Образование **34**, 1467–1481 (2021)

10. Туранов, Х.Т., Илесалиев, Д.И., Джаббаров, Ш.Б., Саидивалиев, Ш.У.: Критический анализ теоретических положений движения вагона с сортировочной горки. Транспорт: наука, техника, управление **4**, 47–53 (2021). ISSN 0236-1914
11. Saidivaliyev, Sh.U., Baxtiyorovich, S.S., Bozorov, R.Sh.: Bo'sh vagonning saralash tepaligi profilida harakati tahlili. IQRO №2 10–16 bet (2023)
12. Saidivaliev, Sh.U., Bozorov, R.Sh., Shermatov, E.S.: A new method of Calculating time and Speed of a carriage during its Movement on the section of the first brake position of a marshaling Hump when exposed headwind. STUDENT EISN: 2658-4964 (2021). № 9. Aida-zade, K.R., Mustafaev, E.E.: About Neural networks' parameters optimization during learning. In: Proceedings of the Scientific Conference "Modern Problems of Cybernetics and Information Technologies", vol. 1, Baku, Azerbaijan, pp. 118–121 (2003)
13. Бозоров, Р.Ш., Расулов, М.Х., Бекжанова, С.Е., Машарипов, М.Н.: Способы эффективного использования пропускной способности участков в условиях пропуска высокоскоростных пассажирских поездов. Текст: непосредственный . Железнодорожный транспорт : Актуальные вопросы и инновации, vol. 2, pp. 5–22 (2021)
14. Khadjimuhametova, M., Merganov, A., Egamberdiev, R.: An innovative method of designing the surface and elements of the hump profiles. AIP Conf. Proc. **2432**, 030046 (2022). https://doi.org/10.1063/5.0089818

Optimization of Tanker Routes Using Hybrid GACM for Oil Terminals

Vyacheslav Kuznetsov and Rahman Aliyev(✉)

Azerbaijan State Oil and Industry University, Azadliq pr. 34, AZ1010 Baku, Azerbaijan
viateslav@mail.ru, rahmanaliyevaz@gmail.com

Abstract. The hybrid genetic ant colony algorithm (GACM) is applied to solve the VRP problems of oil transportation between oil terminals with significant time and cost. The algorithm for selecting ant colony methods and genetic algorithm is used to determine the optimal tank routes considering various constraints such as tank capacity, time window, and distance. The ant algorithm is responsible for selecting routes considering pheromones and heuristic factors, while the genetic algorithm is used to optimize routes through crossover and mutation, which ensures fast solution search and improved results. The performance of the proposed algorithm was evaluated based on oil terminal networks, where real time windows for unloading and refueling tankers, as well as the cost of distance between terminals and shipments were considered. The results lead to improvements compared to classical optimization methods such as nearest neighbor and greedy algorithms. The proposed hybrid approach allows to significantly reduce the transportation time, as well as reduce the cost of logistics operations, which is a necessary condition in the conditions of the modern oil industry. The use of AGKM can be used to optimize processes in various industries where it is necessary to solve complex routing problems with large number of restrictions.

Keywords: Information Processing · Intelligent System · Results Evaluation · Image Processing · Multithread Recognition

1 Introduction

The Vehicle Routing Problem (VRP) is one of the most important problems in logistics and transportation systems. VRP involves optimizing the routes for a group of vehicles to serve a set of customers or terminals with minimal costs, such as travel time or cost. In the oil industry, this problem is of particular importance because optimizing the routes of tankers transporting oil between different oil terminals directly affects the efficiency of operations and reduces overall logistics costs. (Toth, P., & Vigo, D., 2002 Ant colony system: A cooperative learning approach to the traveling salesman problem.)

The solution of such problems becomes especially difficult due to a variety of factors, such as limited tanker capacity, time windows for unloading and refueling, and the need to minimize transportation costs, including fuel and payment for idle time. To solve this problem efficiently, many optimization methods are used, among which the most

A. Abbasov et al. (Eds.): PLMO 2025, CCIS 2767, pp. 121–129, 2026.
https://doi.org/10.1007/978-3-032-13672-5_11

prominent are algorithms using natural selection approaches, such as genetic algorithms, and algorithms inspired by animal behavior, such as ant colony algorithms.

Both approaches have their own characteristics that can be used to solve VRP with various constraints and parameters, such as travel time, transportation cost, terminal and tanker capacity, and environmental requirements. (Ronalds B. F. Applicability ranges for offshore oil and gas production facilities). Hybrid methods that combine the best features of several algorithms are a promising direction in solving routing problems. In this paper, a hybrid algorithm is proposed that combines ant colony and genetic algorithm methods, which allows one to effectively search for optimal solutions considering multiple constraints, including tanker capacity, time windows, and environmental factors.

The ant colony method considers pheromones and heuristic information when choosing a route, while the genetic algorithm, through the use of crossover and mutation, improves the quality of solutions by minimizing the total transportation costs and travel time (Maggi, F., & Fanti, M. P., 2011). An important aspect of this work is also the consideration of time windows that limit the unloading and refueling time of tankers at terminals. These constraints can greatly affect the optimal distribution of tasks among tankers and the determination of the best routes, which makes the problem even more difficult. The proposed algorithm takes into account all of the above constraints and parameters, which allows achieving better results compared to classical optimization methods such as the nearest neighbor method or greedy algorithms.

Figure 1 shows an oil terminal with moored oil tankers.

Fig. 1. Oil terminal with moored oil tankers.

2 Methods

2.1 Problem Statement

The tanker routing problem is to optimize the routes for a group of tankers that must serve a set of oil terminals. Each tanker must visit several terminals, minimizing the total transit time or cost of transportation. Constraints include:

1. Tanker capacity: each tanker has a limited capacity to carry oil.
2. Time windows: each terminal has a certain time to load or unload.
3. Environmental constraints: the need to avoid certain routes, such as through protected natural areas.

Ant Colony Algorithm (ACA)
To find optimal routes, an ant colony algorithm is used. The ants represent possible routes, and each ant chooses a path based on pheromones and heuristic information.

The algorithm updates the pheromones after each iteration, directing the ants to more efficient routes. The probability of choosing a path Pij between two terminals i and j is defined as:

$$p_{ij} = \frac{(\tau_{ij})^{\alpha} \cdot (\eta_{ij})^{\beta}}{\sum_{k \in N_i} (\tau_{ik})^{\alpha} \cdot (\eta_{ik})^{\beta}} \tag{1}$$

where τij is the pheromone level on the route between terminals i and j, ηij is heuristic information (e.g., travel time or cost), and α and β are parameters that control the influence of pheromones and heuristics.

Genetic Algorithm (GA)
To improve the solutions obtained by the ant colony, a genetic algorithm is used. Crossover and mutation are used to create new routes that can lead to a better global solution.

The crossover and mutation operations are defined as:

$$\mathrm{C} = \mathrm{C}_1 \oplus \mathrm{C}_2,\ \ \mathrm{M} \tag{2}$$

where C1 and C2 are the parent routes, C is the new route, ⊕ is a crossover operation combining elements from C1 and C2 to create a new route, M is a mutation operation involving a random change (δ) in the new route C to explore new solutions and increase population diversity.

Scientific Novelty
The scientific novelty of the study lies in the development and application of a hybrid genetic ant colony algorithm to solve the vehicle routing problem in the context of oil logistics. The proposed approach combines the strengths of the ant colony and the genetic algorithm, which leads to a faster and more efficient search for optimal solutions compared to traditional methods. For the first time, the adaptation of this algorithm to specific oil transportation conditions, including capacity restrictions, time windows, and environmental requirements, has been studied.

3 Results and Discussion

3.1 Model, Initial Data and Results of Optimization

A network with 10 oil terminals was used to simulate the tanker routing problem. The table below presents the structure of the input data, including terminals, distances between them, time windows, and tanker capacity:

Figure 2 shows a graph comparing the route costs for the different methods considered (Table 1).

Table 1. Initial Data for the Routing Problem

Terminal i	Terminal j	Distance (km)	Time (h)	Cost of transportation (USD)	Time frames	Tanker capacity (m^3)
1	2	150	3	1333	8:00–12:00	5000
1	3	200	4	1600	9:00–13:00	6000
2	4	100	2	1200	10:00–14:00	4000

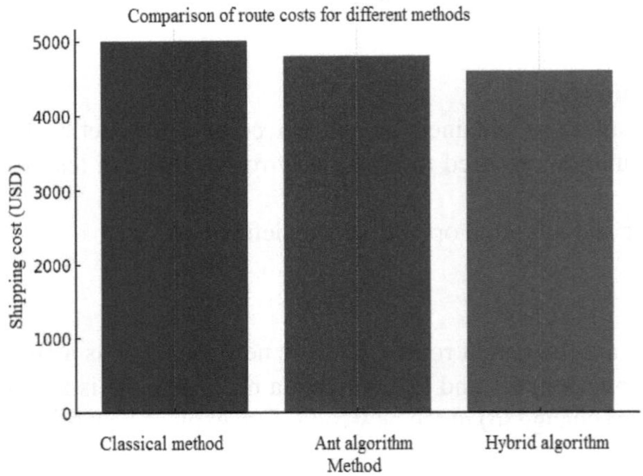

Fig. 2. Graph comparing route costs for different methods

Figure 2 shows a reduction in the cost of transportation using the proposed algorithm compared to classical methods.

Figure 3 shows a graph comparing the execution times for the various methods considered.

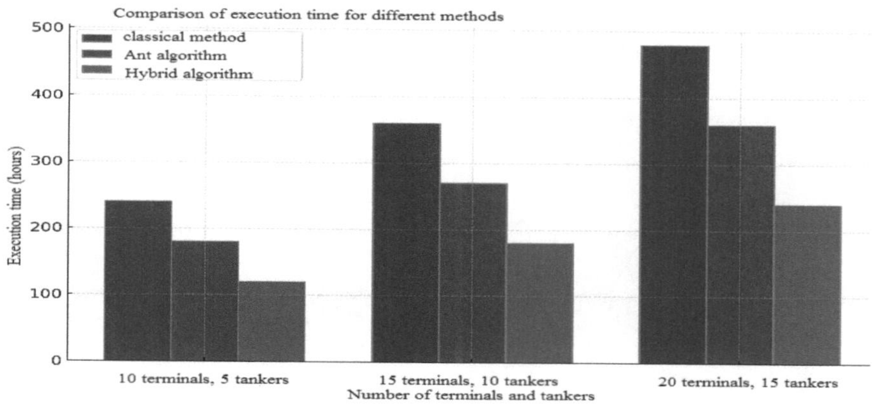

Fig. 3. Comparison graph of execution times for different methods

Figure 3 shows how the execution time of the algorithms varies depending on the number of terminals and tankers (Table 2).

Table 2. Comparison of Routing Results

Method	Completion Time (h)	Cost of transportation (USD))	Total Distance (km)
Classic Method	240	66666	1800
Ant Method (ACA)	180	64000	1750
Hybrid Method (GACM)	120	61333	1700

3.2 Pheromone and Heuristic Parameters

One of the key factors affecting the efficiency of the algorithm is the correct setting of the pheromone parameters and heuristic information.

The tables and graphs above show that the hybrid genetic ant colony algorithm significantly reduces the cost of transportation and the overall execution time compared to classical methods. Using pheromones to find paths and a genetic algorithm to improve global solutions helps to avoid local minima and speeds up the process of finding optimal solutions. In addition, setting the parameters α and β affects the efficiency of the algorithm. The optimal values of these parameters depend on the specific task and should be selected experimentally.

Example of calculating a tanker route using the proposed hybrid algorithm:

Problem Statement. Let's assume that we have three oil terminals and one tanker that must service them, minimizing the total cost of transportation. The following data are given: Terminals: T1, T2, T3.

Figure 4 shows a diagram with terminals T1, T2, T3 for calculating the tanker route using the proposed hybrid algorithm.

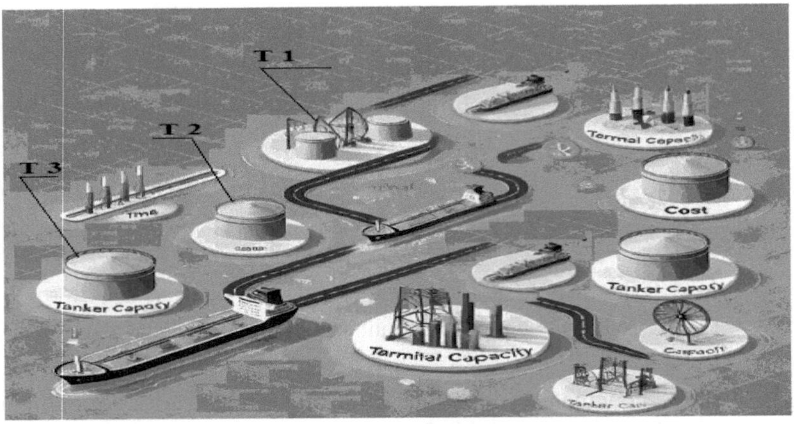

Fig. 4. Scheme with terminals T1, T2, T3 for calculating the tanker route using the proposed hybrid algorithm

- Time windows for terminals: T1: 8:00–12:00, T2: 9:00–13:00, T3: 10:00–14:00
- Distance between terminals (km): T1 → T2: 150 km, T1 → T3: 200 km, T2 → T3: 100 km.
- Travel time (h): T1 → T2: 3 h, T1 → T3: 4 h, T2 → T3: 2 h
- Transportation cost (USD/km): T1 → T2: 106.7 USD/km, T1 → T3: 133.3 USD/km, T2 → T3: 1200 USD/km
- Tanker capacity: 5000 m^3 (this is a limitation for the model, but does not affect the time windows).

3.3 Steps

- Ant Colony Algorithm (ACA)

  Initialization: Create ant paths for all possible routes.
  Each ant chooses a path based on pheromones, heuristic information, and time data.
  Example of calculating a route for a tanker:

1. Route T1 → T2 → T3:

   Start: The tanker starts work at T1 at 8:00 (within the time window 8:00–12:00).
   T1 → T2: Travel time is 3 h. Arrives at T2 at 11:00.
   Time window for T2: 9:00–13:00. The tanker changes in this window.
   T2 → T3: Travel time is 2 h. Arrives at T3 at 13:00.
   Time window for T3: 10:00–14:00. The tanker changes in this window.
   Cost and distance calculation: T1 → T2: 150 km * $1,067/km = $16,005.
   T2 → T3: 100 km * $120.00/km = $12,000.

Total cost = \$16,005 + \$12,000 = \$28,005.
Total distance = 150 km + 100 km = 250 km.

2. Route T1 → T3 → T2: Start: Tanker starts work at T1 at 8:00.

   T1 → T3: Travel time is 4 h. Arrives at T3 at 12:00.
   Time window for T3: 10:00–14:00. Tanker is considering.
   T3 → T2: Travel time is 2 h. Arrives at T2 at 14:00.
   Time window for T2: 9:00–13:00. The tanker is late.
   Since the penetration time at T2 is outside the time window, this route is not allowed.

3. Route T2 → T1 → T3 (to check other options):

   Start: Tanker starts at T2 at 9:00 (within the time window 9:00–13:00).
   T2 → T1: Travel time is 3 h. Arrives at T1 at 12:00.
   Time window for T1: 8:00–12:00. The tanker is considering.
   T1 → T3: Travel time is 4 h. Arrives at T3 at 16:00.
   Time window for T3: 10:00–14:00. Tanker is late.
   This route is also not allowed.

- Use of Genetic Algorithm (GA)

After the ant algorithm has suggested possible routes, the genetic algorithm is used to optimize the routes. It helps to create new routes through crossover and mutation and eliminate those routes that do not meet the time constraints.

- Route evaluation.

For route T1 → T2 → T3:
Total cost: (150 km × 106.7 USD/km) + (100 km × 120.0 USD/km) = 16,005 USD
+
12,000 USD = 28,005 USD.
Total distance: 250 km.
For route T1 → T3 → T2: Total cost: (200 km × 133.3 RUB/km) +
(100 km × 120.0 USD/km) = 26,660 USD + 12,000 USD = 38,660 USD.
Total distance: 300 km.

- Choosing the optimal route.

The route T1 → T2 → T3 with a total cost of \$2805 and distance of 250 km is optimal.

4 Conclusion

The study resulted in the proposed efficient method for solving the vehicle routing problem (VRP) taking into account time windows, tanker capacity limitations and cost minimization. The hybrid algorithm combining the ant colony and genetic algorithm methods demonstrated high efficiency in finding optimal solutions for tanker routes. Empirical results confirm that the proposed approach can significantly improve the performance compared to classical optimization methods. This method can be successfully applied to optimize oil transportation between terminals, which helps reduce costs and improve the efficiency of logistics processes in the oil industry. The proposed hybrid genetic ant colony algorithm has demonstrated good results in the problem of tanker routing between oil terminals, reducing the time and cost of transportation compared to classical methods. It is expected that this approach can be successfully adapted to more complex problems in the field of logistics and oil transportation.

References

1. Dorigo, M., Gambardella, L.M.: Ant colony system: a cooperative learning approach to the traveling salesman problem. IEEE Trans. Evol. Comput. **1**(1), 53–66 (1997)
2. Holland, J.H.: Adaptation in Natural and Artificial Systems. University of Michigan Press (1975)
3. Toth, P., Vigo, D.: The Vehicle Routing Problem. SIAM (2002)
4. Nam, B.W.: Time-domain simulation of berthing problem between FPSO and shuttle tanker in waves
5. Nam, B.W., Kim, Y., Hong, S.Y.: Appl. Ocean Res. **58**, 49–61 (2016). https://doi.org/10.1016/j.apor.2016.03.010
6. Tannuri, E.A., Torres, F.G., Igreja, H., Masetti, I.Q.: FPSO and Monobuoy offloading operation with a conventional shuttle tanker: dimensioning of tugboat based on numerical simulation. IFAC Proc. **42**(18), 134–139 (2009). https://doi.org/10.3182/20090916-3-BR-3001.0031
7. Tannuri, E.A., Morishita, H.M., Vilaça, R., Saad, A.C.: Numerical and experimental analysis of a typical DP shuttle tanker operating in Brazilian waters. IFAC Proc. **43**(20), 324–329 (2010). https://doi.org/10.3182/20100915-3-DE-3008.00049
8. Parul, H.M., Kaur, M.: A novel optical mark recognition technique based on biogeography based optimization. Int. J. Inf. Technol. Knowl. Manag. **5**(2), 331–333 (2012)
9. Queiroz Filho, A.N., Tannuri, E.A., da Cruz, J.J.: A shuttle tanker position cooperative control applied to oil transfer operations based on the LQG/LTR method. IFAC Proc. **45**(27), 67–72 (2012). https://doi.org/10.3182/20120919-3-IT-2046.00012
10. Tannuri, E.A., Saad, A.C., Morishita, H.M.: Offloading operation with a DP shuttle tanker: comparison between full scale measurements and numerical simulation results. IFAC Proc. **42**(18), 249–254 (2009). https://doi.org/10.3182/20090916-3-BR-3001.0021
11. Ronalds, B.F.: Applicability ranges for offshore oil and gas production facilities. Mar. Struct. **18**(3), 251–263 (2005). https://doi.org/10.1016/j.marstruc.2005.06.001
12. Kerkhove, L.P., Vanhoucke, M.: Optimised scheduling for weather sensitive offshore construction projects. Omega **66**, 58–78 (2017). https://doi.org/10.1016/j.omega.2016.01.011
13. Zaikin, D.A., Krestyantsev, A.B., Tarovik, O.V., Topazh, A.G.: Using simulation modeling for analyzing the marine transport and technological system of the "Prirazlomnaya" platform. Transp. Russ. Fed. **1**(68), 44–48 (2017)
14. Zaikin, D.A., Topazh, A.G., Kosortov, A.V.: Modeling the possibility of conducting cargo operations on the "Prirazlomnaya" platform under weather conditions. Bull. Admiral Makarov State Univ. Marit. Inland Shipp. **10**(1), 62–77 (2018). https://doi.org/10.21821/2309-5180-2018-10-1-62-77
15. Kuznetsov, A.L., Kirichenko, A.V., Zaikin, D.A.: Modeling the operation of a marine cargo front. Bull. Admiral Makarov State Univ. Marit. Inland Shipp. **11**(1), 33–42 (2019). https://doi.org/10.21821/2309-5180-2019-11-1-33-42
16. Kiselev, V.S.: Analysis of ship calls as an object of the transport and logistics system of the Arctic zone of the Russian Federation. Transp. Bus. Russ. **2**, 229–233 (2019)

17. Silberholz, M.B., Golden, B.L., Baker, E.K.: Using simulation to study the impact of work rules on productivity at marine container terminals. Comput. Oper. Res. **18**(5), 433–452 (1991). https://doi.org/10.1016/0305-0548(91)90020-R
18. Ozkan, E.D., Nas, S., Guler, N.: Capacity analysis of RO-RO terminals by using simulation modeling method. Asian J. Shipp. Logist. **32**(3), 139–147 (2016). https://doi.org/10.1016/j.ajsl

Features of Non-stationary Heat Exchange in the Combustion Chamber of a Hydrogen Engine

Tamaz Natriashvili, Revaz Kavtaradze(✉), and Merab Glonti

Rafael Dvali Institute of Machine Mechanics (IMM), Mindeli Str.,10, 0186 Tbilisi, Georgia
rzkavtaradze@gmail.com

Abstract. Heat exchange processes in the combustion chamber of hydrogen engines, unlike engines running on traditional hydrocarbon fuels, have the features. A number of authors of experimental works note that heat losses in hydrogen engines tend to increase compared to gasoline engines. In this work, the authors put forward and proved theoretically and experimentally a hypothesis about the possibility of hydrogen flame penetration in micro-gaps in the combustion chamber. Theoretical studies of turbulent combustion processes and the local process were carried out using a 3D mathematical model based on fundamental equations of the Navier-Stokes type. The experimental studies involved direct measurement of the local heat flow in the micro-gap of a running engine using a special heat flow sensor operating on the principle of an "additional wall". Practical recommendations have been developed to reduce heat losses in hydrogen engines. The results obtained should be taken into account when creating new, promising hydrogen engines, as well as when converting traditional engines to hydrogen.

Keywords: Hydrogen Engine · Heat Losses · 3D Mathematical Model · Heat Flow Measurement

1 Introduction

The global problems of modern civilization – energy, environmental and climate problems – are directly related to piston engines, one of the main consumers of natural energy resources, polluters of the environment and sources of greenhouse gas (CO_2) emissions. The time has come when humanity is capable of releasing such a quantity of harmful substances into the environment that the vital conditions on our planet may undergo unpredictable changes. The development and introduction of hydrogen energy into the economy is currently considered a promising way to solve these problems.

A. Abbasov et al. (Eds.): PLMO 2025, CCIS 2767, pp. 130–140, 2026.
https://doi.org/10.1007/978-3-032-13672-5_12

The introduction of hydrogen into transport energy as a fuel for piston engines has a long history, however, it has become most relevant in our century. Serial vehicles have already appeared, in particular trucks and cars of major manufacturers MAN, Daimler-Benz, BMW, Toyota and others, equipped with hydrogen engines. On the other hand, the advantages of piston engines, such as high fuel efficiency, reliability, high-tech industry and developed infrastructure, allow converting serial engines running on hydrocarbon fuels into hydrogen engines with minimal design and technical changes.

Hydrogen as a motor fuel in practical use in piston engines exhibits some features that are not typical of traditional hydrocarbon fuels, such as gasoline, diesel fuel or methane. In this sense, the heat exchange process in hydrogen engines is no exception and has its own characteristics: high combustion temperatures, the absence of solid soot particles in the combustion products - the main generators of thermal radiation, the absence of a heat-insulating layer of carbon on the surface of the combustion chamber, high flame propagation and heat release rates, contributing to increased turbulence and intensification of convective heat exchange. One of the features of the heat exchange process in hydrogen engines is an increase in heat losses, repeatedly noted in the experimental works of a number of authors. This phenomenon is currently accepted as an existing phenomenon that does not have sufficient theoretical justification and explanation. In the proposed work, the main attention is paid to this problem. A hypothesis based on the classical Zeldovich theory of flame extinction/propagation is proposed. Its validity is proven by methods of mathematical modeling and direct measurement of non-stationary heat flows.

2 Flame Quenching/Propagation Conditions in the Combustion Chamber of an Experimental Hydrogen Engine (Problem Statement)

In this work, theoretical and experimental studies were carried out on the serial gasoline engine CA20 of a passenger car, converted to hydrogen with injection of gaseous hydrogen into the intake system. The main technical data of the engine: Number of cylinders $i = 4$; Cylinder diameter/Piston stroke-D/S = 86/86 mm/mm; Compression ratio $\varepsilon = 10$; Power $Ne = 60$ kW (at $n = 5500\ \text{min}^{-1}$); Torque, $M_{max} = 111$ (at $n = 4000\ \text{min}^{-1}$) N·m (at $n = 4000\ \text{min}^{-1}$); The speed of rotation of the crankshaft $n_{max} = 6000\ \text{min}^{-1}$; Cooling – Liquid.

Figure 1 shows the axial (diametrical) section of a 3-dimensional design of a piston engine cylinder. Thermophysical processes (movement, ignition and combustion of the mixture, as well as heat release, formation of nitrogen oxides and heat exchange with the walls) occurring in the combustion chamber and adjacent gap are studied using a 3D mathematical model. Obviously, the processes of hydrogen flame propagation/extinguishing in the annular gap between the piston fire zone, Fig. 1-a, and the cylinder surface, Fig. 1-b (hereinafter, the term "gap" is used for brevity) determine the intensity of heat transfer from burning hydrogen on surfaces with areas F_{SFZ}, F_{SFK} and F_{OFR}. The ratio of the total value F_{GFS} of the specified areas (the inner surface of the annular gap located above the first compression ring of the piston) to the total heat-absorbing surface of the piston F_{GFK} for the hydrogen engine under study

$$\frac{F_{GFS}}{F_{GFK}} = \frac{F_{SFK} + F_{SFZ} + F_{OFR}}{F_{OFK} + F_{SFK} + F_{SFZ} + F_{OFR}} = 0.32 \quad (1)$$

where F_{OFK} is the area of the piston fire bottom. Thus, the area of intense heat transfer from high-temperature gases to the piston in the case of hydrogen flame penetration in the gap increases by 32% compared to the case of extinguishing at the entrance to the gap.

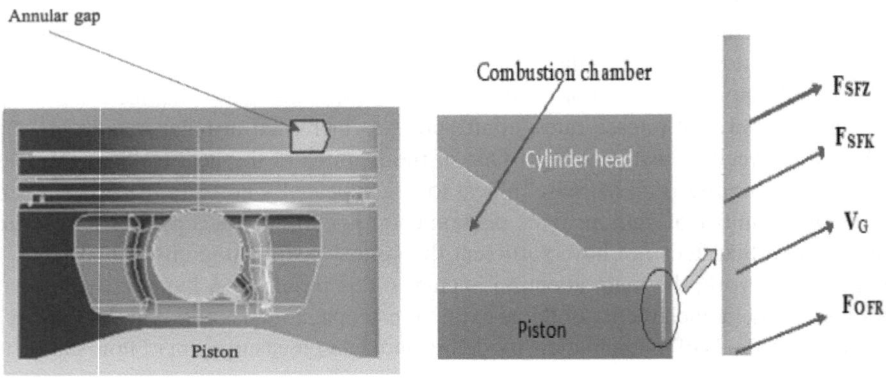

a) b)

Fig. 1. a) The piston fiery belt with a width of 5.5 mm. b) the combustion chamber and the annular gap between the piston and the cylinder above the upper piston ring (axial section). F_{SFZ} - The surface of the cylinder in the gap, F_{SFK} - The surface of the piston in the gap, F_{OFR} - surface of the piston ring in the gap, VG-Gap volume between the piston and cylinder.

The influence of the critical size ℓ_{cr} of hydrogen flame extinguishing on the process of heat exchange with the combustion chamber walls is studied based on the classical results obtained by Ya. B. Zeldovich [1]. The value of the annular gap between the piston and the cylinder above the upper ring for a hot engine operating at maximum load (on a stoichiometric mixture of gasoline with air) $\ell_h = 0.2$ mm, the gap height h = 5 mm (Fig. 1). It was determined for the experimental engine by direct measurement on the heated "cylinder-piston" unit installed on a stand simulating the heat-stressed state of the engine parts. As a result, the condition for flame extinguishing/extinguishing in the annular gap for the experimental engine was formulated [2]:

$$(\ell_{Kr\ Benzin/Diesel} = 0.5\ \text{mm}) > (\ell_h = 0.2\ \text{mm}) > (\ell_{Kr\ H2} = 0.125\ \text{mm}) \quad (2)$$

where $\ell_{Kr\ Benzin/Diesel}$ and $\ell_{Kr\ H2}$ are the critical values (critical distances) of flame propagation/extinguishing during combustion of hydrogen-air and gasoline-air stoichiometric mixtures, respectively. In this case, the value of $\ell_{Kr\ Benzin}$ was established based on the results of experimental values of the critical Peclet number Pe_{kr}, leading to flame extinguishing of a stoichiometric mixture of gasoline with air under the conditions of the combustion chamber of a piston engine: on the wall $Pe_{kr1} = 8$ and in the gaps $Pe_{kr2} = 40$ [3]. The value of $\ell_{kr\ H2}$is established based on the data obtained in [4] during the study of characteristic parameters for the extinguishing/propagation of the flame of a hydrogen-air mixture in gaps depending on the values of pressure and temperature.

Based on relations (1) and (2), it is logical to put forward a hypothesis that the reason for the significant increase in heat losses in hydrogen engines is the intense heat transfer to the walls of the gap of the hydrogen flame, which does not occur in gasoline engines. For the purpose of theoretical and experimental proof of this hypothesis, the following are used:

1. 3D mathematical modeling of turbulent processes of flow, mixture formation, ignition, extinguishing/propagation of flame and local heat exchange between the high-temperature working fluid in the wall (boundary) layers in the combustion chamber and the micro gap of a hydrogen engine;
2. Direct measurement of non-stationary heat flows in the micro gap of an operating engine.

3 3D Mathematical Modeling of Turbulent Processes Occurring in the Volumes of the Combustion Chamber and Annular Gap of a Hydrogen Engine

The turbulent thermophysical processes mentioned above are investigated using a three-dimensional mathematical model based on the fundamental equations of momentum (Navier-Stokes equations), energy (Fourier-Kirchhoff equation), diffusion (Fick equation) and continuity (see Table 1). In these equations, the current time τ is related to the angle φ of rotation of the engine crankshaft by the expression $\varphi = \omega\tau$, where $\omega = \pi n/30$ is the angular velocity, and n is the crankshaft rotation frequency. Since for an arbitrary speed mode of operation $\omega = const$, the parameters φ and τ uniquely determine the crankshaft rotation angle (CRA) and the corresponding moment in time, i.e. in this sense, the terms "CRA φ" and "time τ" are identical. We emphasize that the modeling of thermophysical processes in the combustion chamber and in the gap is not carried out separately, but simultaneously, which corresponds to the real dynamics of flame propagation/extinguishing in the gap.

In the equations from Table 1 the following notation is used: p is the pressure, N/m^2; G_i is the projection of the volume force density vector on the O_{xi} axis of the rectangular Cartesian coordinate system, N/m^3; $\vec{W}$ is the gas velocity vector, m/sec; ρ is the gas density, kg/m^3; C is the concentration, kg/m^3; H is the specific energy, J/kg; $V\mu = 1/3\mu \cdot rad(div\ \vec{W})$ is the volumetric deformation coefficient; μ is the dynamic viscosity, $kg/(m \cdot s)$; c_p is the heat capacity at constant pressure, J/(kg K), wr is the rate of chemical reaction per unit volume, $kg/(m^3s)$, Qr is the amount of heat released per unit mass, J/kg, $q_v = w_rQ_r$ is the internal heat release as a result of the chemical reaction, W/m^3; q_R is the radiative heat flux from the radiation source, W/m^2 (during hydrogen combustion $q_R = 0$, since, unlike carbon fuel, soot, the main generator of radiation, is not released); λ is the thermal conductivity, W/(m K); δ_{ij} is the Kronecker delta; D is the diffusion coefficient, m^2/s; $\dot{m}$ is the power of the mass source (the rate of change in the mass of the chemical component per unit volume, $kg/(m^3s)$. In the equations is used, the rule of summation according to the twice-repeating index $(i, j, k = 1, 2, 3)$, and averaging is realized according to Favre; i.e. the density is used as a weight function, D/Dτ – substantial derivative.

Table 1. The main equations of a mathematical model of the working process of a hydrogen engine

EQUATIONS OF LAWS OF CONSERVATION AS PARTICULAR CASES OF THE GENERALIZED DIFFERENTIAL EQUATION $\frac{\partial}{\partial\tau}(\rho\Phi) + div\left(\rho\vec{W}\Phi\right) = div(\Gamma_\Phi grad\,\Phi) + S_\Phi \Leftrightarrow$ $\frac{\partial}{\partial\tau}(\rho\Phi) + \frac{\partial}{\partial x_j}(\rho W_j\Phi) = \frac{\partial}{\partial x_j}\left(\Gamma_\Phi\frac{\partial\Phi}{\partial x_j}\right) + S_\Phi$		
$\Phi = W_i, \Gamma_\Phi = \mu,$ $S_\Phi = G_i - \frac{\partial p}{\partial x_i} + V_\mu$ Momentum conservation (Navier–Stokes) equation	Initial form	$\rho\frac{DW_i}{D\tau} = G_i - \frac{\partial p}{\partial x_i} + \frac{\partial}{\partial x_j}\left[\mu\left(\frac{\partial W_i}{\partial x_j} + \frac{\partial W_j}{\partial x_i} - \frac{2}{3}\delta_{ij}\frac{\partial W_k}{\partial x_k}\right)\right]$
	Reynolds form New unknown	$\overline{\rho}\frac{D\overline{W}_i}{D\tau} =$ $\overline{G}_i - \frac{\partial\overline{p}}{\partial x_i} + \frac{\partial}{\partial x_j}\left[\mu\left(\frac{\partial\overline{W}_i}{\partial x_j} + \frac{\partial\overline{W}_j}{\partial x_i} - \frac{2}{3}\delta_{ij}\frac{\partial\overline{W}_k}{\partial x_k}\right) - \overline{\rho W_i'W_j'}\right]$ $\overline{\rho W_i'W_j'}$ _ tensor of the Reynolds turbulent stresses determined by the oscillatory components of velocity; $\overline{\tau_{ij}} = \mu\left(\frac{\partial\overline{W}_i}{\partial x_j} + \frac{\partial\overline{W}_j}{\partial x_i} - \frac{2}{3}\delta_{ij}\frac{\partial\overline{W}_k}{\partial x_k}\right)$ - tensor of the viscous (turbulent) stresses determined by the averaged values of the velocity components
$\Phi = H, \Gamma_\Phi = \frac{\lambda}{c_p},$ $S_\Phi = \frac{\partial p}{\partial\tau} + \frac{\partial}{\partial x_i}(\tau_{ij}W_j) +$ $+ G_jW_j + w_rQ_r + \frac{\partial q_{R_j}}{\partial x_j}$ Energy conservation (Fourier-Kirchhoff) equation	Initial form	$\rho\frac{DH}{D\tau} =$ $G_jW_j + \frac{\partial p}{\partial\tau} + \frac{\partial}{\partial x_i}(\tau_{ij}W_j) + \frac{\partial}{\partial x_j}\left(\lambda\frac{\partial T}{\partial x_j}\right) + w_rQ_r + \frac{\partial q_{Rj}}{\partial x_j}$
	Reynolds form New unknown quantities	$\overline{\rho}\frac{D\overline{H}}{D\tau} = \overline{G}_j\overline{W}_j + \frac{\partial\overline{p}}{\partial\tau} + \frac{\partial}{\partial x_j}(\overline{\tau}_{ij}\overline{W}_j) +$ $\frac{\partial}{\partial x_j}\left(\lambda\frac{\partial\overline{T}}{\partial x_j} - c_p\overline{\rho}\overline{T'W_j'}\right) + \overline{w_rQ_r} + \frac{\partial\overline{q}_{R_j}}{\partial x_j}$ $-c_p\,\overline{\rho}\,\overline{T'W_j'}$ - is turbulent enthalpy transfer $\overline{\rho}\,c_p\,T'$ by means of velocity fluctuation W_j';
$\Phi = 1, \Gamma_\Phi = 0,$ $S_\Phi = 0$ Mass (continuity) Conservation equation	Initial form	$\frac{\partial\rho}{\partial\tau} + \frac{\partial}{\partial x_j}(\rho W_j) = 0$
	Reynolds form	$\frac{\partial\overline{\rho}}{\partial\tau} + \frac{\partial}{\partial x_j}(\overline{\rho}\overline{W}_j) = 0$

(continued)

Table 1. (*continued*)

$\Phi = \frac{C_l}{\rho}, \Gamma_\Phi = D_l\rho,$	Initial form	$\frac{DC}{D\tau}\frac{\partial}{\partial x_j}\left(D\frac{\partial C}{\partial x_j}\right) + \overset{\bullet}{m}$
$S_\Phi = \overset{\bullet}{m}_l$ Diffusion (Fick) Equation	Reynolds form	$\frac{D\overline{C}}{D\tau}\frac{\partial}{\partial x_j}\left(D\frac{\partial \overline{C}}{\partial x_j} - \overline{C'W'_j}\right)$
	New unknown quantities	$\overline{C'W'_j}$ - turbulent diffusion transfer of concentration C_l of component ℓ by means of the velocity fluctuation W'_j
In the equations is used, the rule of summation according to the twice-repeating index $(i, j, k = 1, 2, 3)$*, and averaging is realized according to Favre; i.e., the density is used as a weight function*		

The fundamental conservation equations after averaging by the Favre method take the Reynolds form (see Table 1) and form an open system, to which are added the models of turbulence (k-ζ-f-model of Hanjalich), combustion (CFM-Coherent Flame Model), formation of nitrogen oxides NO_x (the thermal mechanism of Zeldovich) and the model of heat transfer in the boundary layer (Wall functions of Spalding-Patankar). These models, as well as the features of their application in engine theory, are described in detail in [5–8]. The solution is carried out by the numerical method of control volumes using 3D CRFD codes AVL-FIRE [7].

4 Some Result of Mathematical Modeling of Thermophysical Processes in the Combustion

The verification of the mathematical model used was carried out by comparing the obtained calculated data with the measurement results carried out on an experimental hydrogen engine under laboratory conditions. The results of modeling non-stationary parameters in the combustion chamber, characterizing the operating modes of the experimental hydrogen engine, such as pressure p(φ), average temperature over the cylinder volume T(φ), Qx(φ) heat release and its speed dQx/dφ = f(φ), were verified. The example of comparing the calculated and experimental indicator diagrams shown in Fig. 2 shows good agreement: the difference between the instantaneous values of the calculated and measured pressures does not exceed 2%.

Figure 3 shows the instantaneous vector fields of the working fluid velocities in the combustion chamber (Fig. 3-a) and in the gap (3-b) at the moment when the piston is in TDC, i.e. during the combustion process. It is evident that the maximum local values of instantaneous velocities (~18–22 m/s) are achieved in the constrictions of the combustion chamber, and in the inlet section its value is almost 2 times less. Note that radiant heat exchange in hydrogen engines is significantly less important than convective heat exchange due to the absence of solid soot particles in the combustion products, which are known to be the main generators of radiation during the combustion of hydrocarbon fuels [8]. Numerical experiments have shown that with an increase in the gap size from

$\ell = 0.2$ mm to $\ell = 0.35$ mm, the velocity in the inlet section of the gap decreases by approximately 1.2 m/s.

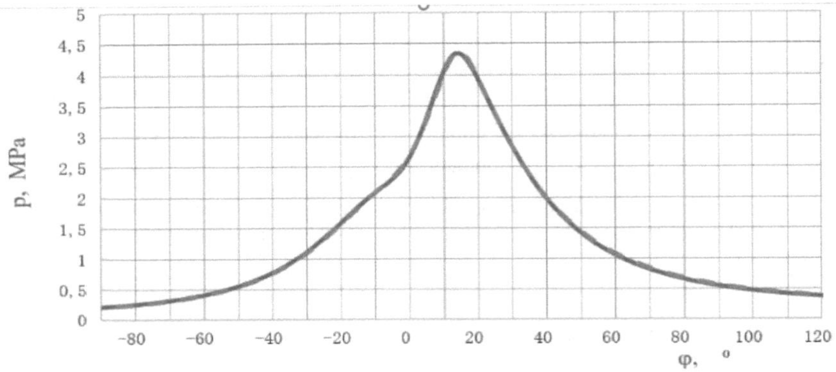

Fig. 2. Comparison of experimental (——) and calculated (– – –) indicator diagrams of a hydrogen engine (rotation speed n = 3000 min^{-1}, ignition advance angle $\varphi_{ign} = 15°$, excess air coefficient $\alpha_{air} = 1.64$). The moment of time $\varphi = 0^0$ corresponds to the top dead center (TDC).

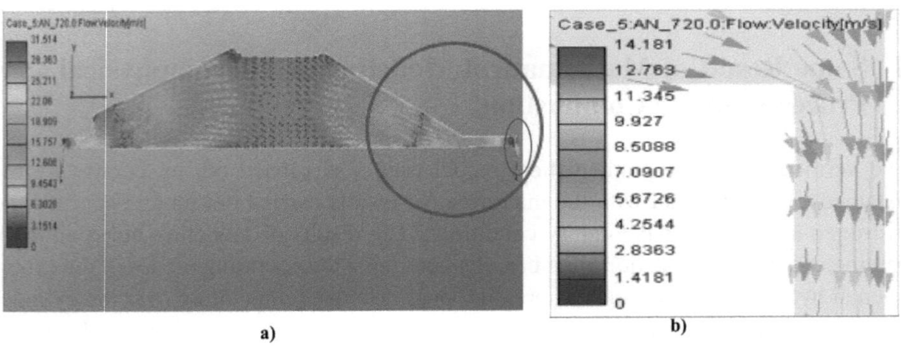

Fig. 3. Instantaneous vector fields of the working fluid velocities in the combustion chamber (a) and in the gap (b) with a size of $\ell = 0.2$ mm at the time $\varphi = 720^{\circ}$ (TDC, $p_z = 4.2$ MPa, n = 3000 min^{-1}, $\alpha_{air} = 1$).

High pressure in the combustion chamber (Fig. 2) ensures that the gap volume is filled with a combustible mixture of air and hydrogen even before the combustion process begins. In this regard, the spread/quenching of the non-stationary flame in the gap can be monitored by the proportions of hydrogen in the working fluid: in the unburned volume of the working fluid, the proportion of hydrogen is maximum at a given value of αair, and in the burnt volume $\alpha_{air} \approx 0$, which is clearly seen from Table 2.

It is evident that at φ = 728° (φ = 720° corresponds to TDC), the hydrogen flame of the stoichiometric mixture enters the gap, spreads throughout its volume, and 50° after

TDC, i.e. at $\varphi = 770^{o}$, almost the entire mass fraction of hydrogen in the gap burns ($\overline{m}_{H2} \approx 0$) and the flame goes out. Thus, at $\alpha_{air} = 1$, the area of the inner surface of the gap, together with the piston's fire bottom, represents a fire surface with intensive heat exchange between the burning working fluid and the walls. It is obvious that when the flame penetrates the gap, heat losses in the wall increase.

Table 2. Flame propagation in the gap

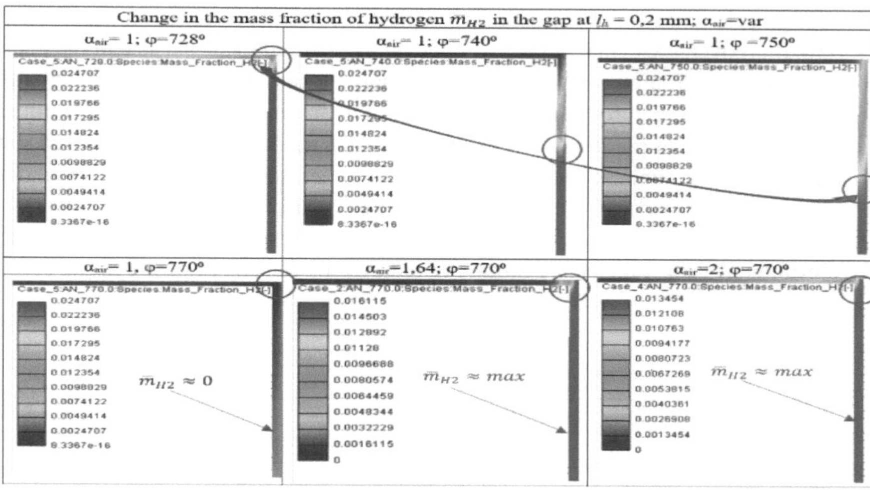

5 Result of an Experimental Heat Exchange in the Gap of Running Engine

The Experimental proof that in the case of hydrocarbon fuel, convective heat exchange in the gap is blocked due to the absence of flame is Fig. 4, which shows the result of measuring the density of non-stationary heat flux in the gap, obtained on a high-speed diesel engine KamAZ-7405. Note that the gap size on this engine in a hot state is $\ell_h = 0,4$ mm. The operating principle of such a sensor, its advantages over surface thermocouples and film resistance thermometers, usually used to measure heat flows in the combustion chambers of piston engines, as well as the features of its installation on the heat exchange surface of a moving piston are described in [8]. As can be seen, the sensor is located in the gap directly above the groove of the upper ring (Fig. 4), i.e. where, according to (2), taking into account the specified gap size, the flame does not penetrate during combustion of hydrocarbon (in this case, diesel) fuel. Indeed, this can be seen in Fig. 4, which shows the change in the local heat flux density during one working cycle: at the beginning (the filling process), a fresh charge (air) enters the gap, the temperature of which is lower than the gap surface temperature, and the heat flux has a negative sign, i.e. it is directed from the surface to the air in the gap.

Then the air in the gap is heated as a result of piston compression, and after the injection of diesel fuel and self-ignition, i.e. after the thermal explosion in the main volume of the combustion chamber - as a result of compression from the expanded combustion products. It is obvious that the air temperature in the gap increases and in the TDC region becomes equal to the wall temperature (at this moment, the instantaneous value of the heat flux $q_w = 0$ and then it changes directions). During the combustion-expansion process, the flame does not penetrate the gap, but the gases in the gap are heated by the hot walls and by compression caused by a sharp increase in pressure after the start of combustion in the main volume of the chamber. The total heat flux value for the working cycle (the sum of negative and positive values) does not differ significantly from zero, moreover, the heat supplied from the working fluid to the surface of the piston flame zone is less (though not by much, Fig. 4) than the heat removed. The fact that the total heat losses in the gap for the cycle when using hydrocarbon fuel are not significant indicates the absence of flame in it. Note also that when modeling the heat-stressed state of pistons of engines running on hydrocarbon fuel, when specifying thermal boundary conditions on the surface of the flame zone, either zero or small values of heat flux densities are specified [8], since only in this case the correspondence of the calculated and experimental values of local piston temperatures in the region of the upper ring is achieved.

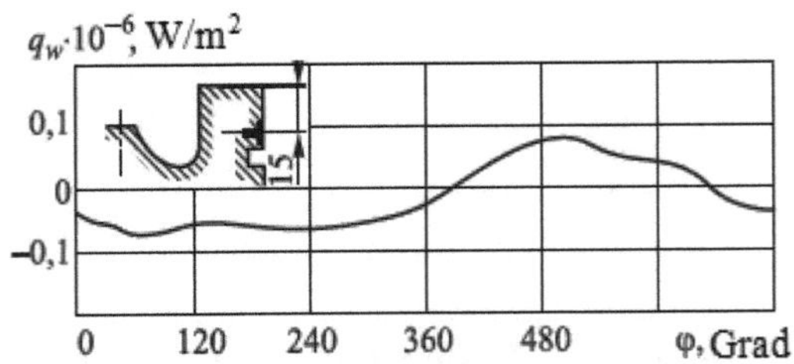

Fig. 4. Change in non-stationary local heat flow in the gap on the piston surface of the KAMAZ-7405 diesel engine. Operating mode: $n = 1800\ \text{min}^{-1}$, $Ne = 163$ kW, gap size on a hot engine $\ell_h = 0.4$ mm. $\varphi = 360°$ corresponds to TDC.

Thus, the results of direct measurement of the non-stationary heat flow (Fig. 4), which are evidence of flame extinguishing when using traditional fuel, and the corresponding results of modeling the thermal state of the piston (Fig. 4), reveal a phenomenon observed in experimental studies [9–11] - an increase in heat losses in the wall of the combustion chamber of a hydrogen engine compared to its basic, gasoline version.

6 Conclusion

1. An important design factor affecting the local heat exchange in the combustion chamber and the thermal state of the hydrogen engine piston is the gap between the surfaces of the piston flame zone and the liner above the upper compression ring. This paper shows that the penetration of the hydrogen-air flame into the gap leads to additional

heat losses and an increase in the heat-stressed state of the piston. Taking this phenomenon into account is especially important when replacing traditional motor fuels (gasoline and diesel fuel, as well as natural gas) with hydrogen. The fact of increased heat losses in a hydrogen engine, repeatedly observed in experimental studies by various authors, which has not yet had a scientific basis, has been studied in detail and substantiated on the basis of the proposed hypothesis;

2. For a gasoline engine converted to hydrogen, it has been established that the critical value of the flame extinguishing distance of the hydrogen-air mixture, i.e. the gap size where the flame cannot penetrate is $\ell_{\text{кр}\, H_2} \approx 0.125$ mm, which is almost two times smaller than the gap in the experimental engine under study when hot ($\ell_{\text{h}} \approx 0.2$). Obviously, in this case, hydrogen combustion takes place in the gap, accompanied by intense heat exchange. In the case of a gasoline-air mixture, $\ell_{\text{кр бенз}} \approx 0{,}5$ mm, which is significantly larger than the gap in the hot experimental engine ($\ell_{\text{h}} \approx 0.2$ mm), the flame in the gap goes out, i.e. there is no gasoline combustion, and the temperature of the mixture and the intensity of convective heat transfer decrease. Obviously, heat losses to the combustion chamber wall in this case will be less than in a hydrogen engine. In the case of the hydrogen engine under study, the heat exchange surface area in the gap is 32% of the entire heat-absorbing surface of the piston along which the flame propagates. In a gasoline engine, in the gap of which there is no flame, this surface is not a surface of active heat transfer from the gas to the wall. In this regard, heat losses in the wall in a hydrogen engine will be significantly higher than in a gasoline engine.
3. Depending on the presence or absence of a flame in the gap, the thermal boundary conditions for the piston and, accordingly, its heat-stressed state change significantly. When a hydrogen-air flame penetrates the gap, the local temperature of the piston in the area of the upper compression ring increases from $t_{or} = 269$ °C to $t_{or} = 316$ °C.
4. As a result of the analysis, we come to an explanation of the phenomenon of increasing heat losses in a hydrogen engine, the existence of which was previously shown only experimentally without theoretical justification.

Acknowledgements. This work was supported by Shota Rustaveli National Science Foundation of Georgia (Grant FR-23-8035).

References

1. Zeldovich, Ya.B.: The theory of the limit of propagation of a silent flame. In: Zeldovich, Ya.B. (eds.) Selected Works. Chemical Physics and Hydrodynamics, pp. 233–246. Publishing House Nauka, Moskow (1984). (in Russian)
2. Kavtaradze, R., Natriashvili, T., Gladyshev, S.: Flame Extinguishing and Heat Transfer in the Combustion Chamber of a Hydrogen Engine. SAE Technical Paper 2025-01-8420, pp. 1–5 (2025)
3. Merker, G., Schwarz, Ch., Stiesch, G., Otto, F.: Verbrennungsmotoren: Simulation der Verbrennung und Schadstoffbildung. Teubner-Verlag, Stuttgart-Leipzig-Wiesbaden (2006)
4. Drell, I.L., Belles, F.E.: Survey of hydrogen combustion properties. Technical Report 1383, pp. 1–5. National Advisory Committee on Aeronautics (NACA), USA (1958)

5. Kavtaradze, R., Natriashvili, T., Gladyshev, S.: Hydrogen-Diesel Engine: Problems and Prospects of Improving the Working Process. SAE International Paper, 2019-01-0541, pp. 1–15 (2019)
6. Kavtaradze, R.Z.: Thermophysical Processes in Diesel Engines Converted to Natural Gas and Hydrogen. Publishing House of Bauman Moscow State Technical University, Moscow (2011). (in Russian)
7. FIRE. Users Manual. Version 2020. AVL List GmbH Graz, Austria (2020)
8. Kavtaradze, R.Z.: Local Heat Transfer in Piston Engines, 3rd edn. Publishing House of Bauman Moscow State Technical University, Moscow (2016). (in Russian)
9. Huang, M., et al.: Experimental investigations of the hydrogen injectors on the combustion characteristics and performance of a hydrogen internal combustion engine. Sustainability **16**, 1929–1940 (2024)
10. Shudo, T.: Improving thermal efficiency by reducing cooling losses in hydrogen combustion engines. Int. J. Hydrog. Energy **32**(17), 4285–4293 (2007)
11. Demuynck, J., De Paepe, M., Verhaert, I., Verhelst, S.: Heat loss comparison between hydrogen, methane, gasoline and methanol in a spark-ignition internal combustion engine. Energy Proc. **29**, 138–146 (2012)

Sustainable Management of Navigation and Sediment Transport on the Danube River

Velizara Pencheva[1], Asen Asenov[1](✉), Ivelin Zanev[2], Mladen Kulev[1], and Valeri Geogriev[1]

[1] Department of Transport, University of Ruse, Ruse, Bulgaria
asasenov@uni-ruse.bg
[2] Executive Agency "Exploration and Maintenance of the Danube River", Ruse, Bulgaria

Abstract. The Danube River is one of the most significant fluvial systems in Europe in terms of navigation, while also exhibiting a complex sediment transport dynamic. Although navigation is indispensable for trade and the transport industry, its impact on sediment transport and river ecosystems should not be underestimated. Sediment transport is a process in which water currents mobilize various particles, such as sand, clay, and gravel, which either accumulate or are displaced in specific river sections. This paper examines the key interactions between navigation and sediment transport, as well as potential management strategies to ensure the sustainable development of inland waterways. For the Bulgarian-Romanian section of the Danube River, an analysis of the days during which navigation was suspended or restricted due to low water levels or freezing was carried out for the period 2010–2024. Additionally, an overview is provided of the objectives and tasks of project 101157942 DANube SEdiment Restoration: towards the deployment and upscaling of sustainable management of the sediments across the Danube catchment basin – DANSER, funded by the European Union under the HORIZON-MISS-2023-OCEAN-01 program. A multicomponent regression–optimization model has been developed for the assessment and management of sediment processes in a transboundary context.

Keywords: Navigation · Danube River · Sediments · Nature-Based Solutions (NBS) · Ecosystem Conservation · Sustainable Waterway Management · Sustainable Navigation · Danube River · Sediments · Transboundary Management · DANSER

1 Introduction

The Danube River is the second longest river in Europe and plays a crucial role in the hydrological and ecological processes of Central and Eastern Europe. The transport of sediments from its headwaters in Germany to its delta in the Black Sea is a defining aspect of its dynamics. Sediment transport in the river is essential for shaping the riverbed, maintaining ecosystems, and ensuring bank stability. In recent decades, human interventions have significantly influenced these processes through the construction of dams, riverbed modifications, dredging, and navigation activities.

A. Abbasov et al. (Eds.): PLMO 2025, CCIS 2767, pp. 141–156, 2026.
https://doi.org/10.1007/978-3-032-13672-5_13

Navigation along the river is of economic importance, however, it must be managed in a way that maintains ecological balance. Ships navigating the river generate hydrodynamic forces that can significantly impact sediment transport and river morphology [1, 2]. Sediment transport and navigation are not only interrelated but also mutually dependent. Understanding the interaction between these two processes is essential for the sustainable management of waterways.

The application of modern technologies, such as digital solutions and the integration of hydrological and engineering approaches, can greatly enhance sediment management, ensuring both the safety and efficiency of navigation in large river systems like the Danube. The DANube SEdiment Restoration: towards the deployment and upscaling of sustainable management of the sediments across the Danube catchment basin (DANSER) project, funded under the HORIZON-MISS-2023-OCEAN-01 program, employs a multidisciplinary, holistic, and science-based approach. This initiative focuses on the Danube River Basin to support its sensitive ecosystem, which is increasingly affected by climate change and human activities.

2 Navigation and River Hydrodynamics

To begin with, a more detailed explanation of the Ship traffic generates specific hydrodynamic processes, including waves, turbulence, and pressure pulsations. These processes influence the movement of sediments along the riverbed and contribute to erosion. The waves created by passing vessels can result in increased sediment displacement and the formation of new features such as sandbanks and meanders [3].

Strong waves generated by ships can lead to bank erosion and sediment displacement. At the same time, as these waves subside, sediment deposition occurs in specific sections of the river, which may alter the natural navigation routes and create new obstacles for shipping [4].

Frequent vessel passage leads to mechanical reshaping of river channels, including the formation of new sand deposits and the removal of sediments from the channels, which can modify the river's profile. This necessitates regular dredging operations to maintain the required depth for the passage of large commercial vessels [5].

The accumulation of sediments in areas with intensive navigation can cause several problems:

- Shallow areas, which reduce the navigational depth of the river and can hinder ship movement, especially for vessels with high displacement [6].
- Congestion and blockages, which can slow down trade and increase maintenance costs.

3 Sustainable Management of Sediment Transport

Sediment transport in the Danube includes both suspended and bedload transport, which depend on hydrodynamic conditions, sediment composition, and the geomorphology of the river basin. The key factors influencing sediment dynamics are:

- river discharge and seasonal variations;

- turbulent flows and wave movements;
- geological and morphological characteristics of the riverbed;
- impact of hydrotechnical facilities (e.g., dams, weirs, ports).

The sediments in the Danube originate primarily from erosional processes in the Alpine and Carpathian regions, as well as from economic and agricultural activities in the ten countries through which the river flows. These sediments include:

- mineral particles – quartz, feldspar, clays, and carbonates
- organic matter – detritus and decomposed plant residues;
- heavy metals and pollutants – resulting from industrial and agricultural activities.

Sediment transport in the river occurs through:

- suspended load – fine particles carried in the water column;
- bedload transport – larger particles moving along the riverbed;
- dissolved substances – chemical elements dissolved in the water.

Factors such as river discharge, channel morphology, and the construction of dams influence the speed and scale of sediment transport.

Sediments play a critical role in:

- habitat preservation – providing suitable conditions for fish and invertebrates;
- soil fertility maintenance – enriching floodplain soils;
- pollutants distribution – potentially threatening ecosystems.

Activities such as dam construction, agriculture, and industrial pollution lead to changes in sediment balance. The reduction of sediment flow to the river delta can result in coastal erosion and the loss of floodplain ecosystems.

Figure 1 presents key strategies for sediment management.

One of the primary methods for sustainable sediment balance management is the optimization of dam, dike, and other hydrotechnical facility operations. Research indicates that mismanagement of water volumes behind dams reduces sediment transport. It is recommended to implement practices for water level and flow regulation to ensure sediment transfer to downstream sections of the river [7]. Additionally, technologies exist for artificially restoring sediment flow by redirecting part of the water and sediments through specialized channels.

Wetlands, which form due to sediment accumulation in river mouths and deltas, are critical for biodiversity conservation. Their restoration and the protection of riverbeds can be achieved through regular dredging operations, careful sediment deposition management, and the use of nature-based restoration methods [8]. Moreover, vegetation planting along riverbanks improves soil stability and reduces erosion.

Continuous monitoring of sediment flow and the condition of river morphology is fundamental for sustainable management. By utilizing modern technologies such as satellite imagery, GIS (Geographic Information Systems), and modeling, it is possible to predict future changes in sediment balance and identify vulnerable sections of the river [9]. Modeling of flows, sediment transport, and erosion provides insights into the most appropriate interventions for maintaining a stable sediment balance.

Although hydrotechnical facilities play a key role in water management, there are also alternative solutions that can help reduce the negative impact on sediment balance. Green

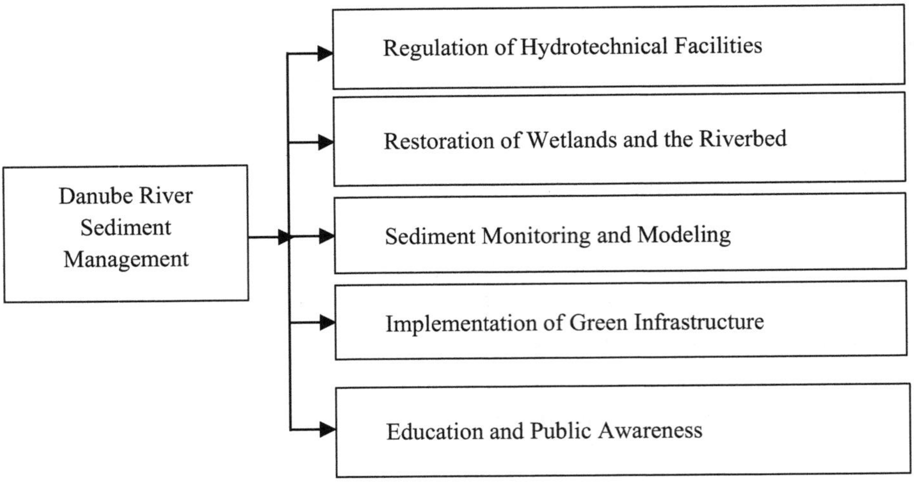

Fig. 1. Key Strategies for Sediment Management.

infrastructure, such as the restoration of wetlands, fishponds, riverbank bioengineering, and other nature-based solutions, can contribute to reducing erosion, increasing sediment retention, and restoring ecosystems [10].

Education and public awareness of the importance of sustainable management of sediment balance and its significance for biodiversity, and the hydrological cycle are essential. This includes educational campaigns, training of local authorities, and involvement of stakeholders in decision-making processes related to water resources and sediment management.

Climate change poses a serious challenge for the river's sediments. It leads to an increase in the intensity of variations and anomalies in water levels, which may affect sediment transport dynamics and to necessitate the adaptation of navigation channels. Changes in river speed and discharge can also increase the amount of sediment that needs to be managed to ensure the safety of navigation [11].

They lead to an increase in the intensity of variations and anomalies in water quantities, which may affect sediment transport dynamics and require adaptation of navigation channels.

A study was conducted on the number of days with restrictions and prohibitions on navigation on the Danube River in the Bulgarian-Romanian section for the period 2010–2024 (Table 1). Also, critical sections were identified where the river level drops below the norm of 2.5 m. The information is collected by the Executive Agency for the Study and Maintenance of the Danube River. Daily information on the state of the shipping route is available on the agency's website [12].

The data presented in Table 1 indicates that the highest number of days with complete navigation bans occurred in 2012, totaling 31 days. Navigation bans were recorded until 2017, primarily due to river freezing and ice drift. Since then, through 2024, no such bans have been imposed, a trend attributed to higher winter temperatures in recent years. Regarding days with navigation restrictions, the peak was in 2015, with a total of 173 days. This was primarily due to low water levels, specifically below the 2.5-m threshold. These restricted days occurred predominantly during summer, although some were observed in other seasons as well. Over the study period, there has been a noticeable year-to-year variability in the number of days with restrictions. This fluctuation has persisted in recent years. Notably, the number of critical segments—areas where navigation is hindered due to insufficient water depth—has increased to 23 in recent years and has remained at that level. This rise is associated with lower river levels, the formation of river islands, and the accumulation of sediments carried downstream during periods of high water.

Table 1. Data on the state of the Danube river in the Bulgarian-Romanian section.

Year	Days with a ban on navigation	Days with limited shipping	Number of critical sections
2010	0	**24**	2
2011	0	**166**	17
2012	**31**	**100**	17
2013	1	**91**	15
2014	1	**35**	7
2015	3	**173**	16
2016	7	**94**	13
2017	21	**116**	17
2018	0	**85**	21
2019	0	**91**	20
2020	0	**26**	22
2021	0	**55**	**23**
2022	0	**120**	23
2023	0	**44**	23
2024	0	**55**	23

A correlation analysis performed using SPSS revealed a weak relationship between the number of days with navigation bans, days with restrictions, and the number of critical river segments (Table 2). This weak correlation can be attributed to the influence of distinct and independent factors affecting each variable. The days with navigation bans are primarily influenced by river freezing and ice drift, phenomena that typically occur during the winter season. In contrast, the number of critical segments is mostly determined by the river's water level, which tends to be low during non-winter seasons. The number of days with navigation restrictions is affected by a wider range of factors, including low water levels, pollution, dredging operations, ice drift, storms, and vessel accidents, among others.

Sustainable management of sediment transport in the context of navigation requires an integrated approach that includes:

- Sediment transport and morphology monitoring using new technologies such as sensor networks and digital twins, which provide real-time information on the state of rivers and channels [13];
- Regular dredging: operations to move accumulated sediments, restoring optimal depth in navigation channels while minimizing environmental impact [14];
- Improvement of river infrastructure by constructing hydrotechnical facilities like dams and sluices to control water levels and prevent excessive sediment accumulation in certain areas.

Table 2. Correlation analysis.

		Days With Ban	Days With limited shipping	Number Of Critical Sections
Days With Ban	Pearson Correlation	1	.234	−.075
	Sig. (2-tailed)		.401	.790
	N	15	15	15
Days With limited shipping	Pearson Correlation	.234	1	.151
	Sig. (2-tailed)	.401		.592
	N	15	15	15
NumberOf Critical Sections	Pearson Correlation	−.075	.151	1
	Sig. (2-tailed)	.790	.592	
	N	15	15	15

Sediment processes are modeled using a variety of mathematical and numerical models, such as HEC-RAS, SWAT, Delft3D, TELEMAC-MASCARET, and others. These models are based on the continuity and mass balance equations, accounting for factors like water discharge, riverbed slope, and sediment grain size composition.

HEC-RAS (Hydrologic Engineering Center's River Analysis System) is one of the most widely used models for simulating river hydrodynamics and sediment transport [9]. It allows the analysis of one- and two-dimensional flows and the assessment of erosion and sedimentation processes. It is used for predicting the effects of dams and levees on sediment balance in the Danube.

SWAT (Soil and Water Assessment Tool) is commonly used for predicting water and sediment outflow in river basins [15]. It incorporates physically-based equations for soil erosion and sediment transport.

Delft3D is a hydrodynamic model used to simulate sediment processes in complex river systems and coastal zones [16]. It enables detailed modeling of the interaction between currents, bottom morphological processes, and climate factors.

TELEMAC-MASCARET is useful for analyzing large river systems like the Danube, offering two- and three-dimensional simulations of hydrodynamics and sediment transport [17].

The use of mathematical models enhances the understanding of sediment processes and supports sustainable sediment balance management.

4 Project Danube Sediment Restoration: Towards the Deployment and Upscaling of Sustainable Management of the Sediments Across the Danube Catchment Basin-Danser

Sustainable sediment balance management is crucial for preserving the health of ecosystems in the Danube River and for preventing negative consequences arising from climatic and hydrological changes. By applying integrated and science-based management strategies that incorporate a range of innovative solutions, a balance can be achieved to ensure riverbed stability, biodiversity conservation, and ecological sustainability.

The project includes three demonstration zones (DEMOs), covering the different sections of the Danube River:

Upper Danube (UD DEMO) – Donau-Auen National Park, with a focus on the long-term dynamics of sediment transport as a model for sustainable river management;

Mid Danube (MD DEMO) – Croatia (Drava River), where efforts are planned to restore the water-sediment connectivity in local ecosystems;

Lower Danube (LD DEMO) – Danube Delta, Iron Gates, and the Friendship Bridge, focusing on dredged sediment management and habitat protection through a combination of active and passive measures to restore, safeguard, and improve local sediment balance.

The main objectives of the project are to:

- Conduct monitoring and restoration activities on the river systems in the demonstration zones;
- Generate evidence on sediment balance and river processes;
- Improve understanding of sediment transport dynamics through advanced monitoring methods, such as satellite observation, modeling, and field research;
- Develop active and passive measures for sediment balance restoration, including nature-based solutions (nbs);
- Identify and establish connections between stakeholders (scientific institutions, local communities, and others) involved in sediment management in the danube river and transboundary regions;
- Collect, assess, utilize, and report necessary data;
- Foster trust and confidence in project analyses and impacts at all implementation stages;
- Synchronize and harmonize project initiatives with the mission ocean, water framework directive (wfd), and danube sediment management plan;
- Support the replication of best practices and their application in demos and associated regions;

- Replication and exploitation based on an evidence-based methodology for impact assessment and technical specifications;
- Integrate digital technologies for data analysis and management, including the creation of an interactive platform for visualizing and analyzing sediment processes.

The DANSER project is designed to implement a multidisciplinary, holistic, and science-based approach, focusing on the Danube River Basin - a vital yet sensitive ecosystem facing the challenges of climate change and human impact.

The project consists of eight main work packages, two of which are horizontal (cross-cutting) (Table 3).

Table 3. Project main work packages.

1. Project Management, Quality, and Ethics					
2. Framework Definition: Baseline Assessment, Require-ments and WFD Compliance [18]	3. DEMOS Preparation: Know-ledge, Data and Moni-toring Approaches	4. DEMOS Implementation: Towards Sustainable Sediment Manage-ment	5. Characterization of Sediment Balance and Key Ecosytem Services	6. Sediment Management: WFD and River Basin Management Plan Contributes	7. Scale-up, Replication and Exploitation
8. Communication and Dissemination					

DANSER includes 35 partners from the scientific, governance, and industrial sectors, seven of whom act as associated partners. These partners are distributed across seven countries as follows: Romania (10), Croatia (9), Austria (7), Bulgaria (4), Ukraine (2), Portugal (2), and Ireland (1).

5 The Impact of Policies and Transboundary Governance on Sustainable Sediment Management

Sediment transport does not recognize national borders—any intervention (e.g., dredging, construction of hydraulic structures) in one country may affect erosion, sediment dynamics, and ecosystems in another.

Sediment management is framed by several strategic documents and legal frameworks:

- EU Water Framework Directive (2000/60/EC). This directive obliges Member States to achieve good ecological status of water bodies, including through controlling morphological alterations, which are often caused by improper sediment management;
- Danube River Protection Convention (1994). The Convention aims to ensure cooperation in the field of transboundary water management in the Danube River Basin,

thereby guaranteeing sustainable and equitable management and use of surface and groundwater resources within the basin. It provides the institutional basis for international cooperation through the International Commission for the Protection of the Danube River (ICPDR), which coordinates joint plans, monitoring, and data exchange;
- EU Strategy for the Danube Region (EUSDR). This strategy defines priorities in areas such as "Improving mobility and multimodality," "Restoring and maintaining the good status of waters," and "Preserving biodiversity," where sustainable sediment management plays a key role.

Despite the existence of a common framework, Danube basin countries often differ in:

- The level of policy implementation – some countries maintain systematic sediment monitoring, while others have scarce data;
- Regulatory regimes for hydraulic works, such as dredging and river channel regulation;
- Management priorities – for example, Austria and Germany focus on ecosystem services, while other countries prioritize improving navigation;
- Stakeholder involvement – ranging from institutionalized consultation mechanisms to limited participation in decision-making processes.

Transboundary sediment management faces numerous practical and institutional challenges:

- Heterogeneous technical standards – lack of harmonized methods for measuring, modeling, and analyzing sediment transport;
- Fragmented data exchange – differences in access, quality, and format of data between countries, which hinder the development of a coherent picture of sediment dynamics;
- Limited interoperability of national water and environmental management systems;
- Insufficient engagement from local and regional authorities, particularly in the eastern part of the basin, where administrative capacity is often limited in terms of resources and/or mandates.

To achieve effective and sustainable sediment management throughout the basin, modern and harmonized governance approaches are required, such as:

- Legally binding interstate agreements to ensure coordinated implementation of sediment management activities;
- Creation of shared databases and early warning systems, enabling all countries to access relevant information on sediment dynamics;
- Development of transboundary digital twins of the Danube river to allow simulations of different scenarios, such as river profile changes, human interventions, and climate impacts;
- Unified indicators and monitoring protocols, applicable across all countries in the basin;
- Integration with climate change adaptation plans, ensuring a direct link between sediment management and measures to mitigate floods, droughts, and erosion.

The **DANSER Project** (Danube Sediment Management – Restoration of Sediment Balance in the Danube River) represents good practice for how transboundary cooperation can be effectively implemented.

The project has the potential to become a platform for sustainable and science-based sediment management, serving as a model for other international river basins.

The quantitative assessment of the impact of national and transboundary policies on key indicators of sustainable sediment management can be achieved through the development of a multicomponent regression–optimization model for evaluating and managing sediment processes in a transboundary context. This model combines quantitative regression analysis with an optimization objective function.

The structure of the model, including its inputs and outputs, is shown in Fig. 2.

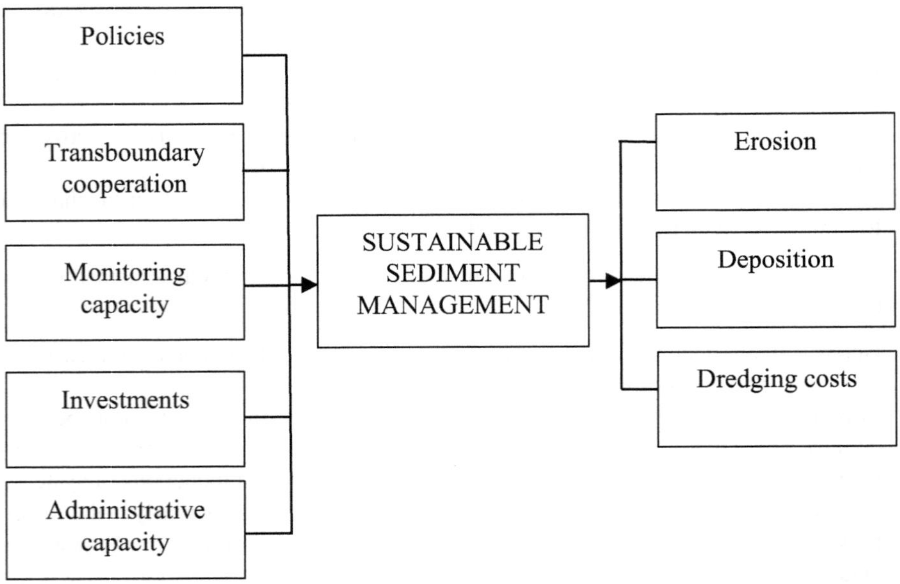

Fig. 2. Block diagram of the multicomponent regression–optimization model for assessing and managing sediment processes in a transboundary context.

Variables:

P_i is presence and strength of policy measures in country i (e.g., sediment management law, strategic plan). The value ranges from 0 (absent) to 1 (fully developed);

$T_{i,j}$ - intensity of transboundary cooperation between countries i and j (e.g., agreements, projects, data exchange), ranging from 0 to 1;

M_i - monitoring capacity in zone i (number of sensors, measurement frequency, data accessibility, etc.);

I_i - investments in nature-based solutions (NbS) or engineering infrastructure (e.g., bank stabilization, wetlands, NbS) that influence sediment control;

C_i - administrative management capacity in zone i (availability of expert staff, institutional structures, coordination mechanisms);

E_i- degree of erosion in zone *I*;

S_i - net sediment balance (deposition – export);

H_i - habitat quality index;

D_i - dredging costs.

Regression model for predicting sustainability in zone i.

The Sediment Management Sustainability Index (U_i) is an aggregated numerical indicator reflecting how well sediment transport and related ecological and hydraulic aspects are managed. A higher value indicates more effective and sustainable management.

$$U_i = \alpha_1 P_i + \alpha_2 \sum\nolimits_j T_{i,j} + \alpha_3 M_i + \alpha_4 I_i + \alpha_5 C_i + \varepsilon, \tag{1}$$

where α_k (k = 1,2,...,5) are weighting coefficients that express how strongly each variable (e.g., policies, cooperation, monitoring) influences the outcome;

U_i - these are determined through empirical calibration, for example, by regression analysis of real data;

$\sum_j T_{i,j}$ - represents the level of transboundary cooperation between zone *i* and all neighboring zones *j*. It captures data exchange, joint actions, agreements, and projects; the summation reflects the overall coordination;

ε - a stochastic error term accounting for unforeseen factors, data imperfections, or local specificities;

This is a linear index model, where each variable contributes to the final score U_i according to its assigned weight (α_k). Higher U_i values indicate more sustainable and effective sediment management; lower values signal weaknesses in policies, coordination, or capacity.

The index Ui is useful for:

- Comparing performance between zones;
- Evaluating the effectiveness of policies and investments;
- Identifying weaknesses in management;
- Serving as an input to optimization models or GIS-based tools.

The Sediment Management Sustainability Index (U_i) is an aggregated numerical indicator reflecting how well sediment transport and related ecological and hydraulic aspects are managed. A higher value indicates more effective and sustainable management.

Performance (Sustainability) Function – Optimization Model

The objective function of the optimization model aims to maximize the benefits of sustainable sediment management under limited resources (e.g., a constrained budget).

$$maxZ = \sum\nolimits_i U_i - \beta_1 E_i - \beta_2 D_i + \beta_3 H_i. \tag{2}$$

This function seeks to:

- Maximize the overall sustainability index U_i for the entire river system;
- Minimize negative effects, represented by E_i (erosion) and D_i (dredging costs);
- Increase positive ecological effects, represented by H_i (habitat/ecosystem quality).

Coefficients β_k: β_1 and β_2 assign weights to the cost/importance of erosion and dredging, while β_3 assigns a positive weight to the value of ecological quality.

Constraints:

Budget constraint: $I_i \leq B$, where B is the total budget. The total investments across all zones must not exceed the available budget B. This reflects the real-world resource limitations in planning.

Bounds on decision variables (management factors)

$$0 \leq P_i,\ T_{ij},\ M_i,\ C_i \leq 1. \tag{3}$$

The decision variables representing management factors (policies, transboundary cooperation, monitoring, and administrative capacity) are expressed as normalized indices within the range [0, 1], where 0 denotes absence and 1 denotes full implementation.

Functional relationships

$$E_i = f\left(P_i, T_{ij}, M_i\right). \tag{4}$$

Erosion is an inverse function of policies, cooperation, and monitoring: higher values of these factors lead to lower erosion.

$$D_i = g(S_i, E_i). \tag{5}$$

Dredging costs depend on sediment accumulation and the level of erosion.

$$H_i = h(M_i, I_i, P_i). \tag{6}$$

Habitat quality depends positively on monitoring efforts, investments, and policy frameworks.

The objective of the model is to allocate limited resources (investments and management efforts) to:

- Improve sustainability (U_i);
- Reduce negative impacts (erosion and dredging);
- Maximize ecological quality.

This is a multi-criteria optimization problem with a linear (or quasi-linear) objective function and non-linear constraints.

Impact Functions

The key dependencies among variables are erosion function; sediment balance; dredging costs; and habitat quality.

- Erosion function

$$\mathrm{E}_i = \gamma_0 - \gamma_1 P_i - \gamma_2 \sum\nolimits_j T_{ij} - \gamma_3 M_i + \delta_1, \tag{7}$$

where γ_0 is baseline erosion level without management measures;

γ_1 – effect of national policies;

γ_2 – effect of transboundary cooperation (good coordination significantly reduces erosion);

γ_3 – effect of monitoring (higher quality and more intensive monitoring lowers erosion);

δ_1 – stochastic noise (local variations such as rainfall, land use).

- Sediment balance

$$S_i = \theta_1 E_i + \theta_2 I_i + \delta_2, \tag{8}$$

where θ_1 is relationship between erosion and sediment transport;

θ_2 – effect of investments, particularly in NbS, which can improve sediment retention and control;

δ_2 – other factors (hydro-meteorological conditions, tributaries, etc.).

- Dredging costs

$$D_i = \lambda_1 S_i + \lambda_1 E_i + \delta_3, \tag{9}$$

where λ_1 is influence of sediment accumulation on dredging requirements;

λ_2 – direct effect of erosion processes on the need for riverbed cleaning;

δ_3 – other administrative or technical factors.

- Habitat quality

$$H_i = \mu_0 + \mu_1 M_i + \mu_2 I_i + \mu_3 P_i + \delta_4, \tag{10}$$

where μ_0 is baseline environmental (habitat) quality without management;

μ_1 – effect of monitoring (a higher coefficient indicates that improved monitoring has a stronger positive impact on habitat conditions);

μ_2 – effect of investments (e.g., habitat restoration, NbS);

μ_3 – effect of policies on ecosystem protection;

δ_4 – external factors (climate, species, human activity, etc.);

γ, θ, λ, μ are coefficients. These coefficients serve two purposes:

- Sensitivity indicators: They quantify how sensitive an output variable (erosion, sedimentation, dredging costs, habitat quality) is to a management factor (policy, investment, etc.);
- Performance evaluation: When calibrated with real data, they allow regression analysis and scenario modeling (e.g., "What happens if we increase investment in monitoring?").

For practical application, these coefficients must be calibrated using real-world data (e.g., from the Danube region) and simulated in an integrated model to assess sustainability under different policy and management scenarios.

Table 4 provides a summary of the model.

Table 4. Multicomponent regression–optimization model for assessing and managing sediment processes in a transboundary context.

Indicator	Formula/Relationship	Dependence on policies
Sustaina-bility U_i	Linear regression The Sediment Management Sustainability Index for zone *i* is modeled as a linear combination of factors: national and transboundary policies, monitoring, investments, and coordination This approach allows a quantitative estimation of the impact of management measures on sustainability in a given zone	Direct – policies directly enter the function for U_i; their effect is explicit and linear
Erosion E_i	Inverse relationship Erosional processes decrease with the presence of effective policies, land-use control, monitoring, and nature-based solutions (NbS) Formally: $E_i = f(P_i, T_{ij}, M_i)$ with an inverse relationship - stronger policies lead to lower erosion	Strong and direct (inverse influence) – policies significantly contribute to reducing erosion
Sediments S_i	Dependence on erosion and investments The amount of sediments entering a zone depends on: the intensity of erosion processes E_i, hydrological conditions, and the level of human interventions (investments, infrastructure) Formally: $S_i = g(E_i, I_i)$.	Moderate – policies have an indirect effect through their influence on erosion and the direction of investments, but are not the sole factor
Dredging D_i	Proportional to S_i and E_i. The need for dredging is linked to sediment accumulation and erosional pressure More sediments → more frequent and intensive dredging operations Formally: $D_i = k(S_i, E_i)$	Indirect – policies do not directly affect dredging, but by controlling the drivers (sediment input, erosion) they can reduce the need for it

(*continued*)

Table 4. (*continued*)

Indicator	Formula/Relationship	Dependence on policies
Habitats H_i	Positive influence of policies and NbS The ecological condition of habitats depends on: the implementation of nature-based solutions (NbS), reducing the intensity of dredging activities, and investments in ecosystem infrastructure Formally: $H_i = f(M_i, I_i, P_i)$.	Direct - environmental policies and the application of NbS have a direct effect on habitats by improving habitat quality and biodiversity

6 Conclusion

This article presents an interdisciplinary approach to the sustainable management of navigation and sediment transport along the Danube River, integrating hydrodynamic, ecological, and governance dimensions. Contemporary policies, instruments, and transboundary initiatives are analyzed, with particular emphasis on the strategic potential of nature-based solutions and digital technologies. The developed sediment balance sustainability model, based on regression analysis and optimization techniques, provides a novel framework for assessing the effects of policies and management actions. The application of the model in a pilot transboundary zone demonstrates its relevance for forecasting and decision-making under uncertainty. A comparative table of the Danube Basin countries reveals differences in capacity and the effectiveness of applied measures. The visualization of the links between sediment transport and ecosystem services highlights the need for integrated management. In conclusion, the proposed model can serve as a basis for policy design aimed at achieving ecologically and economically sustainable navigation on the Danube River.

Acknowledgement. This work is co-funded by the European Union Horizon Europe programme (HORIZON-MISS-2023-OCEAN-01) under Grant Agreement № 101157942 (DANSER).

References

1. Le Hir, P., et al.: Sediment transport dynamics in tidal rivers. Coast. Eng. **39**(2), 89–107 (2000)
2. Figueroa, H., et al.: Hydrodynamics of riverine sediment transport in the presence of shipping traffic. River Res. Appl. **29**(8), 1153–1167 (2014)
3. Meyer, V.: Sediment movement and erosion in river channels under ship traffic. Environ. Eng. Sci. **22**(4), 225–234 (2003)
4. Dorman, P., et al.: Impact of ship traffic on sediment transport in navigable rivers. Environ. Fluid Mech. **20**(3), 313–325 (2016)

5. Gao, X., Mo, Y.: Modeling of sediment transport in river channels under ship-induced disturbances. Water Resour. Res. **57**(10) (2021). e2020WR029557
6. Meyer, V., Millard, M.: Sediment dynamics in shipping channels. Mar. Geol. **391**, 16–30 (2017)
7. Habersack, H., Hauer, C., Holub, M.: Sediment transport processes in large rivers. Geomorphology **270**, 4–19 (2016)
8. Schwarz, U.: Hydromorphological Changes of the Danube River. WWF Report (2010)
9. Brunner, G.W.: HEC-RAS River Analysis System. US Army Corps of Engineers (2016)
10. Liu, J., Yu, D., Li, X.: Green infrastructure for sustainable urban water management. Environ Sci Policy **75**, 45–53 (2017)
11. Mandel, R., et al.: Climate change effects on river morphology and sediment transport. Glob. Environ. Change **55**, 137–149 (2018)
12. Executive Agency "Research and Maintenance of the Danube River", Ruse (2025). https://www.appd-bg.org/index-en. Accessed 10 Mar 2025
13. Zhu, X., et al.: Application of digital twins in river sediment management. Adv. Water Resour. **141**, 103542 (2020)
14. Boer, J., et al.: Sediment transport and dredging in riverine systems. J. Hydrol. **15**(2), 134–150 (2019)
15. Neitsch, S.L., et al.: SWAT theoretical documentation. Texas A&M University Press (2011)
16. Lesser, G.P., et al.: Delft3D: modeling system for rivers, estuaries, and coastal areas. Coast. Eng. **51**, 883–915 (2004)
17. Telemac Mascaret. https://www.ccp-wsi.ac.uk/catalogue/solvers/5dfad67c-60ef-4e43-8aa5-ec9250b130ec. Accessed 10 Mar 2025
18. Water Framework Directive (WFD). https://environment.ec.europa.eu/topics/water/water-framework-directive_en. Accessed 10 Mar 2025

Passenger Carriage with Increased Capacity for Railways of the Republic of Uzbekistan

Rustam Rahimov[1(✉)], Yuriy Boronenko[2], Farida Galimova[1], and Diyor Zafarov[1]

[1] Tashkent State Transport University, 1 Temiryulchilar str., 100167 Tashkent, Republic of Uzbekistan
rakhimovrv@yandex.ru

[2] Emperor Alexander I St. Petersburg State Transport University, 9 Moskovsky pr., 190031 Saint Petersburg, Russian Federation

Abstract. Given the growing importance of developing passenger rail transport in modern economic and social conditions, increasing the passenger capacity of railway rolling stock is becoming a key objective. Enhancing the capacity of passenger wagons not only contributes to more efficient utilization of existing railway infrastructure but also allows for a reduction in the number of required trips. This, in turn, helps decrease operational and maintenance costs, thereby lowering the overall cost of transportation services for the population and improving their affordability and accessibility in the long term. The article provides a scientific rationale for increasing passenger capacity and presents the results of design and engineering work aimed at developing a new model of a long-base passenger wagon. This advanced modification is specifically intended for operation on the railway network of the Republic of Uzbekistan, taking into account the region's unique climatic and operational conditions. Particular attention during the design process was given to ensuring the structural strength, stability, and safety of the wagon. The proposed solution is expected to improve the efficiency of rolling stock utilization, meet the growing demand for passenger transportation, and support the strategic modernization of the national railway infrastructure.

Keywords: Passenger Carriage · Extended base · Increased Passenger Capacity · Body Structure · Wagon Frame · Strength · Stability · Testing · Strain Gauge · Operational Reliability

1 Introduction, Status of the Issue and Objectives of the Work

Passenger transport is an integral part of the country's socio-economic infrastructure. The organization of passenger transportation in modern conditions is one of the most important and in-demand services provided both in large economically developed centers and in remote regions. The main goal of railway passenger transportation is to meet the population's mobility needs while ensuring a high level of safety and service quality [1].

A. Abbasov et al. (Eds.): PLMO 2025, CCIS 2767, pp. 157–169, 2026.
https://doi.org/10.1007/978-3-032-13672-5_14

In the context of the creation of new railway routes and the commissioning of modern routes, the need for optimal organization of the passenger sector of railway transport is increasing. One of the priority tasks is the effective use of passenger complex resources while necessarily meeting the population's demand for high-quality and safe transportation.

One of the possible solutions to this problem is to purchase rolling stock abroad or localize its production in the territory of the Republic of Uzbekistan. The second way is more expedient in terms of long-term economic benefits and the development of national industry. In this regard, since 2009, on the basis of JSC "Tashkent Plant for the Construction and Repair of Passenger Wagons", the production of passenger wagons of the 61–907 model has been mastered, with a length of 24537 mm along the coupling axes, a width of 3105 mm and a base of 17000 mm [2]. On the basis of this design, wagons of various modifications were developed and implemented [3, 4]: wagons with seats of 1 (Business), 2 (VIP) and 3 (Economy) classes; compartment wagons; tourist wagons; specialized measuring and diagnostic wagons (dynamometer, flaw detector, track meter); staff compartment wagons with seats for the disabled; wagons for transportation of special forces and others.

To increase the efficiency of railway passenger transportation, it is necessary to solve the following tasks: increasing the passenger capacity of wagons, increasing the speed characteristics of trains and reducing the cost of transportation per passenger. An analysis of foreign experience in the development and operation of high-capacity passenger wagons shows that achieving this goal is possible through the use of long-wheelbase or double-deck bodies [5–9]. Both options have the common advantage of increasing passenger capacity while reducing costs per passenger. However, double-deck wagons are characterized by a number of significant disadvantages: increased weight, complicated design, high capital costs for manufacturing, increased dimensions, which limits their operation in the conditions of the existing railway infrastructure.

Taking into account these circumstances, at the first stage it was decided to develop a long base passenger wagon capable of meeting modern requirements for traffic safety and operational efficiency.

Thus, the purpose of this study is to develop technical solutions for the design of a passenger wagon with increased passenger capacity, adapted to the conditions of the railways of Uzbekistan.

2 Theoretical Researches

The body structure of an open-type passenger wagon model 61-907, manufactured by JSC "Tashkent Plant for the Construction and Repair of Passenger Wagons", with a passenger capacity of 48 seats, was chosen as the object of the study [10].

For theoretical analysis, a spatial model of the wagon body was created in SolidWorks (Fig. 1) and transferred to ANSYS Workbench for finite element modeling (Fig. 2).

When modeling a body in the form of a plate-rod scheme using the finite element method, the skin elements are represented by thin–layer plates, and the reinforcing elements are represented by rods.

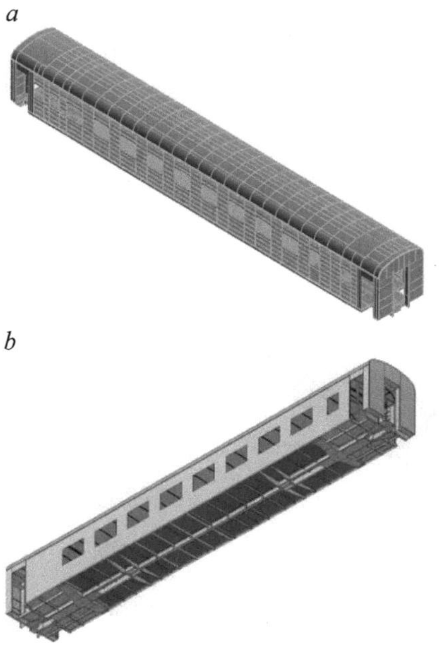

Fig. 1. Spatial calculation model of the passenger wagon body from top (*a*) and bottom (*b*) view

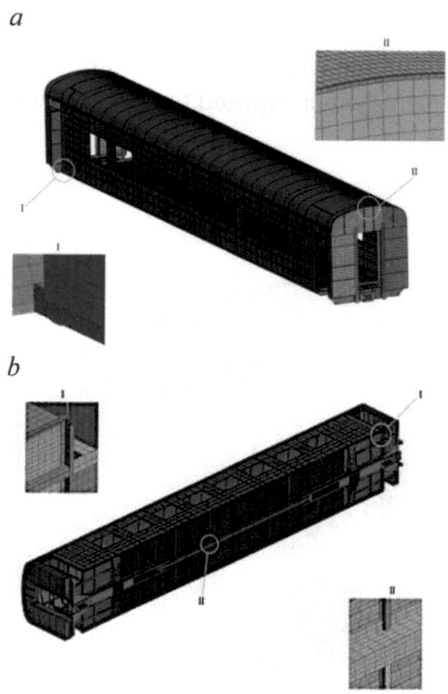

Fig. 2. Finite element model of the passenger wagon body from top (*a*) and bottom (*b*) view

It was assumed that the material of the wagon structure operates in the elastic stage of deformation and has constant mechanical characteristics of Young's modulus $E = 2.1 \cdot 10^5$ MN/m^2 and Poisson's ratio $\mu = 0.3$.

The body elements were imitated by three-dimensional quadratic finite elements (with three degrees of freedom in each node) of the Solid 186 type. The calculated finite element plate-rod passenger wagon model includes 1695631 nodes and 461850 finite elements.

The strength analysis was performed by the finite element method using the ANSYS Workbench software package in accordance with the requirements of regulatory documents on the calculation and design of rolling stock, in particular Norms [11] and GOST 34093-2017 [12].

The developed FE model made it possible to determine the stress-strain state of the body elements under the influence of static and dynamic loads that occur during the operation of the wagon.

To determine the load on the passenger wagon body structure, stress distribution in its elements, and identification of areas requiring reinforcement, the design model provided cross-sections with virtual measuring points placed on them. This made it possible to obtain local stress values at each of the points and conduct a detailed analysis of the stress-strain state of the structure.

As a result of the calculations, the values of the maximum stresses at the virtual measuring points were obtained. Diagrams of the distribution of equivalent Mises stresses that occur when exposed to a longitudinal force of 2.5 MN (compression) are shown in Fig. 3.

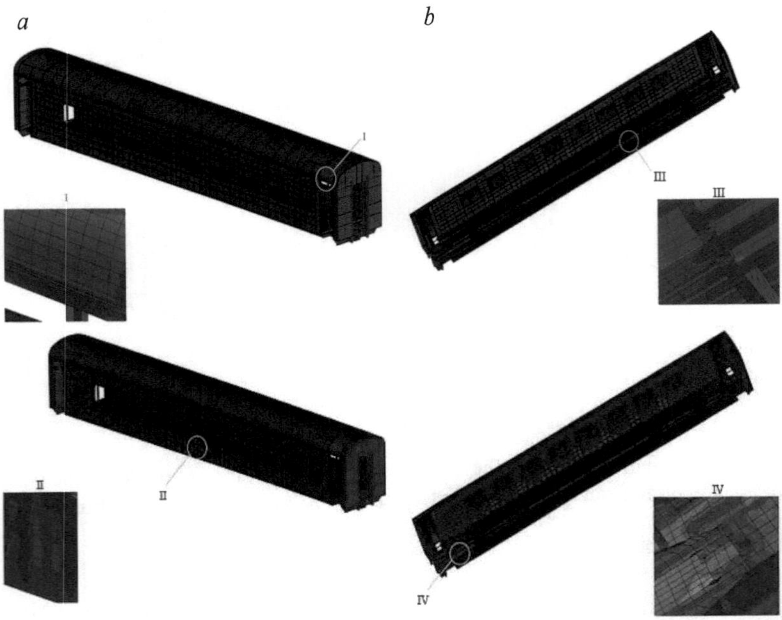

Fig. 3. Fields of equivalent stress distribution (according to Mises) in the passenger wagon body under the influence of a longitudinal compressive force of 2.5 MN from top (*a*) and bottom (*b*) view.

An analysis of the obtained dependencies of the maximum stresses occurring in the elements of the passenger wagon body showed that stress changes in the areas of the side and end walls, as well as the roof, with increasing longitudinal loads are insignificant and do not exceed the established limits. However, the stresses that occur in the elements of the wagon frame in some parts exceed the permissible stresses, which indicates the need for constructive improvement of these areas. In this regard, further research was focused directly on the construction of the wagon frame.

In the course of the research, additional calculations were carried out with a gradual increase in the length of the wagon in the range from 500 to 2500 mm with an interval of 500 mm. At each stage, the maximum stress values were determined at the specified virtual measurement points, which made it possible to trace the effect of geometry changes on the stress-strain state of the structure. Diagrams of the distribution of equivalent Mises stresses in the frame elements with the central interaction of the couplings are shown in Fig. 4.

Thus, with an increase in the length of the carriage by 2500 mm, the maximum equivalent stresses in the ridge beam reach 688.75 MPa, and in the lateral longitudinal beams – 661.13 MPa, which significantly exceeds the permissible stress of 293.25 MPa.

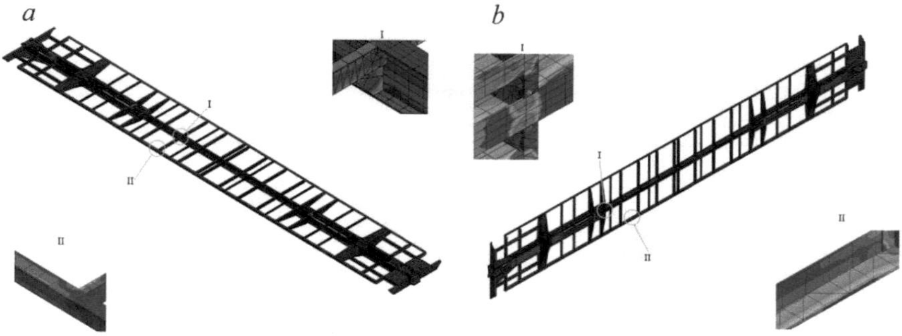

Fig. 4. Fields of equivalent stress distribution in the frame elements from top (*a*) and bottom (*b*) view.

This clearly indicates the need for structural reinforcement of the frame to ensure the safe operation of the extended carriage and to allow for an increased passenger capacity without compromising mechanical integrity or safety standards. Exceeding the stress limits can lead to premature fatigue, deformation, or even failure of load-bearing elements under prolonged service conditions.

Based on the theoretical studies carried out using the finite element method, it was found that in order to meet the strength requirements and ensure adequate stress distribution, the width of the flanges of the central ridge beam of the frame, made from I-beam No. 30, should be increased in the middle section from 135 to 150 mm (Fig. 5). This adjustment provides a substantial increase in the moment of inertia, thereby improving the stiffness and reducing critical stress concentrations. In addition, to increase the overall strength and reliability of the structure, it is recommended to replace the previously used L-profile corner sections in the lateral longitudinal beams with channel No. 18 profiles, which provide better resistance to bending and torsion.

According to the analysis of the theoretical study results, it was also determined that a wagon design with a base extended to 18000 mm (a 1500 mm increase in total length) still meets the requirements for automatic coupling, including conditions at the transition between straight and curved track segments. However, further increasing the length beyond this point results in the violation of coupling adhesion conditions, thereby rendering the structure non-compliant with current regulatory standards.

Thus, based on the results of comprehensive numerical simulations, an improved design of the passenger wagon body extended by 1500 mm is proposed. This enhanced configuration is characterized by the following key engineering solutions aimed at increasing structural performance and safety:

- increasing the width of the I-beam flanges in the central ridge beam from 135 to 150 mm to improve load distribution;
- replacement of the lateral longitudinal beams from L-profile corner sections to channel No. 18 to enhance torsional stiffness and load-bearing capacity.

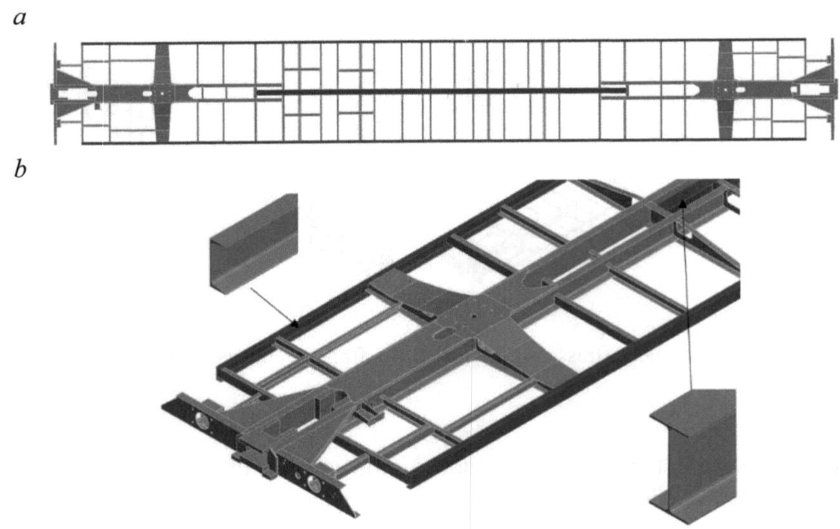

Fig. 5. The frame of an elongated passenger wagon with reinforcing elements: *a* – general appearance; *b* – reinforced elements (ridge beam, lateral longitudinal beams).

After substantiating the selected parameters of the elongated passenger wagon design, calculations were performed for strength, stability, and impact on the railway track, as well as an assessment of the dynamic running parameters of the developed body.

Structural strength analysis according to the requirements of [11, 12] was carried out according to three calculation modes (Table 1).

Table 1. The results of the strength calculation of the body of an elongated passenger wagon

Structural element	Calculation mode		
	I	II	III
Frame elements	219 MPa (74% of the permissible)	237 MPa (80% of the permissible)	96 MPa (51% of the permissible)
Frame elements of side walls	135 MPa (46% of the permissible)	117 MPa (40% of the permissible)	107 MPa (56% of the permissible)
Edge wall frame elements	114 MPa (39% of the permissible)	97 MPa (33% of the permissible)	39 MPa (21% of the permissible)
Roof frame elements	128 MPa (44% of the permissible)	117 MPa (40% of the permissible)	105 MPa (5% of the permissible)

The results of the strength calculation of the body structure of an elongated passenger wagon show that in all design modes, the stresses in the elements are within acceptable values, which confirms the overall strength reliability of the structure. In the most loaded design mode (II), the stresses in the frame are 237 MPa, which is equivalent to 80% of the permissible value. The frame elements of the side and end walls, as well as the roof, exhibit significantly lower stresses, ranging from 21% to 56% of the limit values.

The assessment of the stability of the body elements of an elongated passenger wagon was carried out by comparing the calculated coefficients of the stability margin with the normatively permissible values (Table 2).

Table 2. Stability coefficients of elongated passenger wagon body elements.

Calculation mode	Stability loss zone	Stability reserve factor	
		Estimated	Permissible
Mode I (compression)	Floor sheet at the end of the wagon	2.22	1.1
Mode I (impact)	Floor sheet at the end of the wagon	2.75	1.1
II mode (stretch)	Roof covering in the middle of the wagon	2.90	1.3
II mode (excerpt)	Roof cladding in end part of the wagon	2.38	1.3
Mode III (compression)	Floor sheet at the end of the wagon	1.61	1.5

In addition, studies were conducted to assess the running characteristics of the extended wagon and its impact on the railway track, which revealed that the developed wagon meets regulatory requirements.

3 Static and Dynamic Running Tests

In order to experimentally evaluate the developed design of an elongated passenger wagon, a prototype was made, on which static and dynamic running tests were carried out according to [13].

The purpose of the static tests was to assess the stress-strain state of the body's metal structure elements at control points when exposed to statically applied longitudinal compressive and tensile loads.

The processing of the test results consisted in recalculating the measured deformations at the installation sites of linear strain gages into stresses.

The tests were conducted on the basis of JSC "Tashkent Plant for the Construction and Repair of Passenger Wagons". A specialized stand for loading wagons with static loads was used to create longitudinal forces. The deformations were recorded using strain gages connected to the MIC-185 measuring and computing complex, with the recording of measuring processes on a personal computer.

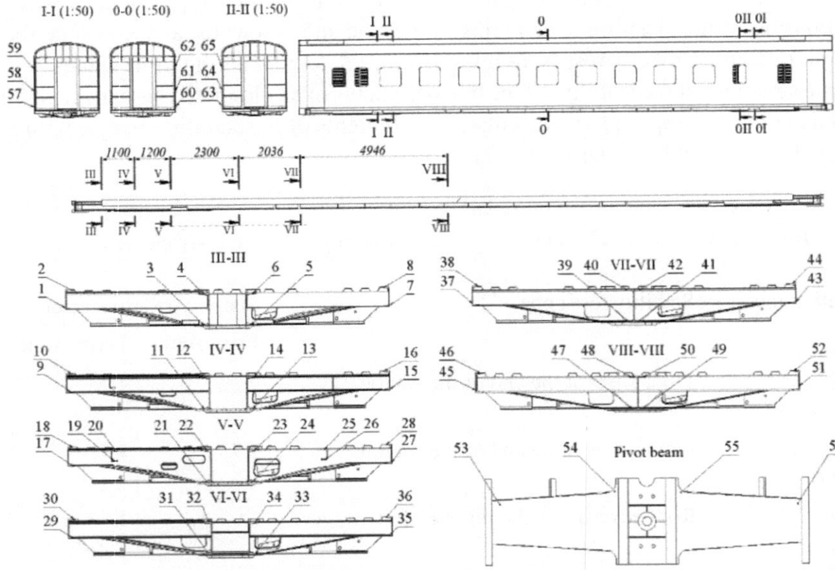

Fig. 6. Arrangement of strain gauges on the body and frame of a prototype wagon of elongated design: *1-65* – strain gauge numbers

Before the start of the tests, strain gages were glued at pre-determined design points of the load-bearing elements of the body (Fig. 6), corresponding to the most loaded sections, established by the results of preliminary finite element calculations.

The tests were carried out by applying a longitudinal static load through the elements of the coupling device with a force of 1.5 MN (tension) and 2.5 MN (compression) using jacks mounted on the loading stand.

During running tests of the wagon, dynamic processes are recorded, based on which the key operational characteristics of the rolling stock are determined. Specifically, the following parameters are evaluated: the vertical dynamic coefficient of the wagon body; the vertical dynamic coefficient of the bogie frame; wagon body accelerations in the vertical and horizontal planes; lateral force acting from the wheelset on the bogie frame (frame force); ride comfort indices in vertical and horizontal directions; the safety factor against wheel derailment on straight track sections; and the safety factor against wagon overturning when passing through curves.

As a result of the static strength tests performed on the prototype of the elongated wagon, the maximum stress values on the ridge beam in the central part were 230.1 MPa; on the lateral longitudinal beam – 83.1 MPa, which does not exceed the permissible value of 293.25 MPa. The distribution of maximum stresses in the body elements is shown in Fig. 7.

Thus, based on the results of complex static tests performed under the influence of longitudinal tensile and compressive loads, it was found that the proposed design of the elongated wagon meets the established strength requirements. The resulting stresses do not exceed the permissible values, no visible damage or residual deformations have been identified in the structure, which confirms its operability and reliability.

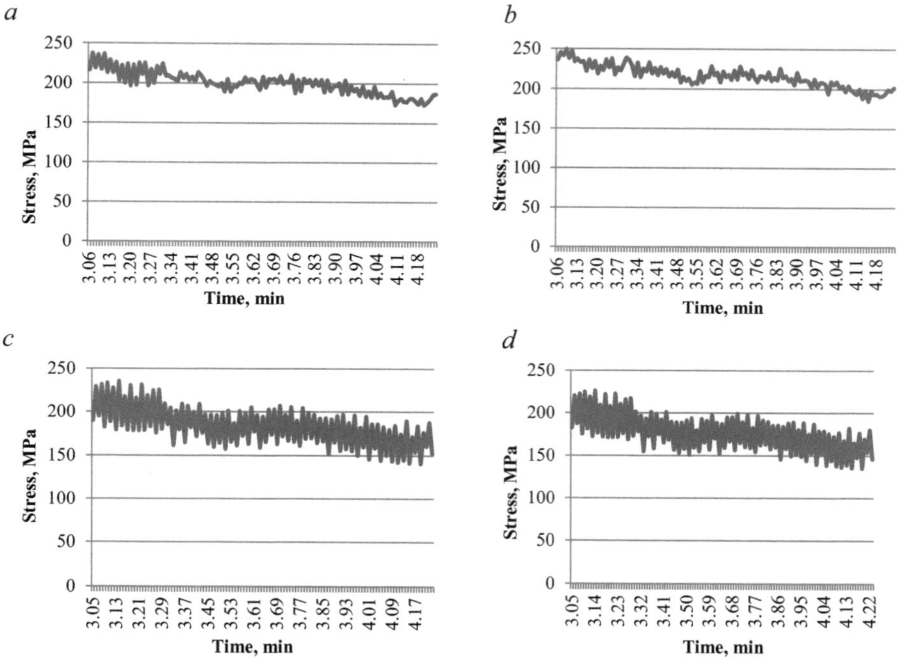

Fig. 7. The maximum stress values obtained in the body elements of an elongated wagon based on the results of static experiments from strain gauge No. 3 (*a*), No. 9 (*b*), No. 17 (*c*) and No. 19 (*d*)

After completion of the static tests, a fully assembled and equipped prototype of an elongated passenger wagon was subjected to dynamic running tests. The purpose of these tests was to experimentally confirm the compliance of the dynamic characteristics of the wagon with the requirements of regulatory documents.

The main objectives of the running test were to determine and evaluate the performance of the wagon when moving at various speeds, including design, in empty and loaded conditions. The tests were carried out on the main section of the Tukimachi-Angren railway line.

Tests to determine the impact of the wagon on the railway track were carried out in accordance with the requirements of GOST 34759-2021. The tests were carried out in the summer (July 29, 2024) on sections of the railway track of the Republic of Uzbekistan under the following conditions: ambient temperature – 26–36 °C, relative humidity – 16–30%, atmospheric pressure – 100.2 kPa.

According to the test results, the following values were established:

- the maximum vertical dynamic coefficient of the wagon body frame was 0.20, which is below the permissible value of 0.35;
- the maximum vertical dynamic coefficient of the bogie frame was 0.22, which is below the permissible value of 0.40;
- the maximum vertical acceleration of the wagon body frame was 0.34 g, which is below the permissible limit of 0.35 g;
- the maximum horizontal acceleration of the wagon body frame was 0.29 g, which is below the permissible limit of 0.30 g;
- the maximum frame force, expressed as a fraction of the static axle load, was 0.19, which is below the allowable limit of 0.25;
- the maximum ride comfort index was 3.10 in the horizontal direction and 3.16 in the vertical direction, which is below the permissible value of 4.0 and corresponds to a "satisfactory" rating (not exceeding 3.25);
- the minimum safety factor against wheel derailment was 2.1, which exceeds the minimum allowable value of 2.0;
- the minimum safety factor against wagon overturning in a curve was 3.13, which exceeds the minimum allowable value of 1.4.

The loaded non-compartment passenger wagon of the extended design was also subjected to running dynamic tests using the same methodology. Based on the recorded dynamic processes, the fatigue strength safety factors of the wagon body structures and the load-bearing elements of the bogie were determined.

The running dynamic tests of the extended non-compartment passenger wagon, carried out in accordance with the approved program and methodology, confirmed that the fatigue resistance of the load-bearing structures during operation at speeds up to 120 km/h complies with the requirements of regulatory documents. In particular, the stresses arising in the bogie structure under the third design loading mode did not exceed 0.72 of the permissible value, while those in the wagon body structure did not exceed 0.74 of the permissible value. The fatigue strength safety factor for the bogie's load-bearing elements exceeded 8.9, significantly higher than the minimum required value of 1.7, and for the wagon body's load-bearing elements, the safety factor exceeded 3.9, also surpassing the minimum required value of 1.7.

As a result of comprehensive tests of the elongated passenger wagon, including the application of static longitudinal compressive and tensile test loads, as well as loads arising during running dynamic tests, it was demonstrated that the proposed car design complies with the established requirements. Furthermore, no visible damage or residual deformations were detected in the structural elements of the tested passenger wagon.

4 Optimization of the Wagon Layout

The developed design demonstrates high operational reliability and provides a significant increase in passenger capacity compared to the base model (48 seats). In the extended Class I and II wagons, the number of seats has been increased by 50% to 72, and in Class III wagons by 87% to 90 seats (Fig. 8).

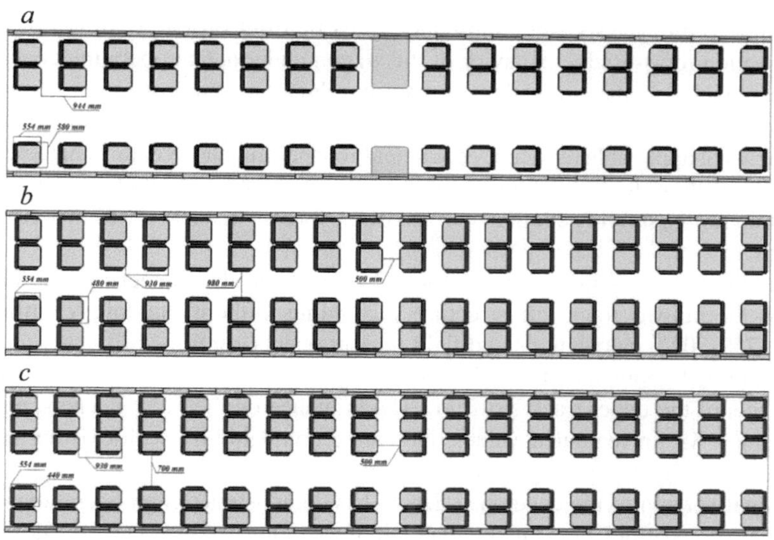

Fig. 8. Layout of open-type passenger wagons with seating: *a* – layout of the existing body structure; *b* – layout of the extended body structure (I and II classes); *c* – layout of the extended body structure (III class)

5 Conclusion

In the course of the work performed, a new design of an elongated passenger wagon body was developed, theoretically justified through numerical analysis, and experimentally validated with the aim of increasing passenger capacity without compromising the strength, dynamic performance, and operational reliability of the vehicle. The proposed solution addresses modern requirements for capacity expansion in passenger transportation while ensuring compliance with safety and performance standards.

Based on detailed theoretical studies carried out using the finite element method (FEM), optimal geometric and structural parameters of the wagon frame components were determined. These parameters ensure the necessary rigidity, strength, and structural stability of the wagon under operational loads while allowing for an increase in the overall body length. As a result of these investigations, an improved design of the wagon body was proposed, extended by 1500 mm in comparison to the standard model. Key structural enhancements included the reinforcement of the central ridge beam by increasing the width of its flanges from 135 mm to 150 mm, and the replacement of the lateral longitudinal frame members – from L-profile corner sections to channel No. 18 sections – to increase stiffness and load-bearing capacity under dynamic conditions.

To validate the numerical model and verify structural integrity, full-scale experimental static tests were conducted on a prototype wagon body. The results demonstrated the adequacy and accuracy of the FEM-based design approach: the experimentally measured stresses in critical load-bearing elements such as the ridge and side beams remained well within the allowable limits defined by the applicable standards. Furthermore, no residual deformations, material damage, or structural failures were detected upon completion of loading cycles, confirming the robustness of the reinforced design.

Dynamic running tests were subsequently carried out on the Tukimachi–Angren railway section to assess the behavior of the wagon under actual operating conditions. These tests included the evaluation of stability, dynamic response, ride quality, and safety indicators. The results confirmed that the elongated wagon design fully meets the requirements of applicable regulatory documents concerning the dynamic characteristics of passenger rolling stock. All dynamic performance indicators – including ride comfort, acceleration levels, stability coefficients, and frame forces – remained within permissible thresholds.

An additional assessment was performed to evaluate the impact of the modified design on the railway track infrastructure. According to the methodology outlined in GOST 34759-2021, calculations and field measurements confirmed that the increased mass and altered geometry of the elongated wagon do not lead to excessive loads on the elements of the upper track structure. The influence on the rails, sleepers, and ballast remained within regulated values, indicating compatibility with existing railway infrastructure without requiring its modernization.

The final version of the developed design has demonstrated high operational reliability and practical efficiency. Implementation of the elongated wagon body allows for a substantial increase in passenger capacity: up to 72 seats (an increase of 50%) for first- and second-class configurations, and up to 90 seats (an increase of 87%) for third-class configurations. This improvement contributes significantly to the economic efficiency of passenger transportation, especially on routes with high demand.

Thus, the comprehensive theoretical and experimental studies conducted throughout the project have confirmed that the proposed elongated wagon body design achieves a significant increase in passenger capacity while maintaining the required levels of structural strength, operational safety, and long-term reliability. The improved design, based on the body of the 61-907 model wagon, was successfully implemented at JSC "Tashkent Plant for the Construction and Repair of Passenger Wagons" for the production of a long-base passenger car with an overall body length of 26 m. Due to the rational selection of optimal structural dimensions and material configurations, it was possible to ensure both increased seating capacity and full compliance with the national and international regulatory framework governing passenger rolling stock. This development represents a meaningful contribution to the modernization and efficiency improvement of the domestic railway transportation system.

References

1. Presidential Decree of the Republic of Uzbekistan No. PP-28 dated January 27, 2025, "On Measures for the Further Development of the Transport and Logistics System of the Republic of Uzbekistan". (In Russian)
2. Compartment Passenger Wagons with Air Conditioning System, Model 61-907. Technical Specifications TU 17923832-013. "TYVQTZ" JSC, Tashkent (2022). (In Russian)
3. Rahimov, R.V.: The first Uzbek long-distance passenger wagon. Heavy Mach. (6), 34–35 (2010). (In Russian)
4. Rahimov, R.V., Khikmatov, F.F., Zafarov, DSh., Galimova, F.S.: Conversion of a passenger wagon into a dynamometric wagon for railways of the republic of Uzbekistan. AIP Conf. Proc. **3265**(1), 070002 (2025). https://doi.org/10.1063/5.0266047

5. Shinkaruk, A.S.: Technical preparation for scheduled preventive maintenance of double-decker rolling stock. World Transp. Transp. **21**(4), 53–61 (2023). https://doi.org/10.30932/1992-3252-2023-21-4-6
6. Kammer, R.: Double-decker passenger coaches of German railways. Zheleznye Dorogi Mira **12**, 34–39 (2008). (In Russian)
7. Piętrowe wagony we Francji na przestrzeni dziejów. transinfo.pl. https://transinfo.pl/inforail/pietrowe-wagony-we-francji-na-przestrzeni-dziejow/. Accessed 26 Apr 2025
8. De to etagers 'Bismarck'. jernbanemuseet.dk. http://www.jernbanemuseet.dk. Accessed 26 Apr 2025
9. Kallee, S.W., Davenport, J.: Trends in design and fabrication of rolling stock. Eur. Railw. Rev. (1), 75–79 (2007)
10. Rahimov, R.V.: New compartment-type passenger wagon for Uzbekistan railways. Proc. PGUPS (2), 286–295 (2010). (In Russian)
11. Standards for the Design and Calculation of New and Modernized Non-Self-Propelled Railway Wagons for 1520 mm Gauge Railways of the Ministry of Railways. VNIIV VNIIZhT, Moscow (1983). (In Russian)
12. GOST 34093-2017: Locomotive-Hauled Passenger Wagons. Requirements for Strength and Dynamic Characteristics. Standartinform, Moscow (2017). (In Russian)
13. GOST 33788-2016: Freight and Passenger Wagons. Methods of Strength and Dynamic Testing. Standartinform, Moscow (2016). (In Russian)

Advance Container Handling

László Vida[1(✉)], Latorcai Zsombor[2], Béla Illés[3], and Antal Véha[4]

[1] Hevterv Ltd, Bethlen Gábor str. 4/E, Budapest 1188, Hungary
vida@t-online.hu

[2] Hungarian Electricity Works AG, Szentendrei str. 207, Budapest 1031, Hungary

[3] Institute of Logistics, University of Miskolc, Egyetemváros, Miskolc 3515, Hungary

[4] Faculty of Engineering, University of Szeged, Tisza Lajos str. 73, Szeged 6725, Hungary

Abstract. This study examines the requirements for container handling procedures that are considered state-of-the-art in continental terminals. The container handling procedures currently used in continental terminals and their characteristics are examined. We also examine the technical solutions that have been developed in recent years to improve continental container handling. We also examine the container handling characteristics that serve the modal shift. Those technical features that are able to facilitate modal shift are considered as perspective. We present a new container handling technology that is considered state-of-the-art and that is in line with robotization and Industry 4.0 methods. We will investigate where on the Asia-Europe route, called the "Silk Road", it is appropriate to deploy advanced container handling technology.

Keywords: Intermodal Freight Transport · Modal Shift · Horizontal Container Transhipment · Sustainable Freight Transport

1 Introduction

Promoting modal shift is an important element of EU and international transport policy. For the EU and the European Transport Area, this means giving preference to rail freight transport, which can significantly reduce CO2 emissions. In the EU Member States, heavy goods vehicle traffic accounts for 4–4.5% of total CO2 emissions [7]. According to the International Maritime Organization (IMO), greenhouse gas emissions related to maritime transport account for approximately 2.5% of global emissions, and their annual emissions exceed 1,000 million tonnes of CO2 [12]. Studies on this topic generally identify electric rail freight as a means of reducing CO2 emissions from land freight transport [4, 6, 8]. The use of electric trucks may be an appropriate answer to unimodal road transport based on fossil fuels, but their mass introduction is still a distant goal and not realistic for intercontinental freight transport. The possibility of modal shift should be explored in the light of the current state of the art. A good way of reducing CO2 emissions in both intercontinental and continental freight transport could be to promote the use of electric rail freight. We believe that the EU targets of "shifting 30% of freight transport over 300 km by road by 2030 and more than 50% by 2050 to other modes

A. Abbasov et al. (Eds.): PLMO 2025, CCIS 2767, pp. 170–181, 2026.
https://doi.org/10.1007/978-3-032-13672-5_15

such as rail or waterborne transport" [4, 6] are not only achievable, but also beyond reach. Research and technical proposals generally provide little concrete information on how this can be achieved. Industry is interested in technically feasible and commercially viable solutions. In order to reduce modal shift and CO2 emissions in the freight sector, customers need to be offered a rail-road combined freight service that is competitive in terms of time and price with current freight modes. Competitiveness in time and price is necessary because the freight market is liberalised, i.e. customer behaviour is essentially determined by the quality of the service offered (competitiveness in time, predictability) and good price.

In Sect. 2, we describe some container management methods that are widely used and partly under development. The concepts of vertical and horizontal container transfer and new types of terminals are reviewed. In Sect. 3, we outline the container handling characteristics that are relevant for modal shift based on our research. In Sect. 4, we present the elements of the proposed freight transport model that, when used together, can ensure modal shift. In Sect. 5, we present a practical example of the application of the proposed intermodal freight transport model in Azerbaijan. Finally, in Sect. 6, we summarise the conclusions.

In our findings and analysis, we draw heavily on research [2], which provided a comprehensive assessment of the situation of intermodal freight transport in the EU. In our opinion, no progress in intermodal freight transport and modal shift can be expected until new technical and organisational solutions are available.

The EU has supported research under the TERMINET project to explore the problems of air pollution and modal shift in the transport sector. Both the EU and national governments are encouraging intermodal freight transport, which is progressing very slowly. In their final study (January 2000) [10], the project authors' team concluded, among other things, that *"the shippers consider the unfavourable cost/quality ratio and the involvement of many actors as obstacles to modal shift"*. Some conclusions of the authoring team:

1. In many cases, the qualitative benefits of new generation terminals and innovative networks are clear and indisputable. This is particularly true when the innovations have a certain synergistic effect on both the network and the terminal. Therefore, terminal and network should always be considered as one system and taken into account at the supply chain level or even at the network level.

2. The fundamental problem with the feasibility of new generation terminals is that the high investment costs occur at the nodes, while most of the benefits are in the network. Therefore, revenue redistribution from terminal nodes is necessary to make next generation terminals feasible."

Although these ideas were made 24 years ago, they are still valid today. It is worth reviewing some CO2 emission data below, especially in the light of the fact that rail traffic on the Silk Road is likely to increase significantly in the coming years. Some thoughts on the relationship between transport mode and GHG (Greenhouse Gas) emissions. The specific CO2 emissions of water transport are 654–718 g/TEU/km depending on the size of the ship, based on data, the transport of a container to the EU by sea results in about 6.6 tonnes of CO2 emissions. In contrast, rail freight has a specific CO2 emission of 18 g/t/km (www.railfreight.com). On this basis, transporting 1 container to the EU from Asia by rail results in CO2 emissions of up to 3.9 tonnes, including CO2 emissions from diesel traction and electricity generation. The lower CO2 emissions are the result of the largely different medium resistance of water and air. The emissions data also show that the ecological footprint of rail transport, even with fossil fuels, is smaller than the ecological footprint of waterborne transport. The ecological footprint of rail transport is further reduced when electric rail traction is used and the electricity is either CO2 neutral (e.g. nuclear power) or from renewable sources (solar and wind).

2 Container Handling Technologies

Examining container handling procedures at continental terminals from a modal shift perspective is not very common. Container handling is most often discussed in the literature in relation to seaports. Container handling procedures in continental terminals justify significant technical differences with respect to container handling in ports due to electrified traction railways. In the following, some of the more important solutions are mentioned, without aiming at completeness, due to space limitations. Vertical and horizontal transhipment procedures are used in continental container terminals. Vertical container handling is defined as those solutions where containers are transferred with a significant lifting height. Such technical solutions are the Gantry crane and the Reach stacker. Both technical solutions are characterised by the fact that they cannot be used under railway catenary lines and are therefore not suitable for modal shifting.

The Gantry crane (Fig. 1) is electric powered, which is an advantage. However, the sway of the wire rope hoist system means that the container has to be lifted to a great height to move, which is a disadvantage. It is widely used at continental terminals with high traffic volumes.

Fig. 1. Gantry crane (source: www.railcargobilk.hu)

The design of the Reach stacker (Fig. 2) requires the container to be lifted high enough for the driver to see the area in front of it. Due to its diesel operation, it is not environmentally friendly. The high front axle load requires a heavy-duty concrete surface. Due to their flexible application, Rech stackers are also widely used at continental terminals.

Fig. 2. Reach stacker (source: www.kalmarglobal.com)

Horizontal container handling and transhipment procedures are technical solutions that ensure the transhipment of containers or unit loads with a low lifting height. These installations are not widespread despite the state-of-the-art technology. We consider MOBILER and ContainerMover (Fig. 3) solutions as such.

In addition to the above, there are countless other horizontal container management procedures that exist at prototype level or only at design level. The PhD dissertation [3] presents 25 technical solutions for increasing the share of combined transport and rail freight.

Fig. 3. ContainerMover (source: www.innovatrain.ch)

Also included in the category of horizontal transhipment are technical solutions for the design of a railway wagon where the truck is not only able to get on and off the wagon at the terminus. This category includes the ModaLohr (Fig. 4) and the Megaswing wagon design.

Fig. 4. ModaLohr system (source: www.modalohr.com)

The study [2] examined the impact of a total of 31 technical solutions on the combined transport price. The reasons for the lack of modal shift were not examined. Based on the freight traffic on the roads, it can be concluded that modal shift has not been achieved by the existing technical solutions. This means that we need to keep looking for a container handling process that can make the modal shift happen in a way that makes business sense.

In addition to container handling, the terminal design is another area that has a major impact on modal shift. Several scientific publications have been published in recent years.

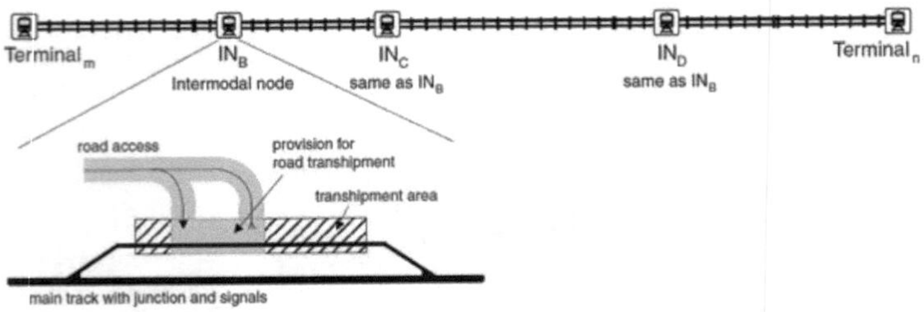

Fig. 5. Layout of new generation terminal [1]

Figure 5 shows the layout of a new generation terminal which, according to experts studying the development potential of intermodal freight transport, could increase the volume of freight transported on the rail infrastructure concerned and the revenue of the railway company operating the transport. According to the authors of the study [1], one of the important prerequisites for the use of new types of terminals is the low cost of container handling technology. Based on our research, a new type of terminal, or intermodal transfer point (ITP), should have the following main characteristics:

- Small area with a road surface with a load capacity adapted to the axle load of the lorries (8.5 tons).
- The loading track has a catenary line which is disconnected from the rest of the network.

- Loading railway track parallel to the main railway line.
- Lack of rail wagon marshalling and diesel traction.
- Minimal checks on rail wagons.
- Container transhipment machine moving on the standard railway line.

3 Container Handling Features to Ensure Modal Shift

Looking at truck traffic on main roads, the low share of rail freight transport, and the countless container handling procedures, it's clear that a complex approach is needed to achieve a modal shift. The first step is to define the requirements that need to be met.

In our research, we have identified the functional elements that need to be satisfied by a container management process that results in a modal shift. In defining the functionalities, we took into account that containers used for continental and intercontinental freight transport are of different designs. It was also considered that the intermodal freight system to be developed should be competitive in time and price with road freight. The container handling technology used in the new type of terminal must have the following characteristics to be competitive:

- Safe application under catenary.
- ISO 668 compliant box container transfer capability (20–45 feet).
- The transhipment capability of different intermodal freight transport units (ILUs, Class C swap bodies compliant with ISO EN 284, stackable Class C swap bodies compliant with EN 13853, stackable Class A swap bodies compliant with EN 14993, containers compliant with EN 1453).
- Electric operation to protect the environment.
- Operation without the presence of an operator.
- Do not require the simultaneous presence of a rail and road transport means.
- Be able to stack containers.
- Do not require new ILU construction, rail wagon construction, or special HGV (Heavy Goods Vehicle) design.

The vertical and horizontal container handling methods mentioned above do not or only partially meet the requirements listed. As a result, the construction practices for continental terminals, container handling procedures, and freight train traffic organization must be rethought.

4 The Freight Transport Model for Modal Shift

The first step is to study known material flow models (batch, continuous) and the technical processes that support them. Studying material handling technologies, it can be concluded that the technology that is most adapted to the given circumstances is the most efficient. In industry, solutions where transport capacity is constantly available have become widespread.

To identify trends, it is necessary to examine the results of technical developments [3], research findings and industrial practice. A well-known variant of intermodal freight modelling is known in the literature as the Physical Internet. The authors of the study

[5] examined intermodal freight transport on a graph-theoretic basis and found that decentralisation helps to manage dynamic logistics networks. This leads to the practical conclusion that the elements of a logistics network, namely terminals and their freight flows, should be de-concentrated rather than concentrated. The intermodal freight transport model proposed in this paper is a deconcentrated network, comparable to the overhead conveyor or roller table freight transport used in industry, with numerous branching points (HUBs, nodes), like real-life rail networks. Some of the characteristics of these material handling systems are highlighted below:

- Delivery capability is always available, the goods are not waiting for a delivery opportunity.
- Material handling does not require human labour.
- The current position of the goods in the system can be accurately calculated.

Based on the above characteristics, a new combined freight transport system model can be created, as shown in Fig. 6.

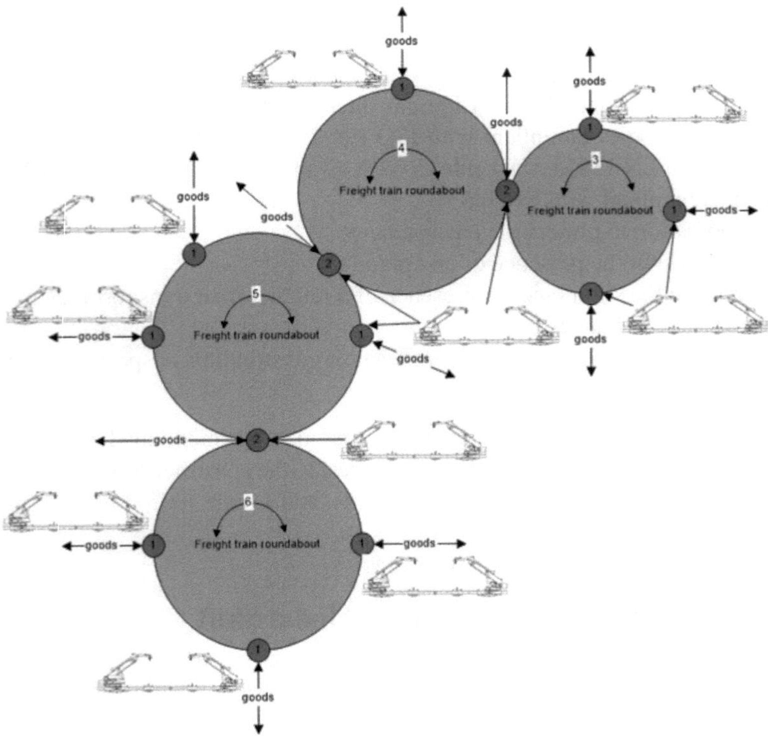

Fig. 6. New combined freight transport model (source: own editing)

In the model shown in Fig. 6, circles 1 - rail-road link, 2 - rail-road and rail-road link, circles 3–6 represent rail traffic. An intermodal freight transport system corresponding to the proposed model can be built using the following elements:

- New generation of intermodal transhipment points, ITP network.
- Efficient horizontal container transhipment technology.
- Railway traffic management to allow freight trains to run at short tracking time.

The ITP is a new type of terminal that differs significantly from the layout and mode of operation of the continental terminals currently in use. Figure 7 shows a cross-section of the ITP when the HCT is serving a rail wagon under the catenary.

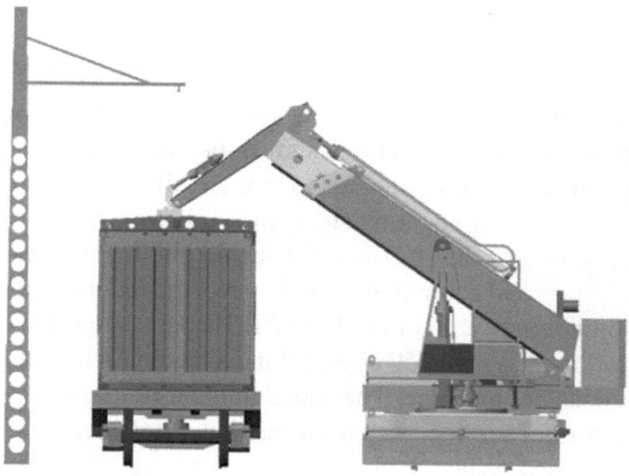

Fig. 7. The ITP section with HCT (source: own editing)

The developed freight transport model shown in Fig. 6, consisting of circular elements, can be the basis for efficient door-to-door (D2D) freight transport. Efficient D2D rail-road intermodal freight transport with the shortest possible payback distance [9] represents sustainable freight transport. The figure does not show the stations of departure and destination of the goods, which are typically 10–20 km away from the ITP. Trains can run in both directions with 1–2 h (or shorter) intervals, regardless of utilization, which is a prerequisite for time competitiveness. The advantage of the model is that it is possible to calculate exactly when the goods will arrive at the destination station after dispatch, and the ILU spends less time in the supply chain than known solutions. The result is a competitive intermodal solution comparable to the flexibility and predictability of current unimodal road transport, as a container picked up from the dispatch point can be on the train within 1–2 h. As there is no compulsory rest period in rail transport, a train travelling between ITPs can cover a significantly longer distance per day (1,200–1,400 km) than a truck (650–700 km) in 24 h. The stopping time of a train at an ITP is 15–20 min, during which time some ILUs may "get on the train" or "get off the train".

A. van Binsbergen et al. (2014) in their article "Innovation in intermodal freight transport: European presentations" [11] analyse some intermodal freight transport concepts, including rail-road variants. They stress the importance of engineering in intermodal freight innovation, **but success is significantly influenced by the state of the host environment and the cooperation of the competing partners.** "*Intermodal freight innovations face a variety of obstacles and challenges during the implementation process. This* *is particularly true for large-scale, system innovations - projects that require large investments and/or fundamental organisational changes in the transport process.".....* ***"The potential success of intermodal transport innovation also depends on the response of competing intermodal actors as well as competing modes of transport, in particular the road transport*** *sector. It is striking that road hauliers, while facing ever-increasing operating costs, have managed to increase their productivity to maintain their strong competitive position against intermodal transport."* Although the article does not address the competitive characteristics of container handling at continental terminals, it does provide relevant findings in terms of the inclusion of complex intermodal freight concepts.

The requirements of the freight transport model shown in Fig. 6 necessitate the development of a new type of horizontal container loading technology. The HCT (Horizontal Container Transhipment) shown in Fig. 7 is a 40-tonne loading capacity transhipment robot with 16 degrees of freedom. The design is patent protected. On the container storage side, it is possible to stack containers for more efficient use of space.

The HCT container transhipment machine shown in Fig. 8 meets the requirements and functions listed above. As the HCT is a distributed intelligence device automatically controlled by IoT devices and camera images, it meets the requirements of Industry 4.0. The average transhipment capacity of HCT is 12 ILUs per hour. If the ITP is open for 14 h and the annual working days are 250 days, [2] the annual yearly transhipment capacity is 42,000 transhipments per machine. The actual number of transhipments is influenced by the priority of the train service, which means that when there is a train on the ITP, the HGV service is paused. When there are no trains on the ITP, there is the possibility to sort ILUs, serving HGVs.

Fig. 8. HCT - container transhipment machine (source: own editing)

5 Azerbaijan ITP Network

Azerbaijan's geographical situation means that the railway infrastructure is not as extensive as the European rail network. The railway network in Azerbaijan is more than 2,500 km long, with a gauge of 1520 mm, and is largely electrified. The main transport corridor runs east-west and is part of the extended European TEN-T transport corridor.

Azerbaijan could be included in the China-EU rail corridor, known as the Silk Road, as it has the rail infrastructure. Rail trains arrive at the Haciqabuli ferry port via the Caspian Sea and travel to Ganja and Tbilisi, shown with read line on Fig. 9.

Fig. 9. Railway network in Azerbaijan (source: www.artway.az)

The ITP network shown in Fig. 10 can be developed along the railway line parallel to the M2 and M5 main roads. The highlighting of the parallel layout is important because modal shift is only possible if there is significant freight traffic on the road parallel to the railway.

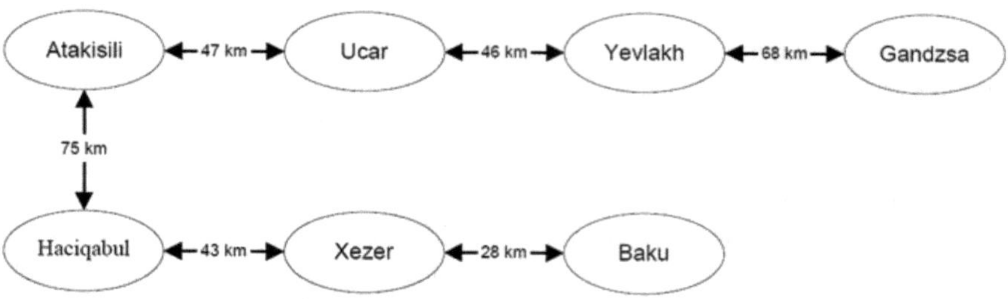

Fig. 10. The proposed Azerbaijan ITP network (source: own editing)

According to the Azerbaijan Statistical Bureau, the volume of land freight transport in 2023 was 152.5 million tonnes. Of this volume, 12% was transported by rail and 88% by road. The country's geography plays a role in the relatively low rail transport share. Inland freight transport in the regions covered by Fig. 10 could certainly be increased by the development of combined transport infrastructure. Road traffic in the regions concerned is on the M2 and M5 motorways, for which no statistics on HGV traffic are available. It is likely that some of the 26,400 articulated lorries in circulation in Azerbaijan are transporting goods on this route. The ITP network shown in Fig. 10, as a result of the modal shift, could take 40–50% of the HGV traffic on the M2 and M5 motorways. This requires a competitive offer in terms of time and price.

Since the China-EU container traffic through Azerbaijan coincides with the route shown in Fig. 9, it can be argued that the proposed ITP network will allow the Azerbaijani economy to cooperate more effectively not only with neighbouring countries but also with the EU economic area.

Data vary by source, according to the Eurasian Railways Association's Index, container volumes transported between EU hubs and China via the Northern (Russia) Corridor decreased by 31.9 percent year-on-year in 2022, from 618,180 TEUs in 2021 to 386,374 TEUs in 2022 [13]. As a consequence, alternative rail freight routes should be explored.

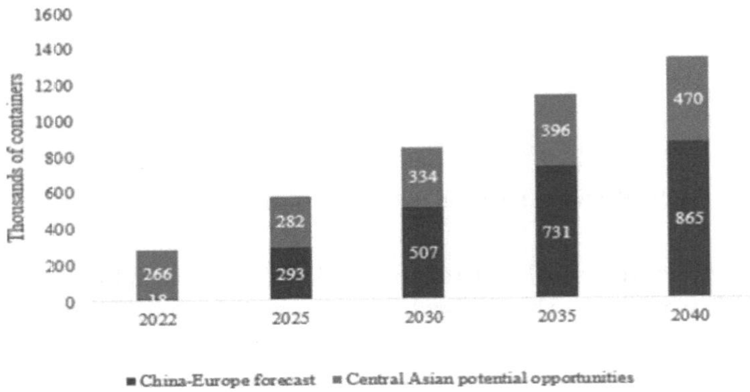

Fig. 11. Container traffic growth between Asia and the EU (source: CPCS)

The European Bank funded a comprehensive study on "Sustainable transport connections between Europe and Central Asia" [14]. The research made recommendations for infrastructure improvements for the extended TEN-T transport corridor in the Central Asian region concerned. The internal and external container transport needs of the Central Asian countries involved in the East-West economic links could increase significantly, as illustrated in Fig. 11. The container traffic forecast for 2025 may correspond to a capacity of 16–18 container trains per day, which cannot be served with the current technology due to the different track gauge. In order for the container traffic growth forecast to become a reality, it may be necessary to develop the container handling technology and ITP network described in the paper.

6 Conclusions

Rail transport between the Asian and European regions is expanding and could be an alternative to containerised freight transport by sea. If technical and rail traffic management solutions are implemented to allow containers to be loaded and unloaded from trains in the region without significant time losses, the economies of the regions concerned could develop significantly. In addition, the creation of conditions for modal shift and the development of electric rail freight could reduce GHG emissions in local economies. It can be concluded that there is a technical (HCT) and organisational (ITP network, rail freight management) solution for modal shift that allows an intermodal freight offer that is competitive in time and price compared to road transport. As a consequence, ambitious modal shift and GHG reduction targets can be achieved. In order to meet environmental requirements, technical solutions should preferably be found that significantly reduce the ecological footprint of the freight sector, thus enabling the economy concerned to operate with lower GHG emissions. We believe that the rail-road intermodal freight solution described in this article meets these criteria.

The proposed intermodal rail-road freight solution cannot be derived from the container handling and intermodal freight solutions currently in use. As a consequence, opposition and aversion from the professional public is to be expected. Technological developments (the electric trucks, driverless vehicles, hydrogen-based transport, automation in material handling, etc.) are a constant challenge for operators. Those actors that are able to respond to these challenges can be successful.

References

1. Flodén, J., Behrends, S.: The effect of transhipment costs on the performance of intermodal line-trains. Logist. Resour. **4**, 127–136. https://doi.org/10.1007/s12159-012-0066-0
2. PWC - Pricewaterhouse Coopers & KombiConsult: Comparative evaluation of transhipment technologies for intermodal transport and their cost. European Union. https://doi.org/10.2832/743839. ISBN 978-92-76-49148-4
3. Vida, L.: The efficient horizontal container transhipment and its impact on intermodal rail-road freight transport. PhD dissertation, Miskolc University. https://doi.org/10.14750/ME.2022.003
4. Islam, D., et al.: How to make modal shift from road to rail possible in the European transport market, as aspired to in the EU Transport White Paper 2011. Eur. Transp. Res. Rev. https://doi.org/10.1007/s12544-016-0204-x
5. Abdenebaoui, L., Kreowski, H.J.: Modelling of decentralized process in dynamic logistic networks by means of graph-transformational swarm. Logist. Res. https://doi.org/10.1007/s12159-016-0147-6
6. Boehm, M., et al.: The potential of high-speed rail freight in Europe: how is a modal shift from road to rail possible for low-density high value cargo? Eur. Transp. Res. Rev. https://doi.org/10.1186/s12544-020-00453-3
7. Delgado, O., Rodríguez, F.: CO2 emissions and fuel consumption standards for heavy-duty vehicles in the European Union. https://theicct.org/wpcontent/uploads/2021/06/Efficiency_standards_HDVs_EU_Briefing_051618.pdf. Accessed 17 Mar 2025
8. Jonkeren, O., et al.: A shift-share based tool for assessing the contribution of a modal shift to the decarbonisation of inland freight transport. Eur. Transp. Res. Rev. https://doi.org/10.1186/s12544-019-0344-x
9. Bierwirth, C., et al.: On transport services selection in intermodal rail/road distribution network. Ger. Acad. Assoc. Bus. Res. **5**(2), 198–212 (2012)
10. TERMINET project final report
11. https://trimis.ec.europa.eu/system/files?file=project/documents/terminet.pdf. Accessed 17 Mar 2025
12. Binsbergen, A.V., et al.: Duin Innovations in intermodal freight transport: lessons from Europe. In: TRB 2014 Annual Meeting. https://doi.org/10.13140/2.1.1918.4329
13. The Silk Road Traffic 2022. RailFreight.com
14. European Bank: Sustainable transport connections between Europe and Central Asia

Author Index

A. Abbasov et al. (Eds.): PLMO 2025, CCIS 2767, p. 183, 2026.
https://doi.org/10.1007/978-3-032-13672-5

FSC
www.fsc.org
MIX
Papier aus verantwortungsvollen Quellen
Paper from responsible sources
FSC® C105338

If you have any concerns about our products,
you can contact us on
ProductSafety@springernature.com

In case Publisher is established outside the EU,
the EU authorized representative is:
Springer Nature Customer Service Center GmbH
Europaplatz 3, 69115 Heidelberg, Germany

Printed by Libri Plureos GmbH
in Hamburg, Germany